English Grammar FOR DUMMIES®

by Lesley J. Ward and Geraldine Woods

BICENTENNIAL
1807
WILEY
2007
BICENTENNIAL

John Wiley & Sons, Ltd

English Grammar For Dummies®

Published by
John Wiley & Sons, Ltd
The Atrium
Southern Gate
Chichester
West Sussex
PO19 8SQ
England

E-mail (for orders and customer service enquires): cs-books@wiley.co.uk

Visit our Home Page on www.wiley.com

For general information on our other products and services, please contact our Customer Care Department within the U.S. at 800-762-2974, outside the U.S. at 317-572-3993, or fax 317-572-4002.

For technical support, please visit www.wiley.com/techsupport.

Wiley also publishes its books in a variety of electronic formats. Some content that appears in print may not be available in electronic books.

British Library Cataloguing in Publication Data: A catalogue record for this book is available from the British Library

ISBN: 978-0-470-05752-0

Printed in the UK

WILEY

About the Authors

Lesley J. Ward has worked in the publishing industry for over thirty years, editing and proofreading books and journals. She is a founder member of the Society for Editors and Proofreaders (SfEP), and regularly leads training courses for SfEP, the Irish Book Publishers' Association and The London College of Communication. She is also a distance-learning tutor for the Publishing Training Centre. Her favourite course is *Brush up your grammar*. She lives in Berkshire and is notorious for being a harmless eccentric/dangerous radical who refuses to have e-mail. She doesn't have a cat.

Geraldine Woods' career as a grammarian began in her elementary school, which in those days was called 'grammar school' for very good reason. With the guidance of a series of nuns carrying long rulers (good for pointing at the board and slapping unruly students), she learned how to diagram every conceivable type of sentence. She has been an English teacher for 25 years and has written 40 books, give or take a few. She loves minor-league baseball, Chinese food, and the novels of Jane Austen.

Dedication

From Lesley: This book is dedicated to Oliver and Francesca, who are going to receive copies from their grammatically obsessed maiden aunt.

From Geraldine: For my husband and son, the hearts of my life.

Authors' Acknowledgements

From Lesley: Most of the people I need to thank will have to remain nameless because I can't remember their names. The primary school teacher who got me hooked on grammar in the first place isn't even a nameless face to me any more, although I can still see the blackboard and remember the weather (rainy) on the day she showed me that language is fascinating. My teachers at grammar school also did a wonderful job. (A special thank-you here to all the members of successive governments who *didn't* decide that I didn't need to know grammar.) Every author who argued with me, and every publishing house that gave me feedback on the work I did for them, helped to hone my skills. And all the experts who have taken the trouble to write grammar books that I could understand. Bless them – I now have a much better idea of how much effort those books took.

Also, thank you to Alison Yates and Simon Bell at Wiley. They were incredibly patient when I missed deadlines. And to Tabby Toussaint, the technical reviewer who saved me from a gaffe or two, and the poor frustrated copy-editor. They tried. Anything that's still wrong is my fault.

From Geraldine: I offer thanks to my students, whose intelligence and curiosity never fail to inspire me. I also thank technical editor Tom LaFarge, whose good sense of humour and knowledge of grammar vastly improved this book. I am grateful to my project editor, Linda Brandon, whose thoughtful comments challenged me to clarify my explanations and whose encouragement changed many a bad day into a good one. I appreciate the hard work of copy editors Billie Williams and Ellen Considine, who constantly reminded me to focus on you, the reader. I am also grateful to acquisitions editors Joyce Pepple, Roxane Cerda, and Susan Decker, who encouraged me at every opportunity. I owe a debt of gratitude to my agent, Carolyn Krupp, who calmed my nerves and answered my e-mails with unfailing courtesy and valuable assistance. Lastly, I thank my colleagues in the English Department, whose passion for teaching and love of our subject make my time at work a pleasure.

Publisher's Acknowledgements

We're proud of this book; please send us your comments through our Dummies online registration form located at www.dummies.com/register/.

Some of the people who helped bring this book to market include the following:

Acquisitions, Editorial, and Media Development

Project Editor: Simon Bell

Content Editor: Steve Edwards

Commissioning Editor: Alison Yates

Copy Editor: Charlie Wilson

Technical Editor: Tabby Toussaint

Executive Editor: Jason Dunne

Executive Project Editor: Martin Tribe

Cover Photo: GettyImages/John Molloy

Cartoons: Ed McLachlan

Composition Services

Project Coordinator: Jennifer Theriot

Layout and Graphics: Carl Byers, Joyce Haughey, Stephanie D. Jumper, Laura Pence, Erin Zeltner

Proofreaders: Jessica Kramer, Susan Moritz

Indexer: Aptara

Brand Reviewer: Janet Sims

Wiley Bicentennial Logo: Richard J. Pacifico

Publishing and Editorial for Consumer Dummies

Diane Graves Steele, Vice President and Publisher, Consumer Dummies

Joyce Pepple, Acquisitions Director, Consumer Dummies

Kristin A. Cocks, Product Development Director, Consumer Dummies

Michael Spring, Vice President and Publisher, Travel

Kelly Regan, Editorial Director, Travel

Publishing for Technology Dummies

Andy Cummings, Vice President and Publisher, Dummies Technology/General User

Composition Services

Gerry Fahey, Vice President of Production Services

Debbie Stailey, Director of Composition Services

Contents at a Glance

Table of Contents

Introduction

*W*hy does grammar make so many people nervous? Many of us weren't taught any at school. (A really great government idea that put us all out of our depth the minute we stepped out of the classroom and into the real world!) Some of us found all the terminology boring. Others have forgotten what they learned because they haven't had much chance to practise. And we can find ourselves in circumstances where our language skills aren't as good as they need to be – in a job interview, writing our first report in a new job, or just trying to please a teacher. This can be stressful and make us very self-conscious. And it's worse if everyone around us seems to be better at it, or if we find to our horror that the boss is one of those people who even seems to *speak* proper grammar. (Were some people *born* knowing this stuff?)

Happily, English grammar is a lot easier than you've been led to believe. You don't have to learn all those technical terms, and if you ignore the terminology you'll find that you already know a lot of it anyway. In this book we tell you the tricks of the trade, the strategies that help you make the right decision when you're facing such grammatical dilemmas as the choice between *I* and *me*, *had gone* and *went*, and so forth. We explain *what* you're supposed to do, but also tell you *why* a particular word is correct or incorrect. You won't have to memorise a list of meaningless rules (well, maybe a couple from the punctuation chapter!) because when you understand the reason for a particular choice you'll pick the correct word automatically.

About This Book

In this book, we concentrate on the common errors. We tell you what's what in the sentence, in logical, everyday (pardon the term) English, not in obscure terminology. You don't have to read this book in order, though you can, and you don't have to read the whole thing. Just browse through the table of contents and look for things that you often get wrong. For example, if you know that verbs are your downfall, check out Chapters 2 and 3 for the basics. Chapters 11 and 18 show you how to pick the correct verb in a variety of situations, and Chapter 22 gives you the equivalent of a doctorate in verbology. You decide how picky you want to be.

How to Use This Book

Each chapter in this book introduces some basic ideas and then shows you how to choose the correct sentence when faced with two or three choices. If we define a term–*linking verbs*, for example–we show you a practical situation in which identifying a linking verb helps you pick the right pronoun. The examples are clearly displayed in the text so that you can find them easily. One good way to determine whether or not you need to read a particular section is to check the pop quizzes that are sprinkled around every chapter. If you get the right answer, you probably don't need to read that section. If you're puzzled, however, backtrack and read the chapter. Also, watch for Demon icons. They identify the little things–the difference between two similar words, commonly misused words and so on–that may sabotage your writing.

What You Are Not to Read

Here and there throughout this book, you see some items marked with the Black Belt icon. No human being in the history of the world has ever needed to know those terms for any purpose connected with speaking and writing correct English. In fact, we recommend that you skip them and do something interesting instead. For those of you who actually enjoy obscure terminology for the purpose of, say, clearing a room within ten seconds, the Black Belt icons define such exciting grammatical terms as *subject complement* and *participial phrase*. Everyone else, fear not: these sections are clearly labelled and completely skippable. Look for the Black Belt icons and avoid those paragraphs like the plague.

Foolish Assumptions

We wrote *English Grammar For Dummies* with a specific person in mind. We assume that you, the reader, already speak English (although you may have learned it as a foreign language) and that you want to speak and write it better. We also assume that you're a busy person with better things to do than worry about *who* and *whom*. You want to speak and write well, but you don't want to get a doctorate in English Grammar. (Smart move. Doctorates in English probably move you up on the salary scale less than any other advanced degree, except maybe Doctorates in Philosophy.)

This book is for you if

- ✔ You want to get better marks for your schoolwork.
- ✔ You aspire to a better-paid or higher-status job.
- ✔ You want your speech and writing to present you as an educated, intelligent person.
- ✔ You want your writing and your speech to be clear and to say exactly what you mean.
- ✔ You want to polish your skills in English as a second language.
- ✔ You simply want to use better grammar.

How This Book Is Organised

The first two parts of this book cover the basics: the minimum for reasonably correct English. Part III addresses the nuts and bolts of writing: punctuation and capital letters. Parts IV and V hit the finer (OK, pickier) points of grammar, the ones that separate regular people from Official Grammarians. If you understand the information in this section, you'll have fun finding mistakes in the daily paper.

Here's a more specific guide to navigating *English Grammar For Dummies*.

Part 1: The Parts of Speech and Parts of the Sentence

This part explains how to distinguish between the three Englishes: the breezy slang of friend-to-friend chat, the slightly more proper conversational language, and I'm-on-my-best-behaviour English. We explain the building blocks of a sentence (subjects and verbs) – and show you how to put them together properly. In this part, we also provide a guide to the complete sentence, telling you what's grammatically legal and what's not. We also define objects and complements and show you how to use each effectively.

Part 11: Avoiding Common Errors

In this part, we describe the remaining members of Team Grammar – the other parts of speech that can make or break your writing. We show you how to join short, choppy sentences into longer, more fluent ones without incurring a visit from the grammar police. We also explain descriptive word and show you how the location of a description may alter the meaning of the sentence. Prepositions – the bane of many speakers of English as a second language – are in this part, too, as well as some tips for correct usage. Finally, in this part we tell you how to avoid mismatches between singular and plural words, by far the most common mistake in ordinary speech and writing. Part II also contains an explanation of pronoun gender. In addition, reading this section may help you to avoid sexist pronoun usage.

Part III: No Garage, But Plenty of Mechanics

If you've ever asked yourself whether you need a comma or if you've ever got lost in quotation marks and semicolons, Part III is for you. We explain all the rules that govern the use of the apostrophe. We also show you how to quote speech or written material and where to place the most common punctuation mark, the comma. Lastly, we outline the ins and outs of capital letters: when you need them, when you don't, and when they're optional.

Part IV: Polishing Without Wax – the Finer Points of Grammar

Part IV inches up on the pickiness scale – not all the way to Grammar Heaven, but at least as far as the gate. In this part, we tell you the difference between subject and object pronouns and pronouns of possession. (No, you don't need an exorcist.) We also go into detail on verb tenses, explaining which words to use for all sorts of purposes. We show you how to distinguish between active and passive verbs and how to use each properly. We illustrate some common errors of sentence structure and tackle comparisons – both how to form them and how to ensure that your comparisons are logical and complete. Finally, we show you how to achieve balance and order in the sentence.

Part V: Rules Even Your Great-Aunt's Grammar Teacher Didn't Know

Anyone who masters the material in Part V has the right to wear a bun and tut-tut a lot. This part covers the moods of verbs (ranging from grouchy to just plain irritable) and explains how to avoid double negatives. Part V also gives you the last word on pronouns, those little parts of speech that make everyone's life miserable. The dreaded *who/whom* section is in this part, as well as the explanation for all sorts of errors with pronouns. We explain subordinate clauses and give you the lowdown on the most obscure punctuation rules.

Part VI: The Part of Tens

Part VI is the Part of Tens, which offers some quick tips for better grammar. Here we show you ten ways to fine-tune your proofreading skills. Finally, we suggest ways (apart from reading *English Grammar For Dummies*) to improve your ear for proper English.

Icons Used in This Book

Wherever you see this icon, you'll find helpful strategies for understanding the structure of the sentence or for choosing the correct word form.

Not every grammar trick has a built-in trap, but some do. This icon tells you how to avoid common mistakes as you unravel a sentence.

Think you know how to find the subject in a sentence or identify a pronoun? Take the pop quizzes located throughout this book to find out what you know and what you may want to learn.

Keep your eye out for these little devils: they point out the difference between easily confused words and show you how to make your sentence say what you want it to say.

Here's where we get a little technical. If you master this information, you're guaranteed to impress your oldest relations and bore all of your friends.

Where to Go from Here

Now that you know what's what and where it is, it's time to get started. Before you do, however, one last word. Actually, two last words. *Trust yourself.* You already know a lot. If you're a native speaker, you've communicated in English all of your life, including the years before you set foot in school and saw your first textbook. If English is an acquired language for you, you've probably already learned a fair amount of vocabulary and grammar, even if you don't know the technical terms. For example, you already understand the difference between

The dog bit Agnes.

and

Agnes bit the dog.

You don't need us to tell you which sentence puts the dog in the doghouse and which sentence puts Agnes in a padded room. So take heart. Browse through the table of contents, take a few pop quizzes and dip a toe into the Sea of Grammar. The water's fine.

Part I
The Parts of Speech and Parts of the Sentence

'I'd like you to seriously consider
my offer of marriage.'

In this part . . .

So it's, like, communication, y'know?

Can you make a statement like that without bringing the grammar police to your door? Maybe. Read Chapter 1 for a discussion of formal and informal language and a guide to when each is appropriate. The rest of this part of the book explains the building blocks of the sentence. Chapter 2 shows you how to find the verb, and Chapter 3 tells you what to do with it once you've got it. Chapter 4 provides a road map to the subject of the sentence and explains the basics of matching subjects and verbs properly. Chapter 5 is all about completeness – why the sentence needs it and how to make sure that the sentence gets it. In Chapter 6, we explore the last building block of a sentence – the complement.

Chapter 1

I Already Know How to Talk. Why Should I Study Grammar?

*Y*ou may be reading this book for a number of reasons. Perhaps you're hoping to impress your English teacher (if so, it's a good idea to let her accidentally catch you reading it). Or maybe you're hoping to become so eloquent that when you pluck up the courage to ask the most beautiful girl in your class out on a date she'll say yes. Or perhaps you want to improve the letters you write at work so that your boss will give you a promotion.

What is grammar anyway?

In the Middle Ages, *grammar* meant the study of Latin, because Latin was the language of choice for educated people. In fact, knowing Latin grammar was so closely associated with being an educated person that the word grammar was also used to refer to any kind of learning. That's why *grammar schools* were called grammar schools; they were places of learning – and not just learning about how Latin and English work.

These days, grammar is the study of language – specifically, how words are put together to create meaning. Because of all those obsessive English teachers and their rules, grammar also means a set of standards that you have to follow in order to speak and write correctly. This set of standards is also called *usage*, as in *standard* and *non-standard usage*. Standard usage is the one that earns an A grade. It consists of the commonly accepted correct patterns of speech and writing that mark an educated person in our society. You'll find standard usage in government documents, in newspapers and magazines, and in textbooks. Non-standard usage draws red ink from a teacher's pen faster than a bullet cuts through butter. Non-standard usage includes slang, dialect and just plain bad grammar.

Whatever your ultimate goal is, you have probably decided that learning better grammar is a good strategy. In this chapter we'll look at how the definition of *better grammar* changes according to your situation, purpose and audience. We'll also tell you what your computer can and can't do to help you write proper English.

Living Better with Better Grammar

The curtain goes up and you step on stage. One deep breath and you're ready. *Ladies and gentlemen, it's an honour to be speaking . . . to speak . . . to have spoken . . . to you this evening.* You clear your throat. *I offer my best efforts to whomever . . . whoever the committee decides . . . will decide should receive the nomination.* You begin to sweat, but you go on. *Now if everyone will rise to his . . . to his or her . . . to their . . . to your feet . . .* Does this sound like you? Do your words twist around themselves until you don't know why you ever thought to open your mouth (or turn on your computer)? If so, you have lots of company. Nearly everyone in your class or office (or book club or squadron or whatever) has the same worries.

Stuck in English class, you probably thought that grammar was invented just to give teachers something to test. But in fact grammar – or, to be more precise, formal grammar teaching – exists to help you express yourself clearly. Without a thorough knowledge of grammar, you'll get by just fine chatting with your friends and family. But you may find yourself at a disadvantage when you're interviewed for a job or a place at university, or when you're trying to convince someone to publish your novel, or when you find yourself having a *slight* disagreement with a customs officer at the airport on your way home from your holiday . . . and heaven help you if your boss turns out to be a *stickler* – one of those people who knows every grammar rule that was ever invented (and thinks that you should know them too) and insists that the English language must never be allowed to change.

Rightly or wrongly, your audience or readers will judge you by the words you use and the way you put them together. Ten minutes at the cinema will show you the truth of this statement. Listen to the speech of the people on the screen. An uneducated character sounds different from someone with five diplomas on the wall. The dialogue reflects reality: educated people follow certain rules when they speak and write. If you want to present yourself as an educated person, you have to follow those rules too.

Deciding Which Grammar to Learn

I can hear the groan already. *Which* grammar? You mean there's more than one? Yes, there are actually several different types of grammar, including *historical* (how language has changed through the centuries) and *comparative* (comparing languages). Don't despair. In *English Grammar For Dummies*, we deal with only two – the two you have to know in order to improve your speech and writing: descriptive grammar and functional grammar.

Descriptive grammar gives names to things – the parts of speech and parts of a sentence. When you learn descriptive grammar, you understand what every word *is* (its part of speech) and what every word *does* (its function in the sentence). There is one important reason to learn some grammar terms – to understand *why* a particular word or phrase is correct or incorrect (and sometimes to be able to explain to someone else why it's wrong).

Functional grammar makes up the bulk of *English Grammar For Dummies.* Functional grammar tells you how words behave when they're doing their jobs properly. It guides you to the right expression – the one that fits what you're trying to say – by ensuring that the sentence is put together correctly. When you're agonising over whether to say *I* or *me*, you're actually solving a problem of functional grammar.

So here's the formula for success: a little descriptive grammar plus a lot of functional grammar equals better grammar overall.

Distinguishing between the Three Englishes

Better grammar sounds like a great idea, but *better* is tough to pin down. Why? Because the language of choice depends on your situation. Here's what I mean. Imagine that you're hungry. What do you say?

Wanna get something to eat?

Do you feel like getting a sandwich?

Will you accompany me to the dining room?

These three statements illustrate the three Englishes of everyday life. We'll call them friendspeak, conversational English and formal English.

Before you choose, you need to know where you are and what's going on. Most important, you need to know your audience.

Wanna get something to eat? Friendspeak

Friendspeak is informal and filled with slang. Its sentence structure breaks all the rules that English teachers love. It's the language of *I know you and you know me and we can relax together.* In friendspeak the speakers are on the same level. They have nothing to prove to each other, and they're comfortable with each other's mistakes. In fact, they make some mistakes on purpose, just to distinguish their personal conversation from what they say on other occasions. Here's a conversation in friendspeak:

> We're gonna go to the gym. Wanna come?
>
> He's, like, I did 60 push-ups, and I go, like, no way.
>
> I mean, what's he think? We're stupid or something? Sixty? More like one.
>
> Yeah, I know. In his dreams he did 60.

I doubt that the preceding conversation makes perfect sense to many people, but the participants understand it quite well. Because they both know the whole situation (the guy they're talking about gets muscle cramps after four seconds of exercise), they can talk in shorthand. It helps, of course, that they're speaking to each other (not just reading the words). The way they say the words helps to communicate their meaning, and if that fails they can wave their hands about or shake their heads in significant ways.

Slang

Psst! Want to be in the in-crowd? Easy. Just create an out-crowd and you're all set. How do you create an out-crowd? Manufacture a special language (slang) with your friends that no one else understands, at least until the media pick it up. You and your pals are on the inside, talking about a *wicked* song that everyone likes (*wicked* means good). Everyone else is on the outside, wondering what you're talking about. Should you use slang in your writing? Probably not, unless you're sending an e-mail or a personal note to a good friend. The goal of writing and speaking is communication (usually with as many people as possible, or your book *won't* become a best-seller). Also, because slang changes so quickly, the meaning may become obscure even a short time after you've written something. Instead of cutting-edge, you sound dated.

When you talk or write in slang, you also risk sounding uneducated. In fact, sometimes breaking the usual rules is the point of slang. In general, you should make sure that your readers know that you understand the rules before you start breaking them (the rules, not the readers) safely.

We don't deal with friendspeak in this book. You already know it. In fact, you've probably created a version of it with your mates.

Do you feel like getting a sandwich? Conversational English

A step up from friendspeak is *conversational English*. Although not quite friend-speak, conversational English includes some friendliness. Conversational English doesn't stray too far from the rules, but it does break some. It's the tone of most everyday speech, especially between equals. Conversational English is – no shock here – usually for conversations, not for writing. Specifically, conversational English is appropriate in these situations:

✔ Chats with family members, neighbours and acquaintances

✔ Informal conversations with teachers and co-workers

✔ Friendly conversations (if there are any) with supervisors

✔ Notes and e-mails to friends

✔ Comments in Internet chat rooms, bulletin boards and so on

✔ Friendly letters to relatives

✔ Novels

Conversational English has a breezy sound. Letters are dropped in contractions (don't, I'll, would've and so forth). You also drop words (*Got a match? Later. On the fridge.* and so on). In written form, conversational English relaxes the punctuation rules too. Sentences run together, dashes connect all sorts of things, and half-sentences pop up regularly. I'm using conversational English to write this book because I'm pretending that I'm chatting with you, the reader, not teaching grammar in a classroom.

Will you accompany me to the dining room? Formal English

You're now at the pickiest end of the language spectrum: formal, grammatically correct speech and writing. Formal English displays the fact that you have an advanced vocabulary and a knowledge of etiquette. You may use formal English when you have less power, importance and/or status than the other person in the conversation. Formal English shows that you've trotted out your best behaviour in someone's honour. You may also speak or write in formal English when you have *more* power, importance or status than the other person (to maintain the distance between you). The goal of using formal English is to impress, to create a tone of dignity, or to provide a suitable role model for someone who is still learning. Situations that call for formal English include:

- Business letters and e-mails (from individuals to businesses as well as from or between businesses)
- Letters to government officials
- Office memos
- Reports
- Homework
- Notes or letters to teachers
- Speeches, presentations and formal oral reports
- Important conversations (for example, job interviews, college interviews, parole hearings, sessions with teachers in which you explain that it wasn't you that did what they think you did, and so on)
- Authoritative reference books

Think of formal English as a business suit. If you're in a situation where you want to look your best, you're also in a situation where your words matter. In business, homework or any situation in which you're being judged, use formal English.

Using the Right English at the Right Time

Which type of English do you speak? Friendspeak, conversational English or formal English? Probably all of them. (See the preceding section for more information.) If you're like most people, you switch from one to another without thinking, dozens of times each day. Chances are, the third type of English – formal English – is the one that gives you the most trouble. In fact, it's probably why you bought this book. (OK, there is one more possibility. Maybe your old maiden aunt gave you your copy of *English Grammar For Dummies* and you're stuck with it. But right now you're obviously reading the book instead of playing computer games, so you've at least acknowledged that you may be able to get something useful from it, and we're betting that it's formal English.) All the grammar lessons in this book deal with formal English, because that's where the problems are fiercest and the rewards for knowledge are greatest.

Which is correct?

A. Hi, Ms Stakes! What's up? Here's the thing. I didn't do no homework last night – too much goin' on. See ya! Love, Lucinda

B. Dear Ms Stakes, Just a note to let you know that I'm not handing in my homework today. I didn't manage to get it done last night! I'll explain later!

> Your friend,

> Lucinda

C. Dear Ms Stakes,

I was not able to do my homework last night. I will speak to you about this matter later.

> Yours sincerely,

> Lucinda Robinson

Relying on grammar checkers is not enough

Your best friend – the one who's surfing the Internet and talking to you while you're trying to read *English Grammar For Dummies* – may tell you that learning proper grammar in the third millennium is irrelevant because computer grammar checkers make human knowledge obsolete. Your friend is wrong about the grammar programs.

It's comforting to think that a little green or red line will tell you when you've made an error and that a quick mouse-click will show you the path to perfection. Comforting, but unreal. English has half a million words, and you can arrange those words a couple of gazillion ways. No program can catch all your mistakes, and most programs identify errors that aren't actually wrong.

Every time I type *I don't think this matters*, the computer objects. It wants me to change *this matters* to *this matter* or *these matters* because it doesn't recognise that *matters* can be a verb.

Spelling is also a problem. The computer can't tell the difference between *homonyms* (words that sound alike but have different meanings and spellings) and doesn't know whether the words I type are the ones I mean. For example, if my fingers type

> He walk son he edges like than ever day. I've told him it he does if and moor and fall sin I'm not polling his out. He's such a pane! I'm going too complain formerly.

(I'm not much good at typing!) the computer underlines nothing. However, I was actually trying to say

> He walks on the edge like that every day. I've told him if he does it any more and falls in I'm not pulling him out. He's such a pain! I'm going to complain formally.

In short, the computer knows some grammar and spelling, but you have to know the rest.

Answer: The correct answer depends upon a few factors. How willing are you to get a failing grade for this piece of work (assuming you do get round to handing it in eventually)? If your answer is very willing, send note A. It's written in friendspeak. Does your teacher come to school in jeans and trainers and have the self-image of a 1960s hippie? If so, note B is acceptable. Note B is written in conversational English. Is your teacher prim and proper, expecting you to follow the rules? If so, note C (which is written in formal English) is your best bet.

Chapter 2

Verbs: The Heart of the Sentence

In This Chapter
- ▶ Knowing the difference between linking verbs and action verbs
- ▶ Finding the verb
- ▶ Using auxiliary verbs correctly and understanding infinitives

*T*hink about a sentence this way: a sentence is a car. You pile all your ideas into the boot, and the car takes the meaning to your audience (your reader or your listener). The verb is a set of tyres. Without the verb, you may get your point across, but you're going to have a bumpy ride.

In other words, every sentence needs a verb. The verb is what the sentence rests on and what gives the sentence movement. Verbs are the heart of the sentence because you start with the verb when you want to do anything to your sentence – including correct it.

Verbs come in all shapes and sizes: linking and action; auxiliary verb and main verb; regular and irregular; singular and plural; and present, past, and future. In this chapter, we'll unravel the first two categories – linking and action, auxiliary verb, and main verb – and show you how to choose the right verb for each sentence.

Linking Verbs: The Giant Equals Sign

Linking verbs are also called *being verbs* because they express states of being – what is, will be or was (and the verb used to express the state of being is often the verb *to be* – no prizes for guessing that one). You can also call one of these verbs a *copulative verb* or *copula* (words derived from a Latin word meaning *to join*). But similar words (derived from the same Latin word) are also used to refer to sex, and we don't want you to be distracted so – if you can just get your mind back on the subject of grammar, please – we'll call them *linking verbs*.

Here's where algebra intersects with English. You can think of linking verbs as giant equals signs in the middle of your sentence. For example, you can think of the sentence

Yasmin *is* a beautiful young woman with an interest in physics.

as

Yasmin = a beautiful young woman with an interest in physics

Or, in shortened form,

Yasmin = a beautiful young woman

Just as in an algebraic equation, the word *is* links two ideas and says that they're the same. Thus, *is* is a linking verb. Here are some more examples:

Bibi *will be* angry if you take away her teddy bear.

Bibi = angry (*will be* is a linking verb)

Sandy *was* the last surfer to leave the water.

Sandy = last surfer (*was* is a linking verb)

Lucinda's red hair and green eyes *were* stunning.

hair and eyes = stunning (*were* is a linking verb)

Bill *has been* depressed ever since United lost last week.

Bill = depressed (*has been* is a linking verb)

Fleas *are* a constant problem for Fido.

fleas = problem (*are* is a linking verb)

You may wonder (OK, only if you're having a no-news day) whether *become* is a linking verb. Grammarians argue this point often (maybe because they tend to have no-news lives). The problem is that *become* is part *being*, part *action*. For example:

Damian's birthmark *becomes* obvious only when he pushes his hair away from his face.

On the one hand, you can say that

birthmark = obvious

but you can also say that the sentence shows action. Damian's birthmark is hidden and then exposed.

So what is *become* – an action or being? A little of each. In the real world, the answer doesn't matter unless you're completing the sentence with a pronoun. (See 'Placing the Proper Pronoun in the Proper Place', later in this chapter.) Frankly, we can't think of any sentence with *become* as a verb that ends with a pronoun. Well, except one:

> 'Moonlight becomes you,' declared Edgar as he strummed a guitar under Yasmin's window.

However, in this sentence the verb means *to look attractive on, to suit*. Therefore, *becomes* in this sample sentence is definitely an action verb.

More linking verbs

In the preceding section, you may have noticed that all the linking verbs in the sample sentences are forms of the verb *to be*. There are other verbs that work in the same way. Check out these examples:

> With his twinkling eyes and shy smile, Damian *seems* harmless.
>
> Damian = harmless (*seems* is a linking verb)
>
> A jail sentence for the unauthorised use of a comma *appears* harsh.
>
> jail sentence = harsh (*appears* is a linking verb in this sentence)
>
> Lucinda's parents *remain* confident that she will pass her exams.
>
> parents = confident (*remain* is a linking verb in this sentence)
>
> Edgar *stays* silent whenever sports are mentioned.
>
> Edgar = silent (*stays* is a linking verb in this sentence)

Seems, appears, remain and *stays* are expressing states of being, so they are linking verbs too. They simply add shades of meaning to the basic concept. You may, for example, say that

> With his twinkling eyes and shy smile, Damian *is* harmless.

But now the statement is more definite. *Seems* leaves room for doubt. Similarly, *remain* (in the third sentence) adds a time dimension to the basic expression of being. Lucinda's parents were confident in her ability *and still are*. (They don't know that she hasn't completed any coursework this year.)

No matter how you name it, any verb that places an equals sign in the sentence is a *linking verb*.

Savouring sensory verbs

Sensory verbs – verbs that express information you receive through the senses of sight, hearing, smell, taste, and touch – may also be linking verbs:

> Even after a bath to remove all the jam, Bibi still *feels* sticky.

> Bibi = sticky (*feels* is a linking verb)

> Edgar's tuba solo *sounds* horrible, like an animal in pain.

> tuba solo = horrible (*sounds* is a linking verb)

> Lucinda *looks* wonderful in her new green dress, which matches her eyes.

> Lucinda = wonderful (*looks* is a linking verb)

> The lasagna that Sandy made *tasted* revolting.

> lasagna = revolting (*tasted* is a linking verb)

> The ten-week-old soup in Sandy's refrigerator *smells* disgusting.

> *soup* = disgusting (*smells* is a linking verb)

Some verbs, especially those that refer to the five senses, may be linking verbs, but only if they act as an equals sign in the sentence. If they aren't equating two ideas, they aren't linking verbs. In the sentence about Bibi and the jam, *feels* is a linking verb. Here's a different sentence with the same verb:

> With her delicate fingers, Yasmin *feels* the silk of Lucinda's new dress.

In this sentence, *feels* is not a linking verb because you're not saying that

> Yasmin = silk

Instead, you're saying that Yasmin is admiring Lucinda's dress and can't help touching the material.

Which sentence has a linking verb?

A. That annoying new clock sounds the hour with a recorded cannon shot.

B. That annoying new clock sounds extremely loud at four o'clock in the morning.

Answer: Sentence B has the linking verb. In sentence B, clock = extremely loud. In sentence A, the clock is doing something – sounding the hour – not being. (It's also waking up the whole neighbourhood, but that information isn't in the sentence.)

Due to a grammatical error

The picnic has been cancelled *due to? because of?* the unexpected blizzard.

OK, which one is correct – *due to* or *because of?* The answer is that this is a highly controversial issue, and more and more people think that both are OK (so you can skip this whole section if you want to). But sticklers think that the answer is *because of.* According to the rule they're following, *due* is an adjective (a descriptive word). So it can be used

- To describe nouns or pronouns. Here are some examples:

    > You will receive your due reward in heaven.

    > Be sure to return your library book by the due date.

- To follow a linking verb if it gives information about the subject (which is always a noun or pronoun). Here are some examples:

    > Payment is due next Thursday. (*due next Thursday* describes *payment*)

    > The closure was due to flood damage. (*due to flood damage* describes *closure*)

    > Lucinda's mania for fashion is due to her deprived upbringing in an all-polyester household. (*due to her deprived upbringing in an all-polyester household* describes *mania*)

(See 'Linking Verbs: The Giant Equals Sign', earlier in this chapter, for more information.) *Because of* describes an action (see 'Lights! Camera! Action Verb!', later in this chapter, for information on action verbs). It usually answers the question *Why? Due to* shouldn't be used in this way. Look at these examples:

The bubblegum gun is no longer being manufactured *because of* protests from dentists.

Why is the gun no longer being manufactured? Because of protests from dentists.

> The shop was closed because of fire damage.

Why was the shop closed? Because of fire damage.

In real life (that is to say, in everyday conversational English), *due to* and *because of* are interchangeable. You only need to be careful when you're using your most formal, most correct language. One easy solution (easier than remembering which phrase is which) is to avoid *due to* entirely in writing and stick to *because of.* But, if you want to demonstrate that you know your grammar, there's a simple test you can use: put *caused by* in the place of *due to* and see what happens. They both work in the same way, but *due to* sounds fine to most people even when it's 'wrong' and *caused by* doesn't:

> The bubblegum gun is no longer being manufactured *caused by* protests from dentists.

See? You'd never say that, would you? There's obviously something wrong with it (and *due to* would be wrong too).

Now try this one:

> Lucinda's mania for fashion is *caused by* her deprived upbringing in an all-polyester household.

That's fine, isn't it? So *due to* would be fine too.

Try another. Which sentence has a linking verb?

A. Damian stays married only for very short periods of time.

B. Mortimer stays only at the most expensive hotels.

Answer: Sentence A has the linking verb. In sentence A, Damian = married (at least for the moment). Sentence B tells us what Mortimer does – stays only in the most expensive hotels (clearly an action).

Linking verbs connect the subject and the subject complement. For more on complements, see Chapter 6.

Here is a list of the most common linking verbs:

- ✔ Forms of *to be:* am, are, is, was, were, will be, shall be, has been, have been, had been, could be, should be, would be, might have been, could have been, should have been, shall have been, will have been, must have been, must be.

- ✔ Sensory verbs: look, sound, taste, smell, feel.

- ✔ Words that express shades of meaning in reference to a state of being: appear, seem, grow, remain, stay.

Completing Linking Verb Sentences Correctly

A linking verb begins a thought, but needs another word to complete it. Unless all your friends have ESP (extrasensory perception), you can't walk around saying things like

President Edwards is

or

The best day for the party will be

and expect people to know what you mean.

There are three possible ways to complete a sentence that begins with a linking verb. The first is a description (an adjective in grammatical terms):

After working seven hours in high heels, Susie's feet are *tired.*

feet = *tired* (tired is a description – an adjective)

Susie's high heels are *painful*, especially when they land on your foot.

high heels = *painful* (*painful* is a description – an adjective)

The second is a person, place or thing (a noun, in grammatical terms). Here are some examples:

Edgar is *president* of the Chess Club.

Edgar = *president* (*president* is a person and therefore a noun)

The best place for the club to meet would be *the park*.

best place = *park* (*park* is a place – a noun)

The most important part of a balanced diet is *pizza*.

part of a balanced diet = *pizza* (*pizza* is a thing – a noun)

The third way to complete a linking-verb sentence is with a *pronoun*, a word that substitutes for the name of a person, place or thing. For example:

The winner of the County Tiddlywinks Championship is *you!*

winner = *you* (*you* is a substitute for the name of the winner, and therefore a pronoun)

Whoever put the frog in my bed is *someone* with a very bad sense of humour.

Whoever put the frog in my bed = *someone* (*someone* is a substitute for the name of the unknown prankster and therefore a pronoun)

You can't do much wrong when you complete linking-verb sentences with descriptions or with nouns. However, you can do a lot wrong when you complete a linking-verb sentence with a pronoun. In the next section, we'll show you how to avoid common errors with linking verbs and pronouns.

Placing the Proper Pronoun in the Proper Place

How do you choose the correct pronoun for a sentence with a linking verb? Think of a linking verb sentence as reversible. That is, the pronoun you put after a linking verb should be the same kind of pronoun that you put before a linking verb. First, however, we look at some examples with a noun, where you can't make a mistake. Read these sentence pairs:

Rashid was a *resident* of Nottingham.

A *resident* of Nottingham was *Rashid.*

Bill has always been a *keen supporter* of his local football team.

A *keen supporter* of his local football team has always been *Bill.*

Both sentences in each pair mean the same thing, and both are correct. Now look at pronouns:

The winner of the election is *him!*

Him is the winner of the election!

Uh oh. Something's wrong. You can't say *him is;* you say *he is.* Because you have a linking verb (*is*), you must put the same word after the linking verb that you would put before the linking verb. Try it again:

The winner of the election is *he!*

He is the winner of the election!

Now you've got the correct ending for your sentence. If you pay attention to linking verbs, you'll choose the right pronoun for your sentence. Subject pronouns are *I, you, he, she, it, we, they, who* and *whoever.* Pronouns that are not allowed to be subjects include *me, him, her, us* and *them.*

The previous examples are in formal English, not conversational English. In conversational English, this exchange is OK:

Who's there?

It's me.

In formal English, the exchange goes like this:

Who is there?

It is I.

Because of the linking verb *is,* you need the same kind of pronoun before and after the linking verb. You can't start a sentence with *me* (unless you're in a Tarzan movie). But you can start a sentence with *I.*

Now you've probably, with your sharp eyes, found a flaw here. You can't reverse the last reply and say

I is it.

I takes a different verb – *am*. Both *is* and *am* are forms of the verb *to be* (one of the most peculiar creations in the entire language). So, yes, you sometimes have to adjust the verb when you reverse a sentence with a form of *to be* in it. But the idea is the same: *I* can be a subject, but *me* can't.

Unfortunately, *The winner of the election is he!* doesn't sound natural with the correct form of the pronoun, does it? There's a good reason for this (apart from the reason that you wouldn't use a pronoun in this sentence in any case): very few people get the pronouns right when they speak. So, when you've learned how to spot the problem, the real solution is often not to use the right pronoun, but to put a noun in instead:

> The winner of the election is Edgar Edwards!

> [Who's there?] It's Damian.

Pronouns are divided into groups called *cases*. One group includes all the pronouns that may be subjects. These are said to be in the nominative, or subject, case. The pronoun that follows the linking verb should also be in the nominative, or subject, case. Another group includes the pronouns that act as objects – those in the accusative, or objective, case. (You'll notice as you read on that grammarians frequently have difficulty agreeing on one name for anything.) Avoid object pronouns after linking verbs. (For more information on pronoun case, see Chapter 17.)

Lights! Camera! Action Verb!

Linking verbs are important, but you're likely to get very bored just sitting around *being* all the time. You have to *do* something eventually. It is here that action verbs come into the picture. Everything that is not *being* is *action*, at least in the verb world. Unlike the giant equals sign associated with linking verbs (see 'Linking Verbs: The Giant Equals Sign', earlier in the chapter), something *happens* with an action verb:

> Yasmin *slapped* Damian when he tried to kiss her. (*Slapped* is an action verb.)

> Edgar *will finish* his pizza as soon as his sneezing fit *ends*. (*Will finish* and *ends* are action verbs.)

> According to Ms Stakes, Lucinda *has made* at least 16 grammatical errors in her first two sentences. (*Has made* is an action verb.)

You can define action verbs as all the verbs that don't express being. Don't let the name *action* fool you. Some action verbs aren't particularly energetic: *think*, *sit*, *stay*, *have*, *sleep*, *dream*, and so forth. Besides describing the perfect lazy vacation, these words are also action verbs! Think of the definition this way: if the verb is *not* a giant equals sign (a linking verb), it's an action verb.

Getting by with a Little Help from My Verbs

You've probably noticed that some of the verbs identified throughout this chapter (such as *slapped* and *ends*) are single words and others (such as *will finish* and *has made*) are made up of several words. The extra words are called *auxiliary verbs*. They have a supporting role. Like the extras in a play or film, they don't get to say anything. But they do help the main verb express meaning, usually changing the time, or *tense*, of the action. (For more on tense, see Chapter 3.)

Here are some sentences with auxiliary verbs:

> Ellie *will have sung* five arias from that opera by the interval.
>
> (In *will have sung*, *sung* is the main verb; *will* and *have* are auxiliary verbs.)
>
> Bill *should have refused* a fifth piece of cake, but his greed simply *would* not *be denied*.
>
> (In *should have refused*, *refused* is the main verb; *should* and *have* are auxiliary verbs. In *would be denied*, *denied* is the main verb; *would* and *be* are auxiliary verbs.)

 Distinguishing between helping verbs and main verbs isn't particularly important, as long as you find all the bits when you're identifying the verb in a sentence. If you find only part of the verb, you may confuse action verbs with linking verbs. You need to keep these two types of verb straight when you choose an ending for your sentence (see 'Placing the Proper Pronoun in the Proper Place', earlier in this chapter).

To decide whether you have an action verb or a linking verb, look at the main verb (not at the auxiliary verbs). If the main verb expresses action, the whole verb is action, even if one of the auxiliary verbs is a form of *to be*. For example:

> is going
>
> will be sung
>
> has been painted
>
> should be strangled

are all action verbs, not linking verbs, because *going*, *sung*, *painted* and *strangled* express action.

Pop the Question: Locating the Verb

When you try to crack a sentence, you should always start by identifying the verb. To find the verb, read the sentence and ask two questions:

- ✔ What's happening?
- ✔ What is? (*or* What word is acting as a giant equals sign?)

If you get an answer to the first question, you have an action verb. If you get an answer to the second question, you have a linking verb. For example, in the sentence

> Archie flew around the room and then swooped into his cage for a birdseed snack.

if you ask 'What's happening?', your answer is *flew* and *swooped. Flew* and *swooped* are action verbs.

If you ask 'What is?', you get no answer because there's no linking verb in the sentence.

Try another:

> Bill's new tattoo will be larger than his previous 15 tattoos.

What's happening? Nothing. You have no action verb. What is? Look for the equals sign: Tattoo = larger. The words that stand for the equals sign are *will be.* So *will be* is a linking verb.

Pop the question and find the verbs in the following sentences. Then identify the verbs as action or linking.

A. Bibi loved the cat, even though the cat had scratched her.

B. After days of inactivity, Sandy is taking a skiing holiday.

C. The twisted frown on Ellie's face seemed strange, but she was listening to Edgar's tuba solo on her headphones.

Answers: A. *loved* and *had scratched* are both action verbs. B. *is taking* is an action verb. C. *seemed* is a linking verb and *was listening* is an action verb.

Strictly speaking, the term *verb* is the name of the part of speech. In the sentence, the action or being is expressed by the *predicate*. (The *subject* is who or what you're talking about and the *predicate* is what you're saying about the subject.) The *complete predicate* is everything that you say about the subject. The *simple predicate* is the plain old verb. We've never been able to figure out why anyone would want to identify the complete predicate. The simple predicate, yes, but the simple predicate is the same as the verb, so you may as well call it the verb and be done with it.

To Be or Not to Be: Infinitives

Here and there in this chapter, we say 'the verb *to be*'. Here, *to be* is an *infinitive*. The verb part (*be*) can be used in two ways: with *to* in front of it (when it's called a *to-infinitive*) and with an auxiliary verb (when it's called a *bare infinitive* because there's no *to*). Here are some examples:

> Ellie likes to sing. (*to sing* is a to-infinitive)

> It isn't too late *to write* your essay. (*to write* is a *to-infinitive*)

> All Bibi did all afternoon was *play* with the box her present had been packed in. (*play* is a *bare infinitive*)

Infinitives are the great-grandparents of verb families. Everything in the verb family descends from the infinitive but, like the retired elderly relative who sits on the porch all day, infinitives don't perform any verb jobs in a sentence. In fact, if they do show up in the sentence, they take on a different job – like a retired plumber who refuses to fix a dripping tap but keeps redecorating the spare room. Infinitives may act as subjects or objects. They may also describe other words in the sentence. (There's more on infinitives in Chapter 24.)

The way it's suppose to be?

Do these sentences look right to you?

> Damian never does anything he's *suppose* to do.

> Rashid *use* to put the rubbish out, but he's so tired when he gets home from work now that he forgets.

If so, look again. They're both wrong. Look more closely at the italicised verbs: *suppose* and *use*. These represent what people hear but not what the speaker is actually trying to say. The correct words to use in these instances are *supposed* and *used* – past tense forms. Here are the correct sentences:

> Damian never does anything he's *supposed* to do.

> Rashid *used* to put the rubbish out, but he's so tired when he gets home from work now that he forgets.

One lump or two?

Here's a spelling tip: some words can be written as one word or two but have a different meaning in each case. Look at these pairs:

> *Maybe* means 'perhaps'.

> *May be* means 'is possibly'.

Example: Mortimer thinks Rashid *may be* the best accountant who has ever worked for him, but Rashid is overwhelmed with work and thinks *maybe* he should have taken the other job he was offered.

> *Sometime* means 'at an unspecified point in time'.

> *Some time* means 'a period of time'.

Example: Edgar asked Yasmin if she'd go out with him *sometime*, but not today because he has promised to spend *some time* with his mother this evening.

(*Someplace* and *some place* work in the same way.)

> *Everyday* means 'ordinary, common'.

> *Every day* means 'occurring daily'.

Example: Edgar loves *everyday* activities such as cooking, cleaning, and sewing. He helps his mother with them *every day*.

> *Anyway* means 'in any event'.

> *Any way* means 'a way, some sort of way'.

Example: Lucinda can't think of *any way* to get Damian to ask her out, so she's thinking of asking him. Yasmin thinks Damian's bad news, but knows that Lucinda will date him *anyway*.

> *Altogether* means 'extremely, totally'.

> *All together* means 'as one'.

Example: Damian was *altogether* disgusted. The prettiest girls were *all together* in the corner and hadn't noticed that he'd arrived.

This last example is particularly interesting, as it belongs to a little group of 'all' pairs, including *all ready* (everybody or everything is ready) *and already* (by a specified time, usually earlier than you were expecting).

Example: It's nine o'clock *already*, so if you're not *all ready* in the next five minutes we're going to miss the train!

But there's one word that the sticklers won't allow to exist at all: *alright*. We're supposed to write *all right*. (You may find that your dictionary is kinder and allows *alright* to be a 'variant spelling' of *all right*.) The sticklers have missed the point, of course. As you well know, if someone asks you how the tricky bit in your solo went last night and you say (with a smile on your face) that you got it *all right* (you didn't make any mistakes), they'll pat you on the back and congratulate you. If you say (glumly) that it went *alright* (. . . ish), they'll know that it was really a bit of a disaster (or, at least, that it should have gone a lot better considering how much hard work you put into it) and that you need to be taken out to lunch to cheer you up. So **I'm** starting a society for the promotion of the rights of *alright* (and the rights of people to buy me lunch), but **you** shouldn't use it if any sticklers are going to read what you've written.

The most important thing to know about infinitives is this: when you pop the question to find the verb, don't choose an infinitive as your answer. If you do, you'll miss the real verb or verbs in the sentence. Other than that, forget about infinitives!

OK, you can't forget about infinitives completely. Here's something else you should know. In (very) formal English, you're not supposed to split them in half (which is why this 'mistake' is called a *split infinitive*). Of course, to split it you have to have *to* in front of it (we're not talking about splitting bare infinitives here), and that makes it two words. And there's no good reason why you shouldn't put another word between them, like this:

> Lucinda vowed *to really study* if she got the chance to take her exams again.

Although this is exactly what most people say, sticklers consider it incorrect. They consider *to study* to be an unsplittable unit – one infinitive. Now that you know this rule, you'll begin to notice that everybody splits infinitives. If you read a newspaper (even the boring ones) you'll find split infinitives. You'll find them in your textbooks and in those programmes on TV that have nothing but brainy people sitting around talking. Why? Well, where else can you put *really?*

> Lucinda vowed really to study if she ever got the chance to take her exams again. (Doesn't sound quite right, does it?)

> Lucinda vowed to study really if she ever got the chance to take her exams again. (Yuk!)

So you have a choice. You can relax and split infinitives all you want, or you can spend hours thinking up inventive places to put words that feel as though they belong in the middle of an infinitive (the end of the sentence is often good) or thinking of other ways to say the same thing (like *Lucinda vowed to study really hard if . . .*) so that you can follow the rule and feel totally superior to the professional journalists. The choice is yours. (If you want to know why we got stuck with this loony rule, see Chapter 3, which tells you a little bit about the history of the English language and this rule in particular.)

See if you can pick the right version from the options given in brackets:

A. 'I can't make head or tail of these accounts, and I have to have this [already/all ready] by Friday,' moaned Rashid.

B. 'You should take a break and go out to lunch,' suggested Alice. 'You work through lunch [everyday/every day].'

C. 'I've eaten my sandwich [already/all ready], and [anyway/any way] I've got too much work to do.'

D. 'Well, I think it's [altogether/all together] too much to expect one person to do,' said Alice. '[Maybe/May be] you should ask Mortimer to get you an assistant.'

E. 'There [maybe/may be] too much to do, but I can't complain when I've only been here a week.'

F. 'But [*everyone/every one*] here complains about their workload [*every-day/every day*]. [*Maybe/May be*] if we went to see Mortimer [*altogether/all together*] [*sometime/some time*] he'd listen.'

G. But Rashid wasn't listening. 'I wonder if there's [*anyway/any way*] to avoid jail for tax evasion,' he mumbled.

ANSWERS: A: all ready; B: every day; C: already; anyway; D: altogether; Maybe; E: may be; F: everyone (OK, that was sneaky as we haven't discussed this one, but if you're getting the hang of these it shouldn't have been too difficult); every day; Maybe; all together; sometime; G: any way.

Chapter 3

Relax! Understanding Verb Tense

. . . .

In This Chapter

▶ Expressing time with verbs

▶ Understanding the meanings of verb tenses

▶ Applying the correct verb tenses

▶ Forming the most common irregular verbs

. . . .

You can tell the time in lots of ways: look at a clock, dial a number and listen to that annoying voice ('At the third stroke the time will be . . .'), or check the verb. The verb shows the action or state of being in the sentence. In English, the verb also shows the time the action or 'being' took place. (For more information on finding the verb in a sentence, see Chapter 2.)

In some lucky languages (Thai, for example), the verb has basically one form. Whether the sentence is about the past, the present or the future doesn't matter – the verb is the same. Extra words – *yesterday*, *tomorrow*, *now* and so forth – indicate the time. Other languages go to the opposite extreme – for example, each verb in Latin has 120 different forms! English isn't as bad as Latin, but it's more complicated than Thai.

English has six tenses. Or two. OK, it depends which grammar books you look in. This is really about arguments between experts and how they think we should describe the language. (They have to have *something* to do.) It's not about how we use the language, so you can stop reading and skip this bit if you like. Here's the deal. If you define a tense as a whole new set of forms for the verb, English only has two: present and past. Everything else is done using these two tenses with a little help from their friends (the auxiliary verbs) and some fancy footwork, and this is all called *aspect* rather than *tense*. Is all this a bit of a shock? If you learned a lot of your grammar by studying a foreign language (one that *does* have lots of tenses), you may think about tenses English by comparing them with the tenses in the foreign languages you've studied. So we stick with the traditional set of six.

Three of the six English tenses (*present*, *past* and *future*) are called *simple*. In this chapter, we explain the simple tenses in some detail, such as the difference between *I go* and *I am going*. The other three tenses are called *perfect* (*present perfect*, *past perfect* and *future perfect*). We touch on the basics of the perfect tenses in this chapter, then dig a little more deeply into the present perfect tense. The other two perfect tenses – past and future – are far less common than the present perfect, so we save them for Chapter 18.

Simplifying Matters: The Simple Tenses

The three simple tenses are present, past and future. Each of the simple tenses (just to make things even *more* fun) has two forms. One is the unadorned, no-frills, plain tense. This form doesn't have a separate name; it is just called *present*, *past* or *future*. It shows actions or states of being at a point in time, but it doesn't always pin down a specific moment. The other form is called *progressive*. The progressive form shows actions or a state of being *in progress*.

Present tense

The present tense tells you what is going on right now. It describes an action or state of being that is occurring now, or that is generally true, or that is always happening. Verbs are sometimes laid out as tables showing what form the verb takes depending who the subject is. (You can see tables for the tenses of the verb *to be* later in this chapter.) But for most English verbs the tables are pretty boring because the verb doesn't change much. It will go something like this: I *work*, you *work*, he (or she or it) *works*, we *work*, you *work*, they *make a fortune* . . . er, they *work*.

As you can see, there's a version with an extra *s* on the end (*works*), which occurs only once, but mostly it's just work! work! work! Take a look at these sentences in the no-frills present tense:

What does Lucinda's cat *want*? It just *sits* there and *stares* at me. (*Want*, *sits* and *stares* are all in the present tense.)

Edgar *plans* nothing for New Year's Eve because he never *has* a date. (*Plans* and *has* are in the present tense.)

The present *progressive* form is similar in that it's talking about things happening now, but it often implies a process (so we're doing it now but we might have started it yesterday and be going to finish it some time tomorrow – if then). Here the verb has a new form (*working* or *making*) but needs a little help from the verb *to be*, and that's the bit that has more than one version of itself (I *am* working, you *are* working and so on).

The –*ing* form of the verb is traditionally called the *present participle* (more on these later in this chapter). Here are two sentences in the present progressive form:

> President Edwards and his beautiful assistant Yasmin *are* arranging a chess tournament for the summer vacation. (*Are arranging* is in the present progressive form.)

> Sandy *is skiing* far too fast down that slope. (*Is skiing* is in the present progressive form.)

> 'I *am doing* my homework,' shouts Lucinda, but her parents know that she *is reading* a magazine instead. (*Am doing* and *is reading* are in the present progressive form.)

The difference between the two is subtle. We go into more details about using these forms in the following sections.

Past tense

The past tense tells you what happened before the present time. This simple tense also has two forms – plain *past* and *past progressive*. The past tense is formed by adding –*ed* to the basic form of the verb (*walk* becomes *walked*). And that's it. There aren't even two forms of the verb in the past tense, just the one (*I walked, he walked*). The bad news is that there are a lot of verbs that have a past that doesn't end –*ed*. We call them *irregular* verbs, and we come back to them in the section 'It's All Highly Irregular' later in this chapter.

Here are some sentences in the plain past tense:

> When the elastic in Ms. Stakes' girdle *snapped*, we all *woke* up. (*Snapped* and *woke* are in the past tense.)

> Sandy *got* a job as a part-time lifeguard at the local swimming pool and *started* last Saturday. (*Got* and *started* are in the past tense – *got* is irregular.)

The past progressive form consists of the present tense of the verb to be (*I am*, *you are* and so on) with the –*ing* form of the verb:

> While Bill *was sleeping*, Rover *was* completely *destroying* the sofa. (*Was sleeping* and *was destroying* are in the progressive form of the past tense.)

> Lucinda's friends *were planning* a surprise party for her birthday. (*Were planning* is in the progressive form of the past tense.)

The *-ing* form of the verb is often called the *present participle*. The examples in the preceding section used it to form the *present* progressive. But in this section the examples use it to form the *past* progressive. (And we're about to use it to form the *future* progessive!) So what's 'present' about it? Nothing. (It would make more sense to call it a *progressive* participle.) The experts are aware of this. Some of them just say that it's 'traditionally' called the present participle and slink off looking a bit embarrassed; others call it the *-ing form* (which is a bit ugly to look at and hard to say, but at least doesn't put on airs and claim to be doing something that it isn't). So, if you know perfectly well what an *-ing* does but can't remember the term *present participle*, don't worry. If challenged, do your best to look superior and explain (looking down your nose if possible) that the experts don't call it *that* any more. This makes you look knowledgeable and up on the latest. But in case you want to be able to talk grammar with people who aren't quite as up-to-date as you are, we go on using both terms to familiarise you with them.

You can't really go wrong with the past tense, but one very common mistake is to mix past and present tenses in the same story. Here's an example:

> So I go to the restaurant looking for Lucinda because I want to tell her about Edgar's date with Yasmin. I walk in and who do I see? Brad Pitt! So I went up to him and asked him for his autograph.

The speaker started in the present tense – no problem. Even though an event is clearly over, the present tense is OK if you want to make a story more dramatic. (See the sidebar 'The historical present', later in this chapter.) But the last sentence switches gears – suddenly we're in the past tense. Problem! Don't change tenses in the middle of a story. And if you *must* ask for his autograph at least have the good manners to wait until he's finished eating!

Future tense

The *future tense* talks about what hasn't happened yet. This simple tense is the only one that always needs helping verbs to express meaning, even for the plain no-frills version. (That's why the experts who say that there are only two tenses say that this isn't really a tense at all.) Future tenses also come in two forms: the *future* and the *future progressive*.

For the plain form of the future put *will* or *shall* (or, informally, *'ll* – which is short for *will* or *shall*) in front of the basic form of the verb (*will make, shall work* and so on). Look at these sentences:

> Damian's wife *will lose* patience with him soon. (*Will lose* is in the future tense.)

Ellie *will sing* at Lucinda's party. (*Will sing* is in the future tense.)

I'*ll make* a cup of cocoa. ('*ll make* is in the future tense.)

For the future progressive, we put *will be* or *shall be* (or '*ll be*) in front of the present participle (the *–ing* form of the verb) like this:

While she waits for her exam results, Yasmin *will be considering* her options for the future. (*Will be considering* is in the progressive form of the future tense.)

I'*ll be eating* out tonight. ('*ll be eating* is in the progressive form of the future tense.)

Find the verbs and sort them into simple present, past and future tenses.

A. When the rain starts, the performance at the open-air theatre stops and everyone runs for cover.

B. Shall I take an umbrella?

C. Spot ate Bill's dinner and buried his slippers in the garden.

Answers: In sentence A, *starts*, *stops* and *runs* are present tense verbs. In sentence B, *shall take* is in the future tense. In sentence C, *ate* and *buried* are in the past tense.

Now find the verbs and sort them into present progressive, past progressive and future progressive forms.

A. Only 65 million years ago, dinosaurs were living on the earth.

B. We are taking the children to their grandparents for the weekend.

C. They will be flying to Bermuda for their honeymoon.

Answers: In sentence A, *were living* is a past progressive verb. In sentence B, *are taking* is in the present progressive form. In sentence C, *will be flying* is in the future progressive form.

Using the Tenses Correctly

What's the difference between each pair of simple tense forms? Not a whole lot. People often interchange these forms without creating any problems. But shades of difference in meaning do exist.

Present and present progressive

The single-word form of the present tense may be used for things that are generally true at the present time but not necessarily happening right now. For example:

Bill *attends* wrestling matches every Saturday.

If you call Bill on Saturday, you'll get the annoying message he recorded on his answering machine because he's at the wrestling match (*attends* is in present tense). You may also get this message on a Thursday (or on another day) and it is still correct, even though on Thursdays Bill stays home to watch football on television. Now read this sentence:

Bill *is playing* hide-and-seek with his dog Spot.

This sentence means that right now as you read this sentence (*is playing* is in the progressive form of the present tense), Bill is running around the living room looking for Spot, who is easy to find because he always hides behind the sofa.

Past and past progressive

The difference between the plain past tense and the past progressive tense is pretty much the same as in the present tense. The single-word form often shows what happened in the past more generally. The progressive form may pinpoint action or state of being at a specific time or occurring in the past on a regular basis.

Lucinda *went* to the shops and *bought* gifts for all her friends.

This sentence means that at some point in the past Lucinda splurged on presents for her friends (*went* and *bought* are in past tense).

While Lucinda *was shopping*, her friends *were planning* the food for her surprise party.

This sentence means that Lucinda has chosen her friends well because, at the exact moment she was spending her pocket money on them, her friends were planning something nice for her (*was shopping* and *were planning* are in the progressive form of the past tense).

Damian *was losing* so much money at the casino that his wife *was feeling* desperate.

The historical present

Not surprisingly, you use the present tense for actions that are currently happening. But you also use the present tense for some actions that happened a long time ago and for some actions that never happened at all. The historical present is a way to write about history or literature:

> On 13 May 1940, Winston Churchill *tells* the nation he has 'nothing to offer but blood, toil, tears and sweat'.

> Harry Potter *faces* three tests when he *represents* Hogwarts in the tournament.

In the first sentence, *tells* is in the present tense, even though the sentence concerns events that occurred decades ago. Here the historical present makes the history more dramatic. In the second sentence, *faces* and *represents* are in the present tense because, for each reader who opens the book, the story begins anew. The book, and therefore the story it contains, always exists for us in the present. The story is always happening, any time we want to read it, even though Harry Potter is a fictional character and the events never happened in real life.

This sentence refers to one of Damian's bad habits, his gambling and the effect it was having on his marriage (*was losing* and *was feeling* are in the progressive form of the past tense). The gambling and the feeling desperate were repeated on a daily basis, over and over again (until, finally, Damian's wife left him).

Future and future progressive

You won't find much difference between the future and future progressive, except that the progressive can give you more of a sense of being in the middle of things. For example,

> Rashid *will play* Hamlet with the local amateur dramatics society.

(where *will play* is in the future tense) may be an official announcement that Rashid has got the part, even if rehearsals haven't started yet and the performances are a few months in the future. But

> Rashid *will be playing* Hamlet with the local amateur dramatics society.

(where *will be playing* is in the progressive form of the future tense) can suggest that we're much nearer to the event (you wouldn't be surprised if this sentence had *tomorrow* on the end of it) or closer to Rashid (he's a friend of ours and we'll go to see him perform and we'll read the review in the local paper).

If you're having difficulty understanding the difference between the two forms of the simple tenses, don't lose sleep over it. You're probably more aware of the differences than you think you are (even if you can't explain them in words) and, for everyday purposes, it's unlikely that any great misunderstandings will arise.

Perfecting Grammar: The Perfect Tenses

Just like the simple tenses, each of these – the *present perfect*, *past perfect* and *future perfect* – has a no-frills version called by the name of the tense and a progressive form. The progressive is a little more immediate than the plain form, expressing an action or state of being in progress.

The plain forms are made up of the present, past, or future of the verb *have* (that's what makes them present, past, or future) with the *past participle* (also called the *–ed* form of the verb, because that's what it is and because, as you can see, it's not just used in the past tense – same problem as with the name of the present participle). This is often exactly the same as the past tense of the verb: in *I walked*, *walked* is the past tense; in *I have walked*, *walked* is the past participle. But it doesn't have to be (more on this when we talk about irregular verbs in the section 'All Highly Irregular' later in this chapter). Here are some examples of these tenses:

> You *have* worked (*have* is the *present* tense of *have*, so this is the *present* perfect tense).

> You *had* worked (*had* is the *past* tense of *have*, so this is the *past* perfect tense).

> You *will have* worked (*will have* is the *future* tense of *have*, so this is the *future* perfect tense).

The progressive forms also start with the present, past, or future of the verb *have*, but then they add *been* and finish with (you've guessed it!) the present participle (or *–ing* form):

> You *have* been working (progressive form of the present perfect)

> You *had* been working (progressive form of the past perfect)

> You *will have* been working (progressive form of the future perfect)

For a full discussion of the correct sequence with past and future perfect tenses, see Chapter 18.

Present perfect and present perfect progressive

The two present perfect forms show actions or states of being that began in the past but are still going on in the present. These forms are used whenever any action or state of being spans two time zones – past and present.

These sentences use the present perfect tense:

> Damian *has lost* almost every penny of his wife's inheritance. (*Has lost* is in the present perfect tense.)

> Bill's dogs *have barked* all night. (*Have barked* is in the present perfect tense.)

Here are some examples of the progressive form:

> Edgar *has been studying* the physics of tiddlywinks for years without winning once. (*Has been studying* is in the progressive form of the present perfect tense.)

> Bill's neighbours *have been trying* to sleep all night. (*Have been trying* is in the progressive form of the present perfect tense.)

Past perfect and past perfect progressive

These forms, the past perfect and past perfect progressive, place an action in the past in relation to another action even further back in the past. Here are a couple of examples of the past perfect tense:

> After she *had sewn* up the wound, the doctor realised that her watch was missing! (*Had sewn* is in the past perfect tense.)

> They *had searched* for it for ten minutes before the doctor remembered that she *had taken* it to be mended that morning. (*Had searched* and *had taken* are in the past perfect tense.)

Compare the preceding sentences with examples of the past perfect progressive:

> The doctor *had been worrying* about the consequences of leaving her watch inside the patient. (*Had been worrying* is in the progressive form of the past perfect tense.)

We *had been thinking* of taking a cruise for a number of years before we finally found the time to do it. (*Had been thinking* is in the progressive form of the past perfect tense.)

For more information about how to use the past perfect, see Chapter 18.

Future perfect and future perfect progressive

The future perfect looks ahead to a point in the future and talks about something that hasn't happened yet but that we expect will have happened by the time in the future that we're thinking of.

Here are some examples of the plain version of the future perfect:

'By then, Lucinda *will have passed* all her exams,' mused her mother. (*Will have passed* is in the future perfect tense.)

'If you go on at this rate, you*'ll have wasted* 14.42 years of your life by the time you retire,' Bill's brother insisted as he checked his calculator. (*'ll have wasted* is in the future perfect tense.)

And here are some sentences using the progressive form of the future perfect tense:

Next Saturday, Lucinda's parents *will have been living* in their house for 25 years. (*Will have been living* is in the progressive form of the future perfect tense.)

Hurry up! They*'ll have been waiting* for us for over an hour by the time we get there! (*'ll have been waiting* is in the progressive form of the future perfect tense.)

For more information on how to use the future perfect tense, see Chapter 18.

So there we are. We've sorted out the six tenses all neat and tidy. But what happens if you really believe that there are only two? Well, you have the present tense and the past tense, and each of these has a *perfective aspect* (what we've been calling the perfect tenses) and all four have *progressive aspects*. And the future doesn't really get included. It's there, but not part of the family. It's as though Mr and Mrs Tense are sitting in their big house with its wonderful aspect and their progressive attitudes and their oh-so-perfect children, and then one of the boys brings home a girl from that awful Future family. You can hear the silence. If she's spoken of at all (and of course she will be, but mostly behind her back), she'll always be just The Future. The poor girl's never going to count as a proper Tense. Ah well, the course of true love never did run smooth, and what's in a name?

Using the Present Perfect Tense Correctly

This mixture of present (*has*, *have*) and past is a clue to its use: the present perfect tense ties the past to the present. There is the suggestion that whatever happened in the past is still going on or still connected in some way to us in the present. Look at this sentence:

> Ellie *has gone* to the cafeteria for lunch every day for six years, and *has* not yet *found* one edible item.

This sentence means that Ellie started eating lunch in the cafeteria six years ago and, although she hates the food, she's *still* eating lunch there every day – this has carried on to the present day. (You have to wonder why!)

Compare these two possible responses to the question 'Where's Yasmin?':

> She *went* to the library.

> She*'s gone* to the library.

The simple past *went* in the first sentence tells us of a completed past act. We know that Yasmin went to the library, but we don't know what she did after that. She may still be there or she may have gone home – her connection to us has ended for the time being. The present perfect *has gone* (shortened to *'s gone*) tells us something a little different: that she went to the library and we have reason to think that she's still there or that we're expecting her back (which connects her to us in the present).

Some tense pairs

Helping verbs, as well as main verbs, have tenses. Some of the most common pairs are *can/could* and *may/might*. The first verb in each pair is in the present tense; the second is in the past tense. If you *can* imagine, you are speaking about the present. If you *could* imagine, you are speaking about the past. More and more people interchange these helping verbs at random, but technically the verbs do express time. So remember:

Now you *may* talk about how much you hate writing school reports.

Yesterday you *might* have had a picnic if it hadn't rained.

After six years of lessons, you *can* finally dance a mean tango.

No one ever danced as well as Fred Astaire *could* in those old musicals.

Which one is correct?

   A. Edgar moved into Lucinda's street in 2003 and lived there ever since.

   B. Edgar has moved into Lucinda's street in 2003 and lived there ever since.

   C. Edgar moved into Lucinda's street in 2003 and has lived there ever since.

Answer: Sentence C has the right combination. You need the simple past for *moved* because his move into a new home is completed (even though he sometimes felt that it never would be) and you need the present perfect for *has lived* to provide a connection to the present because Edgar's still living there now.

Present Participles

Participles are not very mysterious; as you may guess from the spelling, a *parti*ciple is simply a *part* of the verb. Each verb has two participles – a present participle (the *–ing* form) and a past participle (the *–ed* form). The sections earlier in this chapter explain how the *–ing* form of the verb is used in the progressive forms of the tenses. And we've seen how the *–ed* form helps to form the perfect tenses.

If you're thinking that there must be a catch, you're right. The present participle is fairly straightforward (just add *–ing*), but sometimes the spelling isn't quite what you'd expect. A consonant on the end of a verb may be doubled before adding *–ing* (as in *swim* and *swimming*) or a *y* may change to *i* before adding *–ed* (as in *bully* and *bullied*), and an *e* may be lost (as in *file* and *filing*). Table 3-1 shows a selection of regular participles. If you're not sure how to spell a participle, check in a dictionary: the entry for the verb will also give the participles and any other odd things that you may need to know.

Table 3-1	Examples of Regular Participles	
Verb	*Present Participle*	*Past Participle*
ask	asking	asked
beg	begging	begged
call	calling	called
dally	dallying	dallied
empty	emptying	emptied
file	filing	filed
fill	filling	filled

It's All Highly Irregular

So far, we haven't said much about irregular verbs, although we've used one or two in example sentences. You probably didn't think twice about them because you're so used to using them every day. The most used verb of all time is *to be*, which is the most irregular of the lot!

To be

Possibly the weirdest verb in the English language, the verb *to be* changes more frequently than any other. Here it is, tense by tense. Note that the singular forms are in the first column and plural forms are in the second column. Singulars are for one person or thing and plurals for more than one. *You* is listed twice because it may refer to one person or to a group. (This can cause confusion, which is why people sometimes add '. . . I don't mean 'you' personally . . .' to make it clear that they didn't mean any insult to the person they were speaking to – they were just insulting their whole family or all their work colleagues!)

Present Tense

Singular	*Plural*
I am	we are
you are	you are
he, she, it is	they are

Past Tense

Singular	*Plural*
I was	we were
you were	you were
he, she, it was	they were

Future Tense

Singular	*Plural*
I shall be	we shall be
you will be	you will be
he, she, it will be	they will be

Present Perfect

Singular	*Plural*
I have been	we have been
you have been	you have been
he, she, it has been	they have been

Past Perfect

Singular	*Plural*
I had been	we had been
you had been	you had been
he, she, it had been	they had been

Future Perfect

Singular	*Plural*
I shall have been	we shall have been
you will have been	you will have been
he, she, it will have been	they will have been

As you can see, we've given the first person (singular and plural) of the future tenses as *shall*, not *will*. The use of *shall* is gradually being lost (aided, no doubt, by the fact that we usually abbreviate them both to *'ll* when we're speaking). You are still likely to hear *shall* rather than *will* when someone asks a question:

> Shall I open a window?

> Shall we take a taxi?

However, even this is usual only in the south of England – in Scotland or Ireland (to name but two places), *Will I open a window?* and *Will we take a taxi?* are considered correct. So this isn't something to worry too much about.

If this is something that interests you, you may like to know that reversing the usage (putting *will* in the first person and *shall* in the second and third) expresses determination. You should imagine saying the *shall* in this sentence emphatically as you wave your magic wand to make absolutely certain that everything turns out as planned:

> You *shall* go to the ball, Cinderella!

Irregular past tenses and past participles

This is where it gets interesting. Dozens of English verbs have irregular past tense forms, as well as irregular past participles. Sometimes an irregular past tense form is the same as its irregular past participle and sometimes it isn't, and an irregular past participle won't end in *–ed*. (Suddenly, calling them *–ed* form doesn't seem such an easy solution.) Don't panic! If you grew up speaking English, you know most of these already. It's unlikely that you'd ever worry about whether to say *I brought you a present* or *I bringed you (brung you?) a present* (most children figure this one out at a very young age), and because you probably use *eat–ate–have eaten* every day this one won't bother you a bit. It's the verbs we don't use very often that cause most problems (ones like *swim–swam–swum*).

In Table 3-2, the first column is the bare infinitive form of the verb (the form that would go with *to* in the *to-infinitive* – to laugh, to cry, to learn grammar and so on). The second column is the simple past tense. The third column is the past participle (the bit that would be the *–ed* form if it wasn't irregular), which is combined with *has* (singular) or *have* (plural) to form the present perfect tense. The past participle is also used with *had* to form the past perfect tense. (You can make up sentences using them in these tenses to help you get a feel for the ones you're not very familiar with.)

If you have questions about a verb that isn't listed here, check your dictionary.

Table 3-2	Some Irregular Past Tenses and Participles	
Verb	*Past*	*Past Participle*
begin	began	begun
bite	bit	bitten
break	broke	broken
bring	brought	brought
buy	bought	bought
catch	caught	caught
choose	chose	chosen
come	came	come
do	did	done

(continued)

Table 3-2 (continued)

Verb	Past	Past Participle
drive	drove	driven
eat	ate	eaten
fall	fell	fallen
fly	flew	flown
get	got	got
go	went	gone
know	knew	known
lay*	laid	laid
lead	led	led
lend	lent	lent
lie*	lay	lain
lose	lost	lost
ride	rode	ridden
ring	rang	rung
rise	rose	risen
run	ran	run
say	said	said
see	saw	seen
shake	shook	shaken
sing	sang	sung
sink	sank	sunk
sit	sat	sat
speak	spoke	spoken
steal	stole	stolen
swim	swam	swum
take	took	taken
write	wrote	written

For more on the meaning of lie and lay, see Chapter 22.

Who made these rules anyway?

The next time you try to decide whether you *had run* or *had ran* home, thank the Angles and the Saxons. These Germanic tribes invaded England about 1,500 years ago. Their languages blended into Anglo-Saxon, which came to be called Englisc (the *sc* was pronounced *sh*). Nowadays it's called Old English.

Old English lasted about 400 years; this English would look and sound like a foreign language to English-speakers today. Although it's gone, Old English isn't forgotten. Remnants remain in modern speech. You can thank (or blame) the Anglo-Saxons for most of the irregular verbs, including the fact that you say *ran* instead of *runned.*

In the Middle English period (1100 to about 1450) England was speckled with local dialects, each with its own vocabulary and sentence structure. Nobody studied grammar in school, and nobody worried about what was correct or incorrect. (There were a few more important items on the agenda, including starvation and the bubonic plague.)

In the fifteenth century the printing press was invented and the era of Modern English began. At this time, people were more interested than ever before in learning to read and also more interested in writing for publication. But writers faced a new problem. Sending one's words to a different part of the country might mean sending them off to someone whose vocabulary or sentence structure was different. Not to mention the fact that spelling was all over the place! Suddenly, rules seemed like a good idea. London was the centre of government and economic life – and also the centre of printing. So what the London printers decided was right soon *became* right. However, not until the eighteenth century did the rules really become set. Printers, in charge of turning handwriting into type, were guided by 'printers' bibles', also known as the rules.

Schoolmasters tried to whip the English language into shape by writing the rules down. But they grafted Latin concepts onto English, and it wasn't always a good fit. In fact, some of the loonier rules of English grammar come from this mismatch. In Latin, for example, you can't split an infinitive because an infinitive is a single word. In English, the infinitives you aren't allowed to split are formed with two words (*to* plus a *verb*, as in *to dance*, *to dream*) and there's really no reason why you shouldn't put another word between them if you want to. Nevertheless, the rule was handed down: no split infinitives.

Chapter 4

Who's Doing What? Finding the Subject

In This Chapter

▶ Understanding the role of the subject and subject–verb pairs

▶ Spotting the subject and subject–verb pairs in simple sentences

▶ Identifying the subject and subject–verb pairs in more challenging sentences

*I*n Chapter 2, we describe the sentence as a car carrying your meaning to the reader or listener. Verbs are the wheels of the car, and subjects are the drivers. Why do you need a subject? Can you imagine a car speeding down the road without a driver? Not possible, or, if possible, not a pleasant thought!

Who's Driving? or Why the Subject Is Important

All complete sentences contain verbs – words that express action or state of being. (For more information on verbs, see Chapter 2.) But you can't have an action in a vacuum. You can't have a naked, solitary state of being either. Someone or something must also be present in the sentence – the *who* or *what* you're talking about in relation to the action or state of being expressed by the verb. The someone or something doing the action or being talked about is the subject.

A 'someone' must be a person and a 'something' must be a thing, place, or idea. So the subject is usually a noun, because a noun is a person, place, thing, or idea. When it's not a noun, the subject is a pronoun – a word that substitutes for a noun such as *he, they, it* and so forth. (For more on pronouns, see Chapter 10.)

Teaming up: subject–verb pairs

Another way to think about the subject is to say that the subject is the 'who' or 'what' part of the subject–verb pair. The subject–verb pair is the main idea of the sentence, stripped to essentials. Take a look at a few sentences:

> *Lucinda gasped* at the price of the handbag.

In this sentence, *Lucinda gasped* is the main idea; it's also the subject–verb pair.

> *Mortimer will judge* the beauty contest only if *Lucinda competes.*

You should spot two subject–verb pairs in this sentence: *Mortimer will judge* and *Lucinda competes.*

Now try a sentence without action. This one describes a state of being, so it uses a linking verb:

> *Rashid has* always *been* an extremely conscientious worker.

The subject–verb pair is *Rashid has been.* Did you notice that it sounds incomplete? *Has been* is a linking verb, and linking verbs always need something after the verb to complete the idea (refer to Chapter 2 for more about linking verbs). The subject–verb pair in action-verb sentences can usually stand alone, but the subject–verb pair in linking-verb sentences usually can't.

Two for the price of one

Subjects and verbs pair off, but sometimes you get two (or more) for the price of one. For example:

> Bibi *burped* and *cried* after eating the earthworm.

You have two actions (*burped* and *cried*) and one person doing both (*Bibi*). *Bibi* is the subject of both *burped* and *cried.*

Here are some more examples:

> Rashid *worked* through his lunch hour again and *ate* a sandwich at his desk. (There are two verbs: *worked* and *ate.*)

> Edgar *worried* for days about what to buy Yasmin for her birthday and *thought* about flowers but finally *bought* a scarf with Ellie's help. (There are three verbs here: *worried, thought* and *bought.*)

You can also have two subjects (or more) and one verb. Here's an example:

Edgar and *Yasmin* went to the new restaurant on her birthday.

Here there's one action (*went*) and two people (*Edgar*, *Yasmin*) doing the action. So the verb *went* has two subjects.

Now take a look at some additional examples:

Fido and *Rover* ganged up on Spot yesterday. (*Fido* and *Rover* are both subjects, but there's only one verb: *ganged up*.)

Ellie, *Lucinda* and *Yasmin* decided to see a film together on Tuesday. (*Ellie*, *Lucinda* and *Yasmin* are all subjects; the verb is *decided*.)

Pop the Question: Locating the Subject–Verb Pair

Allow me to let you in on a little trick for pinpointing the subject–verb pair of a sentence: pop the question! (No, we're not asking you to propose.) The correct question is vital in the search for information, as all parents know:

WRONG QUESTION FROM PARENT: What did you do last night?

TEENAGER'S ANSWER: Nothing.

RIGHT QUESTION FROM PARENT: When you came in at midnight, were you hoping I wouldn't find out that you went to that club?

TEENAGER'S ANSWER: I didn't go to the club! I went to the cinema.

PARENT: Aha! You went to the cinema on a school night! You're grounded.

The first question to ask about a sentence is *What's the verb?* To find the verb, you need to ask *What's happening?* or *What is?* After you uncover the verb, ask *who* or *what* is doing it to form a new question. The answer to that one is the subject!

Try one:

Edgar practises his tuba every day.

1. Pop the question: What's happening? Answer: *practises*. *Practises* is the verb.

2. Pop the question: Who or what *practises?* Answer: *Edgar practises. Edgar* is the subject.

A pop quiz on popping the question. What are the subjects and verbs in the following sentences?

A. No matter what the weather, Lucinda never even considers wearing a hat.

B. Ellie will soon be smiling because Mortimer wants her to play the lead role in his new musical.

Answers: In sentence A, the verb is *considers* and the subject is *Lucinda.* In sentence B, there are two subject–verb pairs. The first verb is *will be smiling* and its subject is *Ellie.* The second verb is *wants* and the subject is *Mortimer.*

What's a Nice Subject Like You Doing in a Place Like This? Unusual Word Order

In this chapter, all the sample sentences up to this point are in the normal subject–verb order, which is (gasp) subject–verb. In other words, the subject usually comes before the verb. Not every sentence follows that order, though most do. Sometimes a subject hides out at the end of the sentence or in some other weird place.

If you pop the question and answer it according to the meaning of the sentence – not according to the word order – you'll be fine. The key is to put the subject questions (who? what?) in front of the verb. Then think about what the sentence is actually saying and answer the questions. And voilà! Your subject will appear.

Try this one:

Up the avenue and around the park trudged Edgar on his way to tea with Ms Stakes.

1. Pop the question: What's happening? What is? Answer: *trudged. Trudged* is the verb.

2. Pop the question: Who *trudged?* What *trudged?* Answer: *Edgar. Edgar* is the subject.

If you were answering by word order, you'd say *park.* But the *park* did not *trudge, Edgar trudged.* Always find the verb first, then look for the subject. And pay attention to meaning, not to placement in the sentence. Then you can't go wrong.

Me, myself and I

You can use *I* as a subject, but not *me* or *myself*.

> Wrong: Bill and me are going to take the dogs for a run. Bill and myself will soon be exhausted.

> Right: Bill and I are going to take the dogs for a run. Bill and I will soon be exhausted.

> Wrong: Rashid and myself are writing a play. Ellie and me are writing the incidental music.

> Right: Rashid and I are writing a play. Ellie and I are writing the incidental music.

Me doesn't perform actions; it receives actions. To put this rule another way: *me* is an object of some action or form of attention:

> He gave it to *me*.

> I think tea suits *me* better than coffee.

Myself is appropriate only for actions that double back on the person performing the action:

> I told *myself* not to be such a nerd!

> I took *myself* out to lunch to cheer myself up.

Myself may also be used for emphasis, along with the word *I*.

> I'll do it *myself*!

Can you find the subject–verb pair in the following sentence?

> Never am I going to tea with Ms Stakes again!

Answer: The verb is *am* and its subject is *I*.

Find That Subject! Detecting an Implied You

> Be quiet.

> Eat your vegetables.

> Do your homework.

What do these sentences have in common? Yes, they're all nagging comments you've heard all your life. More importantly, they're all commands. The verbs give orders: *be, eat, do*. So where's the subject in these sentences?

If you pop the question, here's what happens:

1. Pop the question: What's happening? What is? Answer: *be*, *eat*, *do*.

2. Pop the question: *Who be*, *eat*, *do*? Answer: Er . . .

The second question appears to have no answer, but you do know who's supposed to be doing these things (or not doing them): *you*. They mean *You* be quiet. *You* eat your vegetables. *You* do your homework. What's that you say? *You* isn't in the sentence? True. *You* is not written, but however much you try to pretend that they weren't talking to you, you know very well they were. *You* is meant. Grammarians say that the subject is *implied*. The subject is *you*, even though *you* isn't in the sentence and even though *you* don't intend to eat those horrible green vegetables.

Pop the questions and find the subject–verb pairs in these three sentences.

A. Lucinda was dancing the cha-cha and forgot to watch her feet.

B. Stop!

C. Over the bandleader and across five violin stands fell Lucinda with a crash.

Answers: In sentence A, *was dancing* and *forgot* are the verbs and *Lucinda* is the subject. In sentence B, *stop* is the verb and *you* is the *implied* subject. In sentence C, *fell* is the verb and *Lucinda* is the subject.

Striking Out on Their Own: Non-finite Verbs

Verbs in English grammar can be a little sneaky sometimes. In Chapter 3 we show how three forms – the basic form, the *–ing* form (the present participle), and the *–ed* form (the past participle) – are used to form tenses. When used in this way, they are called *finite* verbs. But they have a nasty habit of wandering off to do their own thing. The basic form is leader of the gang: it just can't help thinking of itself as an infinitive (often hanging out with a *to*). When they do this they're called *non-finite* verbs. Here are some examples:

To eat like that *is* bad for you, Bill.

Wiping her tears dramatically, Lucinda *blamed* Ms Stakes for her examination failure.

Having been *offered* a leading role, Ellie *was sticking* to a strict diet and *exercised* daily.

Suppose you pop the verb question (*What's happening? What is?*) and get *to eat* or *wiping* or *offered* for an answer. They look like reasonable guesses. But now pop the subject question: *What to eat? Who wiping? Who offered?* There's no real answer in these sentences. (Well, we can guess that Lucinda is probably wiping her own tears, but not because *wiping* is giving anything away.) You need to keep looking for the finite verbs: *is, blamed, was sticking* and *exercised*.

So what are those other verbs doing? *Anything they want!* That's the whole point of getting away from those wrinkly old finite verbs. They can hang out in all sorts of unsavoury joints called clauses and do all sorts of interesting things, like being subjects or objects or . . . (but we'll leave all that for Chapter 24). Why mention these now? Because they can confuse you when you're looking for subject–verb pairs. Until you get round to reading Chapter 24, just learn to recognise them for what they are.

Masquerading as Subjects: Here and There

Someone comes up to you and says, 'Here is a million pounds.' What's the first question that comes into your mind? Obviously, with your burning interest in grammar, it's *What's the subject of that sentence?* Well, try to answer your question in the usual way:

> Here is a million pounds.

1. Pop the question: What's happening? What is? Answer: *is.*

2. Pop the question: Who *is?* What *is?* Answer: ?

What did you say? *Here is?* But *here* can't be a subject (it isn't a noun or a pronoun). Neither can *there*. They're just all dressed up and masquerading as subjects. How can you be sure about this? Because, although they're in the place usually occupied by the subject, *here* and *there* don't decide the form of the verb. You don't know whether to say *is* or *are* until you get to the real subject (which is, of course, what the verb agrees with). Fill in the gaps here and see what the subject really is:

> Here . . . a frog for you to put in Lucinda's bed.

It has to be *Here is a frog;* the verb agrees with *frog*, so that's the real subject. Now try this one:

> There . . . four tickets for *Hamlet* on the fridge.

There are four tickets, so *tickets* is the real subject. Although they sometimes try to disguise themselves as nouns, *here* and *there* are actually adverbs. Adverbs modify verbs, adjectives and other adverbs. They are busy little words. (For more on adverbs, see Chapter 8.)

The moral of this story is: avoid *here* and *there* when searching for the subject of a sentence. And just be sure that the verb agrees with the real subject.

Which sentence is correct?

A. There are seven new kinds of cake for Bill to try.

B. There's seven new kinds of cake for Bill to try.

Answer: Sentence A is correct. In sentence B, *there's* is short for *there is*, but *kinds*, the plural subject, takes a plural verb.

We've been looking at sentences in which *here* and *there* refer to a place (Here in my hand is a frog, There on the fridge are the tickets). Sometimes, *there* isn't talking about a specific place but just saying that things exist (or don't):

There is nothing better than a winter evening by the fire with a glass of wine and a good book.

There are no tickets left for the opening night of *Hamlet*.

Are there any chocolates?

These are called *existential* sentences (because they're about whether things *exist*). You only need to remember that if you really like big words.

Subjects Aren't Just a Singular Sensation: Forming the Plural of Nouns

Distinguishing between singular and plural subjects is harder than you may think, and we go into it in detail in Chapter 11. But before we go any further, we want to explain how to form the plural of nouns (words that name persons, places, or things) because most subjects are nouns. If you learn how to form plurals, you'll also be able to recognise them.

Regular plurals

Plain old garden-variety nouns form plurals by adding the letter *s*. Check out Table 4-1 for some examples.

Table 4-1	Examples of Regular Plurals
Singular	*Plural*
eyebrow	eyebrows
lollipop	lollipops
nerd	nerds
quintuplet	quintuplets
xylophone	xylophones

Singular nouns that end in *s* already, as well as singular nouns ending in *sh*, *ch* and *x*, form plurals by adding *es*. Some examples are shown in Table 4-2.

Table 4-2	Examples of Regular Plurals Ending in s, sh, ch and x
Singular	*Plural*
kiss	kisses
mess	messes
dish	dishes
witch	witches
box	boxes

The *Ies* and *Ys* have it

If a noun ends in the letter *y* and the letter before the *y* is a vowel (a, e, i, o, u), just add *s*. For examples, see Table 4-3.

Table 4-3	Examples of Regular Plurals Ending in a Vowel Plus y
Singular	*Plural*
boy	boys
day	days
monkey	monkeys
turkey	turkeys

If the noun ends in *y* but the letter before the *y* is not a vowel, form the plural by changing the *y* to *i* and adding *es*. For examples, see Table 4-4.

Table 4-4 Examples of Regular Plurals Ending in a Consonant Plus y	
Singular	*Plural*
sob story	sob stories
unsolvable mystery	unsolvable mysteries
one city	two cities
bat-filled belfry	bat-filled belfries
tabby	tabbies

No knifes here: irregular plurals

Plural subjects wouldn't be any fun without irregulars, now would it? OK, you're right. Irregulars are always a pain. However, they're also always around. Table 4-5 gives you examples of irregular plurals.

Table 4-5	Examples of Irregular Plurals	
Singular	*Plural*	
child	children	
goose	geese	(but mongoose, mongooses)
knife	knives	
man	men	
mouse	mice*	
sheep	sheep	
woman	women	

The live variety – it's anybody's guess what the plural of the computer mouse is, so it's a good thing most of us only have one and don't have to worry about this.

Listing all the irregular plurals is an impossible task. Check the dictionary for any noun plural that puzzles you.

The brother-in-law rule: hyphenated plurals

If you intend to insult your relatives, you may as well do so with the correct plural form. Remember: form the plural of hyphenated nouns by adding *s* or *es* to the important word, not to the add-ons. These are all correct plurals:

- ✔ mothers-in-law
- ✔ brothers-in-law
- ✔ vice-presidents
- ✔ secretaries-general
- ✔ dogcatchers-in-chief

When the Subject Is a Number

Numbers are sometimes the subject of a sentence. Check out this example. You're a star footballer and your agent tells you that your favourite team has made an offer. You add up the numbers and send off an e-mail. What do you say?

£10,000,000 is not enough.

No, that's not what you say. Why? Leaving aside the fact that £10,000,000 is more than enough for any human being's work, even work as crucial to the future of civilisation as kicking a ball about, your answer has a more important problem. It's not grammatically correct. Here's the rule: Always begin a sentence with a capital letter. Don't begin a sentence with a number or a symbol, because you can't capitalise numbers, and – to repeat – you must begin every sentence with a capital letter. If need be, write out the amount that you're negotiating:

Ten million pounds a year is not enough.

or reword the sentence:

A mere £10,000,000 a year is not enough.

Here's another example:

WRONG: 1966 was a very good year.

RIGHT BUT CLUMSY: Nineteen sixty-six was a very good year.

ALSO RIGHT: The year 1966 was a good one.

ALSO RIGHT: I had a good time in 1966, at least what I remember of it.

Are you affected? Or effected?

Has the study of grammar *affected* or *effected* your brain? These two words are an annoyance, but once you learn them you're all set. Here are the definitions:

Affect and *effect* can both be verbs. *Affect* means to *influence* (or, sometimes, to *pretend*). And *affected* can also mean *deeply moved*. *Effect* means to *bring about* or *accomplish* (but it's probably better avoided as it tends to sound pompous – there are lots of simpler words that are better).

They can also both be nouns. *Affect* means *the way one relates to and shows emotions* (and you can pretty much forget about it unless you're studying psychology). *Effect* is the *result* of some action. Here are some examples:

Will Rashid's hard work *affect* Mortimer's decision to take on new staff? (*will affect =* a verb, meaning *will influence*)

Yasmin *affected* indifference when she saw Edgar shopping with Lucinda. (*affected* = a verb, meaning *pretended*)

Mortimer was much *affected* by Rashid's performance in *Hamlet.* (*was affected* = a verb, meaning *was emotionally moved*)

Mortimer thinks there may be problems when they effect the changeover to the new accounting system that Rashid recommends. (*effect* = a verb, meaning *carry out; make* would be better here, or just *when they change over*)

Lucinda's parents have told her she needs to work hard and resit her exams, but they don't know what the *effect* of their serious talk will be. (*effect* = a noun, meaning *result*)

Chapter 5

Having It All: The Complete Sentence

*E*veryone knows the most important rule of English grammar: all sentences must be complete.

But everyone breaks the rule. We just did! *But everyone breaks the rule* is not a complete sentence. But you understood it, didn't you? (Another half sentence.) Because what it was trying to say was quite clear. (One more.) In this chapter, we'll explain how to decide whether your sentence is complete. We'll show you how to identify partial sentences, or *fragments*. We'll tell you when fragments are acceptable and when they're not. We also provide everything you need to know about endmarks, the punctuation that separates one sentence from another.

Completing Sentences: The Essential Subjects and Verbs

What is a complete sentence, anyway? First of all, a complete sentence has at least one subject–verb pair; they're a pair because they match. That is, the subject and verb go together. You may think about a subject–verb pair this way: the sentence must include one element expressing action or being, and one element that you're talking about in relation to the acting or being. (For more information on verbs, see Chapters 2 and 3; for more information on subjects, see Chapter 4.) A few subject–verb pairs that match are:

> Edgar scrambled
>
> Sandy runs
>
> Bibi's toy boat will be repaired
>
> Mortimer had decided

Just for comparison, here is one mismatch:

> Edgar scrambling

You may find some mismatches in your sentences when you go subject–verb hunting. Mismatches are not necessarily wrong; they're simply not subject–verb pairs. Take a look at the preceding mismatch, this time inside its sentence:

> Edgar, scrambling for a seat on the plane, dropped the glass vase he'd bought for his mother.

When you're checking a sentence for completeness, ignore the mismatches. Keep looking until you find a subject–verb pair that matches. If you can't find one, you don't have a complete sentence. (For more information, see Chapter 4.) Complete sentences may also include more than one subject–verb pair:

> Alice waited in the shoe shop while Lucinda tried 14 pairs of shoes. (*Alice* = subject of the verb *waited*, *Lucinda* = the subject of the verb *tried*)
>
> Not only did Damian gamble but he also drank. (*Damian* = the subject of the verb *did gamble*, *he* = subject of the verb *drank*)

Complete sentences may also match one subject with more than one verb, and vice versa:

> Ellie appeared in three commercials but sang in only two. (*Ellie* = the subject of the verbs *appeared* and *sang*)
>
> Rover and Spot will fight endlessly over a bone. (*Rover* and *Spot* = the subjects of the verb *will fight*)

Complete sentences that give commands may match an implied subject (*you*) with the verb:

> Give a voucher to everyone who attended the performance that was rained off. (*you* = the implied subject of the verb *give*, *who* = the subject of the verb *attended*)
>
> Write that thank-you letter to your grandmother today. (*you* = the implied subject of the verb *write*)

To find the subject–verb pair, start with the verb. Pop the verb question: *What's happening?* or *What is?* The answer is the verb. Then pop the subject question: ask *who?* or *what?* in front of the verb. The answer is the subject. (For a more complete explanation, see Chapter 4.)

The sentence below contains one true subject–verb pair and one mismatch. Can you find the subject–verb pair?

> The angry driver brought to a standstill by the traffic vowed never to take the M25 again.

Answer: The subject–verb pair is *driver vowed.* The mismatch is *driver brought.* The sentence isn't saying that the *driver brought* something, so *driver brought* is not a match.

In the preceding pop quiz, *to take* is not a finite verb. *To take* is an infinitive, the basic form from which verbs are made. Infinitives are never used as finite verbs in a sentence. (See Chapter 2 for more information on infinitives and Chapter 4 for more on finite and non-finite verbs.)

Complete Thoughts, Complete Sentences

What's an incomplete sentence? It's that moment in a television programme when *the hero slowly edges the door open a few inches, peeks in, gasps, and . . . THE CREDITS ROLL.* In disgust, you realise that it's a two-parter! You're going to have to wait a week to find out what happens next! A complete sentence gets to the end: you know how the story ends. In other words, a complete sentence must express a complete thought.

Check out these complete sentences. Notice how they express complete thoughts:

> Despite Edgar's fragile appearance, he proved to be a tough opponent.
>
> Sandy's biggest ambition is to sail solo around the world.
>
> I can't imagine why anyone would want to ride a roller coaster.

Here are a few incomplete thoughts, just for comparison:

> The reason I wanted a divorce was.
>
> Because I said so.

I can guess what you're thinking. Both of those incomplete thoughts may be part of a longer conversation. Yes, in context those incomplete thoughts may indeed express a complete thought:

> Lucinda: So the topic of conversation was Saturday's football match?
>
> Deborah: No! The reason I wanted a divorce was!

and

> Lucinda: Why do I have to do this dumb revision?
>
> Lucinda's mum: Because I said so.

Fair enough. You can pull a complete thought out of the examples. However, the context of a conversation is not enough to satisfy the *complete thought* = *complete sentence* rule. To be legal, your sentence must express a complete thought.

We can make these incomplete sentences grammatically complete by stating the ideas that the rest of the conversation gave us:

> What we talked about was the reason I wanted a divorce, even though his real interest was Saturday's football match.
>
> You have to do this dumb revision because I said so.

Every complete sentence has at least one subject–verb pair and must express a complete thought.

In deciding whether you have a complete sentence or not, you may be led astray by words that resemble questions. Consider these three words: *who sings best*. A complete thought? Maybe yes, maybe no. Suppose those three words form a question:

> Who sings best?

This question is understandable and its thought is complete. Verdict: legal. Suppose these three words form a statement:

> Who sings best.

Now they don't make sense. This incomplete sentence needs more words to make a complete thought:

> The lead role in Mortimer's new production will go to the person who sings best.

The moral of the story? Don't change the meaning of what you're saying when deciding whether a thought is complete. If you're *questioning*, consider your sentence as a *question*. If you're *stating*, consider your sentence as a *statement*.

Whether or if it rains

Whether and *if* both connect one idea to another in the sentence, but each is used in a different context. *If* describes a possibility. Check out these examples:

> Yasmin will take Bibi to the zoo *if* the sunny weather continues. (The sentence talks about the possibility of sunny weather.)

> *If* Ms Stakes has her way, the Science Fiction Club will be banned. (The sentence talks about the possibility of Ms Stakes getting what she wants.)

But, if you're choosing between two options, select *whether* (as in *whether or not*). Look at the following examples:

Damian is not sure *whether* he should try to talk Deborah out of divorcing him. (He has two choices – to try or not to try.)

He tells himself that *whether* she goes or stays is completely irrelevant to him. (She has two choices – going and staying.)

If you're tempted to add *or not* every time you use the word *whether*, don't. A good general rule is not to add extra words if they don't add any meaning. It will be obvious when you have to add *or not* (because the sentence won't work on its own), as in this sentence:

> Lucinda's parents are going to make her study hard whether she likes it.

Clearly, this needs *or not* on the end.

Which sentence is complete?

    A. Martin sings.

    B. Martin, who hopes to sing professionally some day but can't read music.

Answer: Even though it's short, sentence A is correct. *Martin sings* is a complete idea and includes the necessary subject–verb pair. In sentence B, one subject (*who*) is paired with two verbs (*hopes* and *can't read*), but no complete thought is stated.

Taking an Incomplete: Fragment Sentences

We use incomplete sentences, or fragments, here and there throughout this book and (hope) these incomplete sentences aren't confusing. Especially now, in the Age of the Text Message, short-cuts and quick comments are the rule. Everyone today is much more comfortable with half-sentences than our elderly relatives were.

The most common type of fragment uses the words *and, or, but* or *nor*. These words are called *conjunctions*, and they work like glue: they bind things together. (For more information on conjunctions, see Chapter 7.) Frequently these words are used to combine two (or more) complete sentences (with two or more complete thoughts) into one longer sentence:

1. Mortimer went to his doctor for a cholesterol check, *and* then he rushed home for a large fried brunch.

2. Fido will rule the roost *or* he will die trying.

3. Lucinda's mother was extremely thirsty, *but* she was not fond of camomile tea *and* that was all that Ms Stakes was offering her.

4. She did not want to drink the tea, *nor* did she wish to appear rude.

In example 1, *and* is the glue joining the two sentences:

Mortimer went to his doctor for a cholesterol check. Then he rushed home for a large fried brunch.

In example 2, the glue is *or*, which joins the two sentences:

Fido will rule the roost. He will die trying.

Example 3 contains three sentences, joined by a *but* and an *and:*

Lucinda's mother was extremely thirsty. She was not fond of camomile tea. That was all that Ms Stakes was offering her.

In example 4, you may think that *nor* is joining these two sentences:

She did not want to drink the tea. Did she wish to appear rude.

(That's how *and, but* and *or* worked, after all.) But that's not what's happened here. For the meaning to stay the same, the second sentence would have to have been

She did not wish to appear rude.

So *nor* has taken responsibility for part of the meaning of the original sentence (*not* has disappeared, with its meaning now contained in *nor*), and the word order has changed (because you can't say *nor she did wish*).

You should also note that *nor* doesn't make sense on its own. There has to be another negative first. This sentence isn't grammatically correct:

The biscuits looked delicious, *nor* did she wish to appear rude.

It would have to be

The biscuits looked delicious, *and* she *didn't* wish to appear rude.

Nowadays, more and more writers begin sentences with *and*, *or*, *but* and *nor*, even in formal writing. For example, our four sentences may be turned into:

1. Mortimer went to his doctor for a cholesterol check. *And* then he rushed home for a large fried brunch.

2. Fido will rule the roost. *Or* he will die trying.

3. Lucinda's mother was extremely thirsty. *But* she was not fond of camomile tea. *And* that was all that Ms Stakes was offering her.

4. She did not want to drink the tea. *Nor* did she wish to appear rude.

The connectors (or *conjunctions*) – *and*, *or*, *but* and *nor* – are still there, but they're more like rubber bands than glue. They aren't connecting two or more complete thoughts in *single* sentences. Logically, of course, the conjunctions are still connecting the thoughts. It's just that the second or third thought seems slightly delayed. Sometimes this is exactly right. In fiction, it can suggest that the character is thinking hard and telling us what he's thinking even as he thinks it (and maybe he'll figure it out in time to save the heroine). In a letter to your grandmother it's more likely to convince her that you're struggling to hold two thoughts together. (But, of course, she loves you anyway.) In a report for your boss, it's probably better avoided if you want that promotion.

Could This Really Be the End? Understanding Endmarks

When you speak, your body language, silences and tone act as punctuation marks. You wriggle your eyebrows, stop at significant moments and raise your tone when you ask a question.

When you write, you can't raise an eyebrow or stop for a dramatic moment. No one hears your tone of voice. That's why grammar uses endmarks. The endmarks take the place of live communication and tell your reader how to 'hear' the words correctly. Plus, you need endmarks to close your sentences legally. Your choices are the full stop (.), question mark (?) and exclamation mark (!). The following examples show how to use endmarks correctly.

The full stop is for ordinary statements, declarations and commands:

> I can't do my homework.
>
> I refuse to do my homework.
>
> Do your homework.

The question mark is for questions:

> Why are you torturing me with this homework?
>
> Is there no justice?
>
> Does no one know the trouble trigonometry causes me?

The exclamation mark adds a little drama to sentences that would otherwise end in full stops:

> I can't do my homework!
>
> I absolutely positively refuse to do it!
>
> Oh, the agony of homework!

Don't put more than one endmark at the end of a sentence, unless you're trying to create a comic effect:

> She said my cooking tasted like what?!?!?!

Don't put any endmarks in the middle of a sentence. You may find a full stop inside a sentence as part of an abbreviation, but that isn't considered an endmark:

> Bibi didn't realise that 2 a.m. wasn't a good time to wake her mother.
>
> Susie woke up at once when Bibi cried (even though it was 2 a.m.).

If the sentence ends with an abbreviation, let the full stop after the abbreviation do double duty. Don't add another one:

> WRONG: When Bibi woke Susie, it was 2 a.m..
>
> RIGHT: When Bibi woke Susie, it was 2 a.m.

Ellipsis dots (. . .) aren't end marks. They can be used in the middle of a sentence to show that words have been left out, but if the last words of a sentence are missing you need a full stop to show that you've got to the end. For example, here's Rashid when he was first learning his lines for *Hamlet*:

> To be or not to be . . . slings and arrows . . . outrageous fortune . . . sea of troubles. . . .

Who makes these rules anyway? You do

Listen to yourself talk. What you hear is grammar. You may not be hearing correct grammar but, if enough people talk the way you do, you are hearing *grammar in the making* – at least according to some grammarians.

There are two schools of thought on grammar. In one, teachers and other so-called experts give you a list of rules and tell you to follow them. In the other, grammarians listen and describe what they hear. When enough people speak a certain way, the expression becomes part of standard English. Or, as a grammarian named Lathan said in 1848, "In Language, whatever is, is right."

Take the word *hopefully*, for example. This word originally meant *with hope* and was used to describe the feelings accompanying a specific action (in grammatical terms, it's an *adverb*):

> Yasmin wrote *hopefully*, her mind filled with thoughts of a rosy future.

Some time ago, people began to use *hopefully* in a different way, to mean *it is hoped that:*

> Hopefully Mortimer's new decorator won't decide to redecorate his penthouse apartment in post-modern style.

This means that it isn't behaving like a good little adverb any more. Some people hate it when words take on new roles like this. Many people still frown on this new use of *hopefully*, but most people ignore them – at least in normal speech (and even in some books, but probably not in English tests). Who made the new rule? You did. The *you* above is a collective *you*, not an individual *you*. Don't assume that you can say anything you want and be correct! First a critical mass of speakers (think millions, not you and a bunch of your friends) must accept a new usage before grammarians take notice. And, even then, some will still frown. Know your audience, and be careful in your speech and writing when you are dealing with a known frowner or an unknown audience.

Can you punctuate this example correctly?

> Who's there Archie I think there is someone at the door Archie it's a murderer Archie he's going to

Answer: Who's there? Archie, I think there is someone at the door. Archie, it's a murderer! (A full stop is also acceptable here.) Archie, he's going to. . . .

Chapter 6

Handling Complements

Speeding down the grammar highway, the sentence is a car carrying meaning to the reader. The verbs are the wheels and the subject is the driver. Complements are other common (but not always essential) parts of the car – perhaps the fuel gauge or the signal lights. These words are a little more important than those fuzzy dice some people hang from their rear-view mirrors or bumper stickers declaring *Baby on board*. (What do they think we're going to do about it?)

You can sometimes create a sentence without complements, but their presence is generally part of the driving – sorry, the *communicating* – experience. So sometimes all you need (because it says everything) is the subject and the verb:

   Yasmin phoned.

And sometimes you need a bit more:

   ✔ Yasmin was nervous.

   ✔ Yasmin phoned Edgar.

   ✔ Edgar gave Yasmin a single red rose.

   ✔ Edgar called Yasmin the love of his life.

Each of these four sentences begins with a subject and verb, and each has something more to complete the sentence. The other stuff is called the complement. (*Comple*te the sentence . . . *Comple*ment – get it?) Of course, that's not enough for grammarians. They can see that each of these sentences ends in a slightly different way, and if they can come up with four names instead of one they will. So we'll look at each one in turn to see how it's different (and what it's called).

Before we go any further, let's just clear up one minor confusion. The word *complement* that I used above is a grammatical term and it's spelled with an *e* in the middle. (Compl*e*ment . . . compl*e*te, remember?) There's another word that people confuse it with: *compliment* (spelled with an *i*). This is not a grammatical term; a *compliment* is a remark or act showing your respect or admiration for someone. So, when you can't be bothered to put a whole letter in a package you're posting, you put in a small piece of paper which says *With compliments* (and maybe you sign your name or write a short note on it) to indicate respect (or, at least, more respect than not putting anything in the package but less respect than writing a whole letter). And, if someone gives you complimentary tickets to the theatre, they're giving them to you free because they like you so much. (When you get to the theatre, if your date says that you're looking beautiful, that's a compliment too.)

Being on the Receiving End: Direct Objects

Imagine that you're 14. You're holding a cricket ball, ready to bowl to a friend in your back garden. But, in your imagination, you're at Lords. You go into your run-up and bowl a fastball. The ball arcs gracefully against the clear blue sky – and crashes right through the window in your living room.

You broke the window!

Before you can retrieve your ball, the phone rings. It's your mum, who has radar for situations like this. *What's going on?* she asks. You mutter something containing the word *broke*. (There's the verb.) *Broke? Who broke something?* she demands. You concede that *you* did. (There's the subject.) *What did you break?* You hesitate. You consider a couple of possible answers: *your habit of biting your nails* maybe, or *the world record for the hundred metre dash*. Finally you confess: *the window*. (There's the complement.) *Broke* is an action verb because it tells you what happened. The action came from the subject (*you*) and whatever's on the receiving end of the action (*the window*) is called a *direct object* (because it receives the action directly from the verb). So, in the sentence

Yasmin phoned Edgar.

phoned is an action verb because it expresses what's happening in the sentence. The action goes from the subject (*Yasmin*) to the object (*Edgar*). In other words, *Edgar* receives the action of *phoning*. Or, in grammatical terms, Edgar is the *direct object* of the verb *phoned*.

Here are two more examples of sentences with direct objects:

> The X-ray machine took *pictures* of Bill's broken leg. (*X-ray machine* = subject, *took* = verb)

> Lucinda squashed the *frog*. (*squashed* = verb, *Lucinda* = subject)

You may be able to recognise direct objects more easily if you think of them as part of a pattern in the sentence structure: subject (S) – action verb (AV) – direct object (DO). This S–AV–DO pattern is one of the most common in the English language.

> machine took pictures

> Lucinda squashed frog

Of course, just to make your life a little bit harder, a sentence can have more than one DO. Check out these examples:

> Rashid autographed *programmes* and *copies* of the play for his many admirers.

> The new president of the Science Fiction Club immediately phoned *Edgar* and *Yasmin*.

> Lucinda bought *orange juice*, *tuna*, *aspirins* and the expensive *handbag*.

Some sentences have no DO. Take a look at this one:

> Throughout the endless afternoon and into the lonely night, Nurse Oduwole sighed sadly.

No one or nothing receives the sighs, so the sentence has no direct object. But it has a verb and expresses a complete thought.

One Step Removed: Indirect Objects

Another type of object is the indirect object. This one is called *indirect* because the action doesn't flow directly to it. The *indirect object*, affectionately known as the IO, is an intermediate stop along the way between the action verb and the direct object. Read this sentence, in which the indirect object is italicised:

> Edgar gave *Yasmin* a single red rose.

The action is *gave*. *Edgar* performed the action, so *Edgar* is the subject. What received the action? The *rose*. *Rose* is the direct object. That's what was given, what received the action of the verb directly. But *Yasmin* also received the action, indirectly. *Yasmin* received the giving of the rose. *Yasmin* is called the indirect object.

The sentence pattern for indirect objects is subject (S) – action verb (AV) – indirect object (IO) – direct object (DO). Notice that the indirect object always precedes the direct object: S–AV–IO–DO. Here are a few sentences with the indirect objects italicised:

> Inspector Barker will tell *his boss* the details of his investigation so far. (*will tell* = verb, *Inspector Barker* = subject, *details* = direct object)

> Inspector Barker took his brother *Bill* some grapes. (*took* = verb, *Inspector Barker* = subject, *grapes* = direct object)

> Nurse Oduwole sent *Yasmin* a text message when Ms Stakes died. (*sent* = verb, *Nurse Oduwole* = subject, *message* = direct object)

> The crooked official offered *Lucinda* a bribe for dropping out of the beauty contest. (*offered* = verb, *official* = subject, *bribe* = direct object)

Indirect objects don't appear very often. When indirect objects do arrive, they're always in partnership with a direct object. You probably don't need to worry about knowing the difference between direct and indirect objects (unless you're an English teacher). As long as you understand that these words are objects, completing the meaning of an action verb, you recognise the basic composition of a sentence.

A fight about indirect objects is tearing apart the world of grammar. (Did you gasp or was that a yawn?) Read these two sentences:

> Bill gave the doctor his grapes.

> Bill gave his grapes to the doctor.

According to one school of thought, the first sentence has an indirect object (*doctor*), and the second sentence doesn't. This thinking assumes that, because *to* is present in the second sentence, *doctor* isn't an indirect object. (If you're into labels, *to the doctor* is a prepositional phrase.) According to another group of grammarians, both sentences have indirect objects (*doctor*) because, in both sentences, *doctor* receives the action of the verb indirectly; the presence of the word *to* is irrelevant. What's really irrelevant is this discussion. You may side with either camp or, more wisely, ignore the whole thing.

No Bias Here: Objective Complements

Sometimes a direct object doesn't get the whole job done. A little more information is needed (or just desired), and the writer doesn't want to bother adding a whole new subject–verb pair. Look at this sentence:

Edgar called Yasmin . . .

Edgar isn't phoning Yasmin, he's saying something about her and we want to know what. Like this:

Edgar called Yasmin the love of his life.

The love of his life finishes the sentence, so it's some sort of complement, right? It's called an *objective complement* because it adds more information about the direct object. The objective complement (italicised in the following sentences) may be a person, place, or thing. In other words, the objective complement may be a noun:

The reviews declared Ellie's performance *the highlight of the evening.* (*declared* = verb, *the reviews* = subject, *Ellie's performance* = direct object)

The club members elected Martin *chairman of the Science Fiction Club.* (*elected* = verb, *the club members* = subject, *Martin* = direct object)

The objective complement may also be a word that describes a noun. (A word that describes a noun is called an *adjective*; see Chapter 8 for more information.) Take a peek at some sample sentences:

Mike considered Lucinda *lazy* at best. (*considered* = verb, *Mike* = subject, *Lucinda* = direct object)

The doctor proclaimed Bill *well enough to go home.* (*proclaimed* = verb, *the doctor* = subject, *Bill* = direct object)

Deborah called Damian *heartless.* (*called* = verb, *Deborah* = subject, *Damian* = direct object)

As you see, the objective complements in each of the sample sentences give the sentence an extra jolt – you know more with it than you do without it. But the objective complement is not a major player in the sentence.

Finishing the Equation: Linking-Verb Complements

Linking-verb complements are major players in sentences. A *linking verb* begins a word equation: it expresses a state of being, linking two ideas. (For more on linking verbs see Chapter 2.) The complement completes the equation, like this:

Yasmin was *nervous.*

Because a complement following a linking verb expresses something about the *subject* of the sentence, it is called a *subject complement.* In fact, of all the complements, these are the only ones that are likely to cause you any problems. So when people talk about 'the complement' this is the one they mean.

In each of the following sentences, the first idea is the subject, and the second idea (italicised) is the complement:

Susie was *upset* when she heard the news. (*Susie = upset*)

Rashid will be a company director before he's 40. (*Rashid = company director*)

Natasha is an interior designer. (*Natasha = interior designer*)

Subject complements can take on several forms. Sometimes the subject complement is a descriptive word (an *adjective*) like *upset* in the first sentence. Sometimes the subject complement is a *noun* (person, place, thing, or idea) like *company director* and *interior designer.* And sometimes it's a *pronoun* (a word that substitutes for a noun). Pronouns cause problems, so we'll leave them until later in this chapter. As long as you can find the subject complement, you're grasping the sentence structure.

Don't mix types of subject complement in the same sentence, completing the meaning of the same verb. It's better style to stick to all descriptions (adjectives) or all nouns and pronouns. Take a look at these examples:

WRONG: Clarence is grouchy and a patron of the arts.

RIGHT: Clarence is a grouch and a patron of the arts.

ALSO RIGHT: Clarence is grouchy and arty.

WRONG: Sandy's sister can be annoying and a real nuisance.

RIGHT: Sandy's sister can be an annoyance and a nuisance.

ALSO RIGHT: Sandy's sister can be annoying and irritating.

Pop the Question: Locating the Complement

In Chapter 2, we explain how to locate the verb by asking the right questions. (*What's happening? What is?*) In Chapter 4, we show you how to pop the question for the subject. (*Who? What?* before the verb.) Now it's time to pop the question to find the direct object or the complement. You ask these questions after both the verb and the subject have been identified. The complement questions are

Whom?

What?

Try popping the questions in this sentence:

Mortimer maintains the cleanest car in town.

1. Pop the verb question: What's happening? Answer: *maintains. Maintains* is the action verb.

2. Pop the subject question: Who or what *maintains?* Answer: *Mortimer maintains. Mortimer* is the subject.

3. Pop the object/complement question: *Mortimer maintains* who/whom? No answer. *Mortimer maintains* what? Answer: Mortimer maintains *the cleanest car in town* (*car* for short). Because *car* is receiving the action of the verb, *car* is the direct object.

Remember that objects (direct or indirect) follow action verbs.

Time for you to try another:

The ancient garden gnome appeared tired and worn.

1. Pop the verb question: What's happening? No answer. What is? Answer: *appeared. Appeared* is the linking verb (so we're looking for a complement, not a direct object).

2. Pop the subject question: Who or what *appeared?* Answer: *gnome appeared. Gnome* is the subject.

3. Pop the object/complement question: *Gnome appeared* who? No answer. *Gnome appeared* what? Answer: *tired* and *worn. Tired* and *worn* are the complements.

Remember that complements follow linking verbs.

Pop the Question: Finding the Indirect Object

You can check for indirect objects with another question. After you locate the action verb, the subject and the direct object, ask:

> To whom? For whom?
>
> To what? For what?

If you get an answer, it should reveal an indirect object. Here's an example:

> Mildred will give Inspector Barker a clue soon.

1. Pop the verb question: What's happening? Answer: *will give. Will give* is an action verb.

2. Pop the subject question: Who will give? Answer: *Mildred. Mildred* is the subject.

3a. Pop the DO question: *Mildred will give* whom? or what? Answer: *Mildred will give a clue. Clue* is the direct object.

3b. Pop the IO question: *Mildred will give a clue* to whom? Answer: to *Inspector Barker. Inspector Barker* is the indirect object.

You may come up with a different answer when you pop the DO question in number 3a (*Mildred will give* whom? or what?). You may answer *Mildred will give Inspector Barker*. True. The only problem is that the sentence then has *clue* flapping around with no label. So your attempt to determine the sentence structure has reached a dead end. Does this matter? Not really, because you aren't likely to make any mistakes with these. As long as you understand that both *Inspector Barker* and *clue* are objects, you can leave the grammarians to worry about which one is direct and which one is indirect.

Object or complement? Identify the italicised words.

> Sandy seemed *soggy* after his marathon, so we gave *him* a *towel*.

Answer: *Soggy* is the complement. (*Seemed* is a linking verb.) *Him* is the indirect object. *Towel* is the direct object. (*Gave* is an action verb.)

Pronouns as Objects and Subject Complements

He told I? He told me? Me, of course. Your ear usually tells you which pronouns to use as objects (both direct and indirect), because the wrong pronouns sound funny. The object pronouns include *me, you, him, her, it, us, them, whom* and *whomever*. Check them out in context:

> Bibi splashed *her* with icy water.

> The Inspector gave *them* a warning.

> He told *us* everything.

But your ear may not tell you the correct pronoun to use after a linking verb. That's where you want a *subject* pronoun, not an *object* pronoun. (Just for the record, the subject pronouns include *I, you, he, she, it, we, they, who* and *whoever*.) Why do you need a subject pronoun after a linking verb? Remember the equation: what's before the verb should be equal to what's after the verb (S = SC). You put subject pronouns before the verb as subjects, so you put subject pronouns after the verb, as complements.

DEMONS

You gotta problem with grammar?

Do you possess an ear for grammar? Do you recognise proper English, distinguishing it from the way everyone else around you speaks? If so, you probably don't say *gotta* or *gonna* or any of the many other unofficial abbreviations that we all use among friends. Although these are OK when you're just chatting, they can give the wrong impression when you're speaking to a teacher, a boss, a television interviewer, or the police. Thus,

> WRONG: We *gotta* go. Are you *gonna* leave that chocolate cake? *'Cos* I *ain't* eaten since last night. If you don't *wannit*, give it *'ere*.

RIGHT: We have to go. Are you going to leave that chocolate cake? Because I haven't eaten since last night. I'll eat it if you don't want it.

ALSO RIGHT: We're running a little late. Aren't you going to eat that delicious-looking chocolate cake? It seems such a pity to waste it. I can wrap it in a paper serviette and put it in this convenient plastic sandwich bag that I happen to have with me.

We'd add another example, but it's almost time for lunch. We gotta go.

Which sentence is correct?

A. According to the witness, the burglar is her, the one with the bright orange hat!

B. According to the witness, the burglar is she, the one with the bright orange hat!

Answer: Sentence A is acceptable in conversation. Sentence B is correct if you're writing formally. *Is* is a linking verb and must be followed by a subject pronoun, *she.* But would you ever say that? Or feel comfortable writing it? We're betting you wouldn't. Instead, you could say *the burglar is the woman with the bright orange hat* and avoid the whole nasty problem. (There are some more examples in the section 'Placing the Proper Pronoun in the Proper Place' in Chapter 2.)

Part II
Avoiding Common Errors

'It was the way he would have
wanted it – He was a terrible
English grammar teacher.'

In this part . . .

Want to build a castle? You can build one that has thick walls with slits to fire arrows through, but how much more interesting it is to throw in a moat and a drawbridge and a round tower or two! Communication is the same. You can get by with the basics, but to express yourself with any flair you'll need to add descriptions, joining words and an occasional exclamation to your sentences. In this part, we explain a few more parts of speech – conjunctions, adjectives, adverbs, prepositions and interjections. This part also contains a field guide to the pronoun, a useful little part of speech that resembles a minefield when it comes to possibilities for error. Finally, we delve a little further into the complexities of subject–verb agreement, also a minefield. Not to worry: we have some handy little mine detectors to help you.

Chapter 7

Getting Hitched: Marrying Sentences

Listen to the nearest toddler and you may hear something like, 'I played with the clay and I went to the zoo and Mummy said I had to take a nap and . . .' and so forth. Monotonous, yes. But – surprise, surprise – grammatically correct. Take a look at how the information would sound if that one sentence turned into three: *I played with the clay. I went to the zoo. Mummy said I had to have a nap.* The information sounds choppy. When the sentences are combined, the information flows more smoothly. Granted, joining everything with *and* is not a great idea. Read on for better ways of gluing one sentence to another.

Matchmaking: Combining Sentences Legally

Although combining sentences may improve your writing, it can be dangerous. You may easily end up with a *run-on sentence,* which is two or more complete sentences faultily run together. A run-on (a grammatical felony, by the way) is like a dinner speaker who's supposed to entertain the guests during the appetizer but instead talks right through the entrée, the dessert, and the kitchen cleanup. You don't want run-ons in your writing! The best way to avoid these sentences is to figure out how to connect sentences legally.

Connecting with co-ordinate conjunctions

The words used to join clauses are called *conjunctions*. You're familiar with these common words: *and*, *but*, *yet*, *so*, *for* and *or*. (*And* is the most popular, for those of you keeping track.) These little powerhouses, which are called *co-ordinate conjunctions*, eat their spinach and work out every day. They're strong enough to join complete sentences. (They can do other things as well. *Yet* and *so* can be adverbs, for example, and *for* is more often used as a preposition.) They may use their strength to join all sorts of equal grammatical elements. Here they are in action joining equal clauses:

> Mortimer told Alice to call all the numbers on the Rolodex, *but* Alice had no idea what a Rolodex was.

> You can take a hike, *or* you can jump off a cliff.

> Clarence did not know how to shoe a horse, *nor* did he understand equine psychology.

> The rain pelted Bill's grey hair, *and* his green velvet shoes were completely ruined.

The co-ordinate conjunctions give equal emphasis to the elements they join. In the preceding sentences, the ideas on one side of the conjunction have no more importance than the ideas on the other side of the conjunction.

If you learned grammar at school recently, you may be worrying about the comma in front of the *and* in the last of these examples. You have probably been told *never* to put a comma in front of *and*. Well, you can relax. A comma before *and* is perfectly legal when the *and* is joining two complete sentences. If you are still at school and have (oh, joy!) more examinations to come, **do not** tell your teachers that they're wrong. This is called 'rudeness' and is a punishable offence. **Do** leave out all the commas before *and* in your coursework and your exams. This is called 'exam technique' and is a valuable skill.

Although combining sentences may improve your writing, it can be dangerous. You may easily end up with a *run-on sentence*, which is two or more complete sentences faultily run together (usually with a comma trying to do the work of a conjunction – more on this later in the chapter). A run-on sentence (a grammatical crime, by the way) is like a dinner speaker who's supposed to entertain the guests during the first course but instead talks on through the dessert and the clearing up afterwards. You don't want run-ons in your writing! The best way to avoid these sentences is to figure out how to connect sentences legally.

Pausing to place commas

A few special rules govern the use of commas in joined sentences:

- When you join two complete sentences, put a comma in front of the conjunction.

- These same conjunctions – *and, but, or, nor, for, yet, so* – may also unite other things. For example, these words may join two nouns (*Yasmin and Edgar*) or two verbs (*sing or dance*) and so forth. Use the comma only when joining two complete sentences. Here are a few examples:

    WRONG: Little Jack Horner sat in the corner, and then pulled a plum out of his pie.

    WHY IT'S WRONG: *And* joins two verbs, *sat* and *pulled*.

    RIGHT: Little Jack Horner sat in the corner and then pulled a plum out of his pie.

Take a look at another set:

    WRONG: Edgar, and the chairman of the local Noise Abatement Society propose to take action against Bill because his dogs are keeping everyone awake all night.

    WHY IT'S WRONG: *And* joins two nouns, *Edgar* and *chairman*.

    RIGHT: Edgar and the chairman of the local Noise Abatement Society propose to take action against Bill because his dogs are keeping everyone awake all night.

And just to make sure you're with us on this point:

    WRONG: Blind mice seem to spend a lot of time running up clocks, and singing nursery rhymes.

    WHY IT'S WRONG: *And* joins two descriptions, *running* and *singing*.

    RIGHT: Blind mice seem to spend a lot of time running up clocks and singing nursery rhymes.

- Don't send a comma out all by itself when you want to join two complete sentences. Commas are too weak to glue one sentence to another. Despite the fact that these puny little punctuation marks can't hold anything together, every single day people try to use commas for just that purpose. So many people, in fact, that this sort of error actually has a name: a *comma splice*. (You know a grammatical error has made it to the major leagues when the error has its very own name.) A comma splice always produces a *run-on sentence* (remember them?). Here are some comma splices and their corrections:

WRONG: Glue sticks fascinate Bibi, glitter attracts Lucinda.

WHY IT'S WRONG: The comma joins two complete thoughts.

RIGHT: Although glue sticks fascinate Bibi, glitter attracts Lucinda.

ALSO RIGHT: Glue sticks fascinate Bibi, but glitter attracts Lucinda.

RIGHT AGAIN: Glue sticks fascinate Bibi; glitter attracts Lucinda.

Another example for you to consider:

WRONG: As usual, the boys dived off the board without looking, Sandy hopes to convince them of the value of caution.

WHY IT'S WRONG: The comma joins two complete thoughts.

RIGHT: As usual, the boys dived off the board without looking, but Sandy hopes to convince them of the value of caution.

ALSO RIGHT: Although the boys dived off the board without looking (as usual), Sandy hopes to convince them of the value of caution.

RIGHT AGAIN: As usual, the boys dived off the board without looking. Sandy hopes to convince them of the value of caution.

Now you're getting the hang of these:

WRONG: The monkeys see, the monkeys do.

WHY IT'S WRONG: Though short, each statement about the monkeys is a complete thought.

RIGHT: The monkeys see, and the monkeys do.

ALSO RIGHT: The monkeys see and the monkeys do.

WHY IT'S ALSO RIGHT: When the sentences you are joining are very short, you may omit the comma before the conjunction.

RIGHT AGAIN: Primates imitate.

Which sentence is correct?

A. The professor sat sedately on his sofa inhaling the fragrance of the roses, and coffee dripped quietly from his saucer onto the cat.

B. The professor sat sedately on his sofa inhaling the fragrance of the roses and coffee dripped quietly from his saucer onto the cat.

C. The professor sat sedately on his sofa inhaling the fragrance of the roses, coffee dripped quietly from his saucer onto the cat.

D. The professor sat sedately on his sofa inhaling the fragrance of the roses. And coffee dripped quietly from his saucer onto the cat.

Answer: Sentence A is correct because two complete thoughts are joined by the word *and*, which is preceded by a comma. Sentence B is incorrect because the comma is missing. Missing out the comma makes the reader think, to begin with, that the professor was inhaling *the fragrance of the roses and coffee*. So don't miss out the comma in a sentence like this. Sentence C is wrong (a comma splice): you can't join two complete thoughts only by a comma. The second sentence in D is incorrect in formal English because it begins with *and*, which is technically an error. See the following paragraph for a more complete explanation of sentence D.

Beginning a sentence with a word that joins equals (particularly *and* and *but*) is increasingly popular. This practice is perfectly acceptable in conversational English and in informal writing (which is the sort you're reading in this book). It is sometimes used deliberately in fiction to make the story more exciting. (Do you think that there's a stronger feeling of time passing when the sentence is split into two as in D?) It can become irritating when it's overdone, though, so it's best not to do this too often. In formal English, beginning a sentence with a conjunction may still be considered incorrect. Be careful! (For more on sentence fragments, see Chapter 5.)

Attaching thoughts: semicolons

The semicolon is a funny little punctuation mark. It gets its name from another punctuation mark: the colon. (These days, the colon is frequently used to create smiley faces in e-mail messages.) The semicolon is no less important and no less powerful than its relative. This punctuation mark is strong enough to attach one complete sentence to another, and it has some other useful abilities in lists. (See Chapter 15 for more information on lists.)

The thing about semicolons is that some people express strong feelings about them. Some writing manuals proclaim, 'Never use semicolons!' with the same intensity of feeling as, say, 'Don't blow up the world with that nuclear missile.' Other people can't get enough of them, sprinkling them like confetti. You don't have to use them at all if you're not happy about them, but they can help to make your writing more interesting.

If you do put a semicolon in your sentence, follow two general guidelines. First, attach equals – that is, two complete sentences – with a semicolon. Don't use the semicolon to join nouns (except in lists – see Chapter 15). Second, use the semicolon only to attach related ideas. When your reader encounters a semicolon, he or she pauses a bit, but not for long. The semicolon says, 'More information coming'. So the reader has a right to expect a logical train of thought – not something completely new. Here's an example:

RIGHT: Bill and Mike were born in Manchester; they moved to Chipping Norton when Bill was four.

WRONG: I put non-fat yogurt into that soup; I like Stephen King's books.

Avoiding false joiners

Some words appear to be strong enough to join sentences, but in reality they're just a bunch of seven-stone weaklings. Think of these words as guys who stuff socks in their sleeves, creating biceps without all the hassle of going to the gym. These fellows may look good, but the minute you need them to pick up a truck or something, they're history. False joiners include *however*, *consequently*, *therefore*, *moreover*, *also* and *furthermore*. Use these words to add meaning to your sentences but not to glue the sentences together. For more information on the proper placement and punctuation associated with these false joiners, see Chapter 15.

In the first example, both parts of the sentence are about where Bill and Mike grew up. In the second, the two ideas are, to put it mildly, not in the same universe. (At least not until Stephen King writes a book about killer yogurt.)

Here are some logical semicolon sentences, just to give you some role models:

> Bill visits that tattoo parlour regularly; when he retires he plans to start a second career as a tattoo designer.

> Alice mowed the lawn yesterday; she cut the electric cord in half twice.

> Sandy thinks that tea is best when it tastes like battery acid; no one drinks anything at Sandy's house any more.

> Lucinda detests purple pens; she once tore up her vocabulary homework because the teacher marked it in a lovely shade of lilac.

> The pearl box is harder to open than an oyster; here's a pair of pliers for the job.

Punctuate the following, adding or subtracting words as needed:

> Edgar will clip the thorns from that rose stem he is afraid Yasmin may scratch herself.

Answer: Many combinations are possible:

> Edgar will clip the thorns from that rose stem. He is afraid Yasmin may scratch herself.

> Edgar will clip the thorns from that rose stem; he is afraid Yasmin may scratch herself.

> Edgar will clip the thorns from that rose stem because he is afraid Yasmin may scratch herself.

Boss and Employee: Joining Ideas of Unequal Ranks

In the average company, the boss runs the show. The boss has subordinates who play two important roles. They must do at least some work. They must also make the boss feel like the centre of the universe. Leave the boss alone in the office and everything's fine. Leave the employees alone in the office and pretty soon things start to go wrong.

Some sentences resemble companies. The 'boss' part of a sentence is all right by itself; it expresses a complete thought (it's an *independent clause*). The 'employee' can't stand alone; it's an incomplete thought (also known as a fragment or *subordinate clause*). For more information on independent and subordinate clauses see Chapter 24. Together, the 'boss' and the 'employee' create a more powerful sentence. Check out some examples:

> BOSS: Martin ate the cake.
>
> EMPLOYEE: After he had picked out all the raisins.
>
> JOINING 1: Martin ate the cake after he had picked out all the raisins.
>
> JOINING 2: After he had picked out all the raisins, Martin ate the cake.

Try these:

> BOSS: Inspector Barker made a list of all the suspects and their alibis.
>
> EMPLOYEE: Because he was getting nowhere with the case.
>
> JOINING 1: Inspector Barker made a list of all the suspects and their alibis because he was getting nowhere with the case.
>
> JOINING 2: Because he was getting nowhere with the case, Inspector Barker made a list of all the suspects and their alibis.

Here's another:

> BOSS: Bill's dogs will start barking at exactly four o'clock.
>
> EMPLOYEE: Although he tries to keep them quiet.
>
> JOINING 1: Bill's dogs will start barking at exactly four o'clock, although he tries to keep them quiet.
>
> JOINING 2: Although he tries to keep them quiet, Bill's dogs will start barking at exactly four o'clock.

And another example:

> BOSS: The book is puzzling the inspector.
>
> EMPLOYEE: that Edgar left behind at the scene of the crime
>
> JOINING: The book that Edgar left behind at the scene of the crime is puzzling the inspector.

The joined example sentences are all grammatically legal because they all contain at least one complete thought (the 'boss', also known as an independent clause). In several of the sample sentences, the less important idea is connected to the rest of the sentence by a subordinate conjunction, indicating that the ideas are not of equal importance. See the next section for more information on subordinate conjunctions.

Choosing subordinate conjunctions

The conjunctions in the boss–employee type of sentence do double duty. These conjunctions emphasise that one idea ('boss' or independent clause) is more important than the other ('employee' or subordinate clause), and they also give some information about the relationship between the two ideas. These conjunctions are called *subordinate conjunctions*. Here are some common subordinate conjunctions: *while, because, although, though, since, when, where, if, whether, before, until, than, as, as if, in order that, so that, whenever* and *wherever*. (Phew!)

Check out how subordinate conjunctions are used in these examples:

> Sentence 1: Martin was shaving. (not a very important activity)
>
> Sentence 2: The earthquake destroyed the city. (a rather important event)

If these two sentences are joined as equals, the writer emphasises both events:

> Martin was shaving, *and* the earthquake destroyed the city.

Grammatically, the sentence is legal. Morally, this statement poses a problem. Do you really think that Martin's avoidance of five-o'clock shadow is equal in importance to an earthquake that measures seven on the Richter scale? Better to join these clauses as unequals, making the main idea about the earthquake the boss:

> *While* Martin was shaving, the earthquake destroyed the city.

or

The earthquake destroyed the city *while* Martin was shaving.

The *while* gives you *time* information, attaches the employee sentence to the boss sentence, and shows the greater importance of the earthquake. Not bad for five letters.

Here's another:

> Sentence 1: Isolde must do her homework now.
>
> Sentence 2: Mum is on the warpath.

In combining these two ideas, you have a few decisions to make. First of all, if you put them together as equals, the reader will wonder why you're mentioning both statements at the same time:

> Isolde must do her homework now, *but* Mum is on the warpath.

This joining may mean that Mum is running around the house screaming at the top of her lungs. Although Isolde has often managed to concentrate on her history homework while playing CDs of Wagner operas at mirror-shattering levels, she finds that concentrating is impossible during Mum's tantrums. Isolde won't get anything done until Mum settles down with a cup of tea. That's one possible meaning of this joined sentence. But why leave your reader guessing? Try another joining:

> Isolde must do her homework now *because* Mum is on the warpath.

This sentence is much clearer: Isolde's mother just got a note from her daughter's teacher about her missed homework. Isolde knows that, if she wants to survive long enough to leave school, she'd better get to work now. One more joining to check:

> Mum is on the warpath *because* Isolde must do her homework now.

OK, in this version Isolde's mother has asked her daughter to help clean the house. She's been asking Isolde every ten minutes for the last three hours. Now Isolde's grandparents are about to arrive and Mum's really upset. But Isolde has told her that she can't clean up now because she has to do her homework (which, of course, she has **not** spent the last three hours doing). The Third World War breaks out!

Do you see the power of these joining words? These subordinate conjunctions strongly influence the meanings of the sentences.

Steering clear of fragments

Remember: Don't write a sentence without a 'boss' or independent clause, the section that can stand alone as a complete sentence. If you leave an 'employee' all by itself, you've got trouble. An 'employee' all by itself is called a sentence fragment. A *sentence fragment* is any set of words that doesn't fit the definition of a complete sentence. Like run-on sentences, sentence fragments are crimes in formal English. Don't let the number of words in sentence fragments fool you. Not all sentence fragments are short, though some are. Decide by meaning, not by length.

Here are some fragments, so you know what to avoid:

When it rained pennies from heaven

As if he were king of the world

After the ball was over but before it was time to begin the first day of the rest of your life and all those other clichés that you read every day in magazines on your way to work

Whether Mortimer likes it or not

Whether you like it or not, and despite the fact that you don't like it, although I am really sorry that you are upset

If hell freezes over

Further to your letter of the 17th

and so on.

Which of these is a sentence fragment? Which is a complete sentence? Which is a comma splice (a run-on sentence)?

A. Edgar sneezed.

B. Because Edgar sneezed in the middle of the opera, just when the women in those helmets with the little horns on top were putting down their spears and shields and taking off their armour.

C. Edgar sneezed, I pulled out a handkerchief.

Answers: Sentence A is complete. Sentence B is not really a sentence; it's a fragment with no complete idea. Sentence C is a comma splice because it contains two complete thoughts joined only by a comma.

The reason being is that I like grammar

Many people say *the reason being is that* to introduce an explanation. But the idea of *is* is there already in *being*, so saying *is* as well is like saying *the reason is is that*. Say *the reason is* if the reason is the 'boss' in the sentence and *the reason being* if it's the 'employee'. Or try a simpler way of saying the same thing (like *because*). Here are some examples:

RIGHT: The reason *is that* I don't like her boyfriend, but I didn't like to say so.

ALSO RIGHT: She wasn't going with them, the reason *being that* she doesn't like his girlfriend.

EVEN BETTER: She said she wasn't going with them *because* Damian drinks and drives.

WRONG: Bill bought a turkey, the reason being is that it was Christmas.

RIGHT: Bill bought a turkey, the reason being that it was Christmas.

ALSO RIGHT: It was Christmas, so Bill bought a turkey.

And *being that* on its own isn't acceptable in formal English. For example:

WRONG: The turkey shed a tear or two, *being that* it was Christmas.

RIGHT: The turkey shed a tear or two, *because* it was Christmas.

You may like the sound of *since* in the following sentences. The dictionaries now say that *because* is one meaning of *since*, and so far civilisation as we know it hasn't crumbled. The grammarians who like to predict the end of the world because of such issues prefer to use *since* only for time statements like these:

Bill realised suddenly that he hadn't seen the turkey *since* he brought it home and left it on the table.

Since she left Damian, Deborah has begun an affair with Bill.

Another grammatical no-no is *irregardless*. I think *irregardless* is popular because it's a long word that feels good when you say it. Those *r's* just roll right off the tongue. Sadly, *irregardless* is not a conjunction. It's not even a word, according to the dictionary. Use *regardless* (not nearly so much fun to pronounce) or *despite the fact that* – or, if you want a long, impressive-sounding word, *irrespective*.

WRONG: Irregardless, we are going to eat you, you turkey!

RIGHT: Regardless, we are going to eat you, you turkey!

ALSO RIGHT: Despite the fact that you are a tough old bird, we are going to eat you, you turkey!

RIGHT AGAIN: Irrespective of your feelings about the matter, we are going to eat you, you turkey!

Employing Pronouns to Combine Sentences

A useful trick for combining short sentences legally is the *pronoun connection*. (A *pronoun* substitutes for a noun, which is a word for a person, place, thing, or idea. See Chapter 10 for more information.) Check out these combinations:

Sentence 1: Lucinda read the book.

Sentence 2: The book had a thousand pictures in it.

Joining: Lucinda read the book *that* had a thousand pictures in it.

Sentence 1: Damian's master plan stuck to Edgar's shoe.

Sentence 2: He's going to use the plan to break the bank at Monte Carlo.

Joining: Damian's master plan, *which* he's going to use to break the bank at Monte Carlo, stuck to Edgar's shoe.

Sentence 1: Mildred wants to hire a bricklayer.

Sentence 2: The bricklayer will build a big wall between her garden and her neighbour Bill's.

Joining: Mildred wants to hire a bricklayer *who* will build a big wall between her garden and her neighbour Bill's.

Sentence 1: Mortimer wants to marry Lucinda.

Sentence 2: He has been adoring her from afar for two weeks.

Joining: Mortimer, *who* has been adoring her from afar for two weeks, wants to marry Lucinda.

An even better joining: Mortimer, *who* has been adoring Lucinda from afar for two weeks, wants to marry her.

Sentence 1: The Budget was announced yesterday.

Sentence 2: The Budget lowers taxes for 0.00009 per cent of people.

Joining: The Budget *that* was announced yesterday lowers taxes for 0.00009 per cent of people.

Alternative joining: The Budget *that* was announced yesterday lowers taxes for billionaires.

That, *which* and *who* are pronouns. In the combined sentences, each takes the place of a noun. (*That* replaces *book*, *which* replaces *master plan*, *who* replaces *bricklayer*, *who* replaces *Mortimer*, and *that* replaces *Budget*.) These pronouns serve as glue, firmly attaching a subordinate or less important idea to the main body of the sentence.

That, *which* and *who* (as well as *whom* and *whose*) are pronouns that may relate one idea to another. When they do that job, they are called *relative pronouns*. Relative pronouns often serve as subjects or objects of the subordinate or dependent clause. For more information on clauses see Chapter 24.

Where and *when* can also be used to join things together in this way.

Rewrite these notes by a reporter from Bill's local paper to make them into one sentence.

> Sentence 1: Inspector Barker has not been removed from the case.
>
> Sentence 2: The victim lived next door to Bill.
>
> Sentence 3: Bill is Inspector Barker's brother.

Answer: Inspector Barker, whose brother, Bill, lived next door to the victim, has not been removed from the case. (The pronoun *whose* replaces *Inspector Barker's*.)

Another answer: Although Bill Barker, who lived next door to the victim, is Inspector Barker's brother, the inspector has not been removed from the case. (The pronoun *who* replaces *Bill*.)

What the paper isn't mentioning is that Bill isn't a suspect because he was in hospital with a broken leg at the time of the murder.

Now help the Inspector to make his notes flow smoothly for his report by joining the sentences.

> Sentence 1: Lucinda was shopping with Alice at the time of the murder.
>
> Sentence 2: Lucinda tried on most of the shoes in her size.
>
> Sentence 3: Staff in the shoe shop remembered Lucinda.
>
> Sentence 4: Susie was looking for Lucinda at the restaurant.
>
> Sentence 5: Lucinda works in the restaurant part time.
>
> Sentence 6: The waiters remembered Susie.
>
> Sentence 7: The day of the murder was the day Brad Pitt had lunch in the restaurant.

Answer: There are lots of ways to join these sentences together. Here are two:

At the time of the murder, Susie was looking for Lucinda at the restaurant where Lucinda works part time. The waiters remembered because that was the day Brad Pitt had lunch there. Lucinda was shopping with Alice. Staff in the shoe shop remembered her because she tried on most of the shoes in her size.

or

Because Lucinda tried on most of the shoes in her size, the staff there remembered she was shopping with Alice at the time of the murder. The waiters at the restaurant where Lucinda works part time remembered that Susie was looking for her on the day Brad Pitt had lunch in the restaurant.

Chapter 8

Do You Feel Bad or Badly? The Lowdown on Adjectives and Adverbs

In This Chapter

▶ Identifying adjectives and adverbs

▶ Deciding whether an adjective or an adverb is appropriate

▶ Understanding why double negatives are wrong

▶ Placing descriptive words so that the sentence means what you intend

*W*ith the right nouns (names of persons, places, things, or ideas) and verbs (action or being words) you can build a pretty solid foundation in a sentence. In this chapter we explain the two basic types of descriptive words of the English language – *adjectives* and *adverbs*. We also show you how to use each correctly to add meaning to your sentence.

You may be wondering whether these words really matter. If you've ever wished that a book you're reading would stop describing the scenery and get on with the story, you probably think that descriptive words just hold up the action. But sometimes they can be the key to expressing your meaning. If you don't believe that, take a look at this sentence:

> Lucinda was sauntering past Harrods when the sight of a Ferragamo Paradiso Pump paralysed her.

Would you understand this sentence? What do you need to know in order to make sense of it? Apart from the meaning of words like *saunter* (which you could find in a dictionary if you weren't sure what it meant), you'd need some background information. For example:

✔ Harrods is a department store. (You probably do know that.)

✔ Ferragamo is an expensive shoe label. (Maybe you know that.)

✔ A Paradiso Pump is a type of shoe. (You couldn't know that because we made it up.)

It would also help to know that Lucinda is obsessed with shoes. If you knew all this, or if you have a good imagination and the ability to use context clues when reading, you probably understood it.

But what if you didn't know all this to start with? That's when descriptions can be useful. Here's version two:

> Lucinda was sauntering past the *famous* Harrods *department* store when the sight of a *fashionable green low-heeled dress* shoe with the *ultra-chic Ferragamo* label paralysed her.

OK, it's overloaded a bit, but you get the point. The descriptive words help to clarify the meaning of the sentence, particularly for the fashion-challenged.

Now that you realise that descriptions can be essential to the meaning of a sentence, I know you're dying to find out more. Read on.

Adding Adjectives

An *adjective* is a descriptive word that adds information on number, colour, type and other qualities to your sentence.

Where do you find adjectives? Most of the time you find them in front of a noun (the one the adjective is describing), but they roam about a bit. You may find them after the noun sometimes, or after a pronoun (when they're describing the pronoun). And sometimes you find them connected to their noun by a linking verb. We'll look at all these ways of using adjectives in turn.

Adjectives describing nouns

The most common job for an adjective is describing a noun. Here are some sentences with the adjectives in italics:

> There is a *poisonous* snake on your shoulder.

> There is an *angry poisonous* snake on your shoulder.

> There is a *rubber* snake on your shoulder.

All the adjectives are describing the noun *snake* and they're all in front of the noun. The second sentence has two adjectives and they're stuck together without anything connecting or separating them. (You're allowed to put a comma between them, but that's one of those things that people disagree about. These commas aren't very fashionable any more, but some people like them.)

In these three sentences, those little descriptive words certainly make a difference. They give you information that you would really like to have. See how diverse and powerful adjectives can be?

Now here's an example with the adjectives after the noun:

> Edgar, *sore* and *tired*, pleaded with Sandy to release him from the headlock she had placed on him.

Sore and *tired* tell you about *Edgar*. Note that when more than one adjective is used after a noun they need to be joined by an *and*. You can't just say *Edgar, sore tired* (or at least not without changing the meaning – *sore* doesn't seem to be describing *Edgar* any more). If there are more than two adjectives, you should punctuate them like a list:

> Edgar, *sore, tired and thirsty*, pleaded with Sandy to release him from the headlock she had placed on him.

(There's more on punctuating lists in Chapter 14.)

Adjectives describing pronouns

Adjectives can also describe *pronouns* (words that substitute for nouns):

> There's something *strange* on your shoulder. (The adjective *strange* describes the pronoun *something*.)

> Everyone *conscious* at the end of the play made a quick exit. (The adjective *conscious* describes the pronoun *everyone*.)

> Anyone *free* should report to the meeting room immediately! (The adjective *free* describes the pronoun *anyone*.)

As you can see, these adjectives usually go after their pronouns.

Attaching adjectives to linking verbs

Adjectives may also follow *linking verbs*, in which case they describe the subject of the sentence (which can, of course, be a noun or a pronoun). Linking verbs join two ideas, associating one with the other. They are like giant equals signs, equating the subject (which comes before the verb) with another idea after the verb. (See Chapter 2 for a full discussion of linking verbs.)

Sometimes a linking verb joins the subject to an adjective (or a couple of adjectives):

> The afternoon appears *dull* because of the smoke from Damian's cigars. (The adjective *dull* describes the noun *afternoon*.)

> Lucinda's dress is *long* and *purple*. (The adjectives *long* and *purple* describe the noun *dress*.)

You'll notice that there has to be an *and* between the adjectives *long* and *purple* when they come after a linking verb (just as there does when two or more adjectives come *after* a noun).

Find the adjectives in this sentence.

> Gentle Martin always has a kind word for everyone exhausted by rehearsals even though he is tired and hungry too.

Answer: *gentle* (describing *Martin*), *kind* (describing *word*), *exhausted* (describing *everyone*), *tired* and *hungry* (describing *he*).

When adjectives are positioned before a noun (*the red rose*) they are called *attributive* adjectives. When they follow a linking verb (*the rose is red*), they are called *predicative* adjectives. Most adjectives in English can be used in both ways (like *red*), but some can't. For example, *alive* and *asleep* can't be used attributively – you can say *the children are asleep* and *the snake is alive* but not *the asleep children* or *the alive snake*. And *mere* and *latter* can't be used predicatively – you can say *a mere infant* and *the latter half* but not *the infant is mere* or *the half is latter*. Weird, huh! OK, you can forget that now.

Pop the question: identifying adjectives

To find adjectives, go to the words they describe (nouns and pronouns). Start with the noun and ask these three questions:

- ✔ How many?
- ✔ Which one?
- ✔ What kind?

Take a look at this sentence:

> Lucinda placed the three short red skirts in her new wardrobe.

You see three nouns: *Lucinda*, *skirts* and *wardrobe*. You can't find answers to the questions *Which Lucinda?* and *What kind of Lucinda?* No words in the sentence provide that information, so no adjectives describe *Lucinda*.

But try the three questions on *skirts* and *wardrobe* and you do come up with something. How many skirts? Answer: *three*. *Three* is an adjective. What kind of skirts? Answer: *red* and *short*. *Red* and *short* are adjectives. The same goes for *wardrobe*. What kind? Answer: *new*. *New* is an adjective.

Her answers one of the questions. (Which *wardrobe*? Answer: *her wardrobe*.) *Her* is working as an adjective, but *her* is also a pronoun. Don't worry about the distinction, unless your goal is to be an authority on the subject (sure to be a conversation stopper at parties). Some English textbooks call *her* a pronoun, and others call *her* an adjective. Whatever you want to call it, *her* functions in the same way in the sentence. This kind of completely irrelevant discussion gives English teachers a bad reputation.

Look at another sentence:

> Damian's interested glance thrilled Lucinda's innocent little heart.

This sentence has four nouns. Two (*Damian's* and *Lucinda's*) are possessive. If you ask how many *Lucinda's*, which *Lucinda's*, or what kind of *Lucinda's*, or ask the same questions about *Damian's*, you get no answer. So there are no adjectives here. The other two nouns, *glance* and *heart*, do yield an answer. What kind of glance? *Interested*. What kind of heart? *Innocent*, *little*. So *interested*, *innocent* and *little* are all adjectives.

You may notice that a word changes its part of speech depending on how it's used in the sentence. In the last sample sentence, *glance* is a noun, because *glance* is clearly a thing. Compare that sentence with this one:

> Yasmin and Edgar *glance* casually at the giant television screen.

Here *glance* isn't a thing, it's an action that Yasmin and Edgar are performing. In this example sentence, *glance* is a verb. The moral of the story? Read the sentence, see what the word is doing, and then – if you like – give it a name.

Stalking the Common Adverb

Adjectives aren't the only descriptive words. Adverbs are also descriptive words. These alter the meaning of a verb, an adjective, or another adverb. Check these out:

> The boss *regretfully* said no to Rashid's request for a raise.

The boss *furiously* said no to Rashid's request for a raise.

The boss *never* said no to Rashid's requests for a raise.

If you're Rashid, you care whether the word *regretfully*, *furiously* or *never* is in the sentence. *Regretfully*, *furiously* and *never* are all adverbs. Notice how adverbs add meaning in these sentences:

Ellie *sadly* sang Martin's latest song. (Perhaps Ellie is feeling sad or perhaps it's a sad song.)

Ellie sang Martin's latest song *reluctantly*. (Ellie doesn't want to sing this song or she doesn't feel like singing at all.)

Ellie *hoarsely* sang Martin's latest song. (Ellie has a cold.)

Ellie sang Martin's latest song *quickly*. (Ellie is in a hurry.)

Pop the question: finding the adverb

Adverbs mostly describe verbs, giving more information about an action. Nearly all adverbs (enough so that you don't have to worry about the ones that fall through the cracks) answer one of these four questions:

- How?
- When?
- Where?
- Why?

To find the adverb, go to the verb and pop the question. (See Chapter 2 for information on finding the verbs.) Look at this sentence:

Mortimer happily financed Martin's new musical yesterday.

There's one verb here: *financed*. *Financed* how? Answer: *happily*. *Happily* is an adverb. *Financed* when? Answer: *yesterday*. *Yesterday* is an adverb. *Financed* where? No answer. *Financed* why? Knowing Mortimer, I'd say he hopes to make a lot of money out of the enterprise, but you won't find that information in the sentence.

Here's another example:

'I've finally solved the mystery of the book,' said the sergeant quickly as he was just going home.

First, identify the verbs. There are three: *solved, said* and *was going.* Then ask the questions. Solved how? Answer: *finally. Finally* is an adverb. Solved when? Solved where? Solved why? No answers. Now for *said.* Said how? Answer: *quickly. Quickly* is an adverb. Said where? Said when? Said why? No answers. And finally, *was going.* Was going how? No answer. Was going when? Answer: *Just. Just* is an adverb. *Was* going where? Answer: *home. Home* is an adverb. Was going why? No answer. The adverbs are *finally, quickly, just* and *home.*

Adverbs can be in lots of places in a sentence. If you're trying to find them, rely on the questions *how, when, where* and *why,* not the location. Similarly, a word may be an adverb in one sentence and something else in another sentence. Check these out:

> Lucinda went *home* in a huff.
>
> *Home* is where the heart is.
>
> *Home*-cooking was something Mortimer longed for.

In the first example, *home* tells you where Lucinda went, so *home* is an adverb in that sentence. In the second example, *home* is a place, so *home* is a noun in that sentence. In the third example, *home* is an adjective, telling you what kind of *cooking* it is.

Adverbs describing adjectives and other adverbs

Adverbs also describe other descriptions, usually making the description more or less intense. (A description describing a description? Give me a break! But it's true.) Here's an example:

> Lucinda was extremely unhappy when Damian didn't phone her.

How *unhappy?* Answer: *extremely unhappy. Extremely* is an adverb describing the adjective *unhappy.*

Sometimes the questions you pose to locate adjectives and adverbs are answered by more than one word in a sentence. In the previous example sentence, if you ask *Was when?* the answer is *when Damian didn't phone her.* Don't panic. These longer answers are just different forms of adjectives and adverbs. For more information, see Chapters 9 and 24.

Now back to work. Here's another example:

> She quite sensibly put it out of her mind and reorganised her clothes.

This time an adverb is describing another adverb. *Sensibly* is an adverb because it explains how Lucinda *put*. In other words, *sensibly* describes the verb *put*. How *sensibly?* Answer: *quite sensibly. Quite* is an adverb describing the adverb *sensibly*, which in turn describes the verb *put*.

In general, you don't need to worry too much about adverbs that describe adjectives or other adverbs; only a few errors are associated with this type of description. See 'Sorting out adjective/adverb pairs' later in this chapter for some tips.

Distinguishing Between Adjectives and Adverbs

Does it matter whether a word is an adjective or an adverb? Some of the time, no. You've been talking and writing happily for years, and you've spent very little time worrying about this issue. In your crib, you demanded, 'I want a bottle NOW.' You didn't know you were adding an adverb to your sentence. For that matter, you didn't know you were making a sentence. You were just hungry. But some of the time knowing the difference is helpful. In this section we tell you how to apply the *–ly* test to sort adjectives from adverbs and how to decide between some commonly confused pairs of adjectives and adverbs.

Sorting adjectives from adverbs: the –ly test

Strictly is an adverb, and *strict* is an adjective. *Nicely* is an adverb, and *nice* is an adjective. *Generally* is an adverb, and *general* is an adjective. *Lovely* is a . . . gotcha! You were going to say *adverb*, right? Wrong. *Lovely* is an adjective. But you can use the *–ly* test for lots of adverbs. Just bear in mind that not all *–ly* words are adverbs and that lots of words (like *soon, now, home* and *fast*) are adverbs even though they don't end in *–ly*. The best way to tell if a word is an adverb is to ask the four adverb questions: *how, when, where* and *why.* If the word answers one of those questions, it's an adverb.

Not is an adverb because it reverses the meaning of the verb from positive to negative. While I'm speaking of *not*, I should remind you to avoid double negatives. In many languages (Spanish, for example), doubling or tripling the negative adjectives and adverbs or throwing in a negative pronoun or two simply makes your denial stronger. In Spanish, saying 'I did not kill no victim' is OK. In

English, however, that sentence is a confession. English grammar, supremely irrational in a million ways (see Chapter 3 on irregular verbs!), decides that strict logic is best in sentences with negatives. If you *did not* kill *no* victim, you must have killed at least *one* victim. In other words, two negatives equal a positive (there's maths rearing its ugly head again). You can put a lot of negatives together – just don't put them in the same sentence. (Other types of double negative may trip you up. See Chapter 22 for more information.)

Identify the adjectives and adverbs in the following sentences.

A. Thank him for the lovely presents he so kindly gave you yesterday.

B. Her knitting, folded neatly in her old work basket, will not be finished.

Answers: In sentence A, *lovely* is an adjective describing *presents. Kindly* is an adverb describing the verb *gave*, and *so* is an adverb describing the adverb *kindly. Yesterday* is an adverb describing when he *gave* the presents. In sentence B, *neatly* is an adverb describing the verb *folded. Old* and *work* are adjectives describing *basket. Not* is an adverb reversing the meaning of the verb *will be finished.* (And you can call *her* an adjective if you want to.)

Sorting out adjective/adverb pairs

Time for some practice in choosing between adjectives and adverbs. A lot of common adverbs are distinguished from their adjectives by the letters *–ly*:

There was a *sudden* gasp when Ophelia tripped as she walked on stage.

Clarence stopped *suddenly* when the stop sign loomed.

Sudden is an adjective describing the noun *gasp. Suddenly* is an adverb describing how Clarence *stopped* (a verb).

Take a look at these examples (we'll begin with some easy pairs, to allow you to apply the *–ly* test):

WRONG: Damian grins *casual* when he's bluffing.

RIGHT: Damian grins *casually* when he's bluffing.

WHY IT'S RIGHT: The adverb *casually* describes how Damian *grins.*

ALSO RIGHT: Damian's *casual* grin gives him away every time.

WHY IT'S ALSO RIGHT: The adjective *casual* describes the noun *grin.*

Don't stop now! Check these examples:

> WRONG: The syrup tasted *sweetly* when Bill tried it.
>
> RIGHT: The syrup tasted *sweet* when Bill tried it.
>
> WHY IT'S RIGHT: The adjective *sweet* describes the noun *syrup*. *Tasted* is a linking verb, so the adjective that follows the verb describes the subject.
>
> ALSO RIGHT: Bill drowns his pancakes in *sweet* syrup.
>
> WHY IT'S ALSO RIGHT: The adjective *sweet* describes the noun *syrup*.

One last set:

> WRONG: I did really *bad* on the test, Dad.
>
> RIGHT: I did really *badly* on the test, Dad.
>
> WHY IT'S RIGHT: The adverb *badly* describes how I *did* (a verb).Confusing *bad* and *badly* is a common error. But, as you can see, the *–ly* test works.

Also, watch out for verbs that can be linking or non-linking depending on the sense of the sentence. Are you feeling *bad* or *badly*? You feel *bad* if you do something wrong. *Feel* here is a linking verb (I = bad). You feel *badly* if for some reason – an anaesthetic at the dentist, perhaps – you've suddenly become unable to feel properly. Here, *feel* is a non-linking verb. (For more on the difference between linking and non-linking verbs, see Chapter 2.)

Remember: Adjectives describe nouns or pronouns, and adverbs describe verbs, adjectives, or other adverbs. The sentences in this section were easy. Your ear for good English probably told you the proper word choice. However, sometimes your ear may not automatically tell you which word is correct. In the next sections we'll look at some confusing pairs, including good/well and continual/continuous.

Choosing between good and well

Do you ever think it would be a good idea to abolish all those irregular forms? Then the adjective *good* could have an adverb *goodly*. Oh, wait a minute – we already have the word *goodly* (although you probably don't use it much) and it's an adjective! Curses. Back to plan A.

Good is an adjective, and *well* is an adverb (except when you're talking about your health):

> What's that book you're reading? Is it any *good?*
>
> Edgar plays the piano *well.*
>
> I'm *well.*

In the first sentence, *good* is an adjective describing *it*. In the second sentence, *well* is an adverb. It describes how Edgar *plays* (a verb). In the third sentence, *well* is an adjective describing *I* (*'m*, short for *am*, is a linking verb). The sentence means *I am not sick*. Now look at this one:

> I'm *good*.

In this sentence, *good* is an adjective. Unfortunately, it's anybody's guess what the sentence really means. Said in pious tones, it could mean *I have the qualities of goodness (they're proposing me for sainthood next week)*. It could mean *I am in a good mood*. But it's generally used to mean *I haven't finished the drink I've got, thanks*, or *I think that's a good idea, count me in*, or even *Go away, I don't feel like talking to anybody*. So it's fine to use it when chatting to friends – they know you and have your body language and tone of voice as well as the context of the conversation to help them understand what you mean. In writing, try to think of another word to replace *good* – a more interesting one that will make your meaning clear.

Which sentence is correct?

A. When asked how he was feeling, Damian smiled at his ex-wife Hazel and replied, 'Not well.'

B. When asked how he was feeling, Damian smiled at his ex-wife Hazel and replied, 'Not good.'

Answer: Sentence A is correct because Damian's ex is inquiring about his health.

Now fill in the spaces in these sentences with *good* or *well*.

A. Sandy skates . . . doesn't she?

B. She has really . . . skates.

Answer: Sentence A needs *well* (an adverb) because *well* describes *skates* (and in this sentence *skates* is a verb). *Skates* how? Answer: *skates well*. Sentence B needs *good* (an adjective) because *good* describes *skates* (which is a noun here). What kind? Answer: *good*.

Choosing between continuous/continuously and continual/continually

A pair of words that may confuse you is *continuous* and *continual*. Read this paragraph:

> The continual interruptions are driving me crazy. Every ten minutes someone barges in and asks me where the coffee machine is. Do I look like a coffee house? I've been working *continuously* for seven hours. Perhaps I'll stop for a while and find that coffee machine.

Continual refers to events that happen over and over again, but with breaks in between. *Continuous* means without stopping. *Continuous* noise is steady, uninterrupted, like the drone of a refrigerator that's about to die but is making a heroic effort round the clock to keep your drinks cold until it does. *Continual* noise is what you hear when someone with a pneumatic drill is digging a hole in the street outside your window. Every time the noise stops for five seconds, you hope they've finished. But then they start again. Both words have an adjectival and an adverbial form. Here are some examples:

> WRONG: Bibi screamed *continually* until Susie trapped the bee and took it outside.

> WHY IT'S WRONG: Bibi's screams don't come and go. When she's upset, she's really upset, and nothing shuts her up until she gets what she wants.

> RIGHT: Bibi screamed *continuously* until Susie trapped the bee and took it outside.

> WHY IT'S RIGHT: In this version, Bibi takes no breaks.

Check out another set of examples:

> WRONG: Mortimer's *continuous* attempts to impress Lucinda were fruitless, including the substantial raise he gave Rashid on Monday and the lunch menu with Ellie's favourite foods that he introduced in the theatre restaurant on Tuesday.

> WHY IT'S WRONG: Mortimer's attempts stop and start. He does something on Monday, goes away to think when that doesn't work, and then does something else on Tuesday.

> RIGHT: Mortimer's *continual* attempts to impress Lucinda were fruitless, including the complimentary tickets he gave her parents on Wednesday and the sponsorship deal he offered Sandy on Thursday.

> WHY IT'S RIGHT: Now the sentence expresses a recurring action.

Adjectives and adverbs that look the same

Odd words here and there (and they are odd) do double duty as both adjectives and adverbs. They look exactly the same, but they take their identity as adjectives or adverbs from the way that they function in the sentence. Take a look at these examples:

> Upon seeing the stop sign, Clarence stopped *short.* (adverb)

> Clarence did not notice the sign until the last minute because he is too *short* to see over the steering wheel. (adjective)

> Mildred's advice is *right:* Clarence should not drive. (adjective)

> Clarence turned *right* after his last-minute stop. (adverb)

Clarence came to a *hard* decision when he turned in his licence. (adjective)

Mildred tries *hard* to schedule some time for Clarence, now that he is carless. (adverb)

The English language has too many adjectives and adverbs to list here. If you're unsure about a particular word, check the dictionary for the correct form.

Which sentence is correct?

A. It was real nice of Damian to send you flowers.

B. It was really nice of Damian to send you flowers.

Answer: B. How *nice? Really nice. Real* is an adjective and *really* is an adverb. Adverbs answer the question *how.*

Avoiding Common Mistakes with Adjectives and Adverbs

A few words – *even, almost, only* and others – often end up in the wrong spots. If these words aren't placed correctly, your sentence may say something that you didn't intend.

Placing even

Even is one of the sneaky modifiers that can land anywhere in a sentence – and change the meaning of what you're saying. Take a look at this example:

It's two hours before the grand opening of Mortimer's musical, and the star of the show goes down with food poisoning. What will Mortimer do? Lucinda has a suggestion:

✔ Possibility 1: Lucinda shouts, 'We can still go on! *Even Alice* knows the dances.'

✔ Possibility 2: Lucinda shouts, 'We can still go on! Alice *even knows* the dances.'

✔ Possibility 3: Lucinda shouts, 'We can still go on! Alice knows *even the dances.*'

What's going on here? These three statements look almost the same, but they aren't. Here's what each one means:

- Possibility 1: Lucinda isn't worried. She knows several people who could step in and save the day because the role isn't very demanding. In particular, the dances are very easy. Alice is very slow at learning dance steps, but *even Alice* knows the dances.

- Possibility 2: Lucinda knows that a replacement must be found, and suddenly she realises that there's an obvious candidate: Alice not only knows all the songs – she *even knows* the dances.

- Possibility 3: One person who may be able to take over the role is Alice because she can handle the songs and already know the dialogue. But can she manage the dances? It doesn't take long to find out, to everyone's relief, that Alice knows *even the dances.*

Got it? *Even* is a description; *even* describes the words that follow it. To put it another way, *even* begins a comparison:

- Possibility 1: *even* Alice (as well as everyone else)

- Possibility 2: *even* knows (doesn't have to learn)

- Possibility 3: *even* the dances (as well as the songs and words)

So here's the rule. Put *even* at the beginning of the comparison implied in the sentence.

Placing almost

Almost is another tricky little modifier to place. Here's an example:

> Last night Lucinda wrote for *almost* an hour and then went skating.

and

> Last night Lucinda *almost* wrote for an hour and then went skating.

In the first sentence, Lucinda wrote for 55 minutes and then stopped. In the second sentence, Lucinda intended to write, but every time she sat down at the computer, she remembered that she hadn't watered the plants, called Yasmin, made a sandwich and so forth. After an hour of wasted time and without one word on the screen, she grabbed her skates and left.

Farther and further

Here we have two words and two meanings and another really pointless argument. The meanings are: 1) a longer distance away; 2) more or additional. Most people dislike *farther* and don't use it. (They use *further* for both meanings – and everyone seems to know what they mean.) Sticklers like to use *farther* when distance is involved and *further* for *more* or *additional*. There's no historical reason for this. *Further* is the older word (*farther* was a later variant which had the *same* meaning). You can now forget all this. All it means is that you're safe using *further* and forgetting *farther* completely if you want to. If your boss doesn't like it, use *farther* when talking about distances but tell him that 'Fowler doesn't agree'. *Fowler* is one of the books that sticklers like to quote at people (you can find out more about it in Chapter 27). It does them good to have it quoted back at them, as it gives them something to do, checking up on what you've said. They really enjoy that. Here are a couple of examples in case you have a boss who insists you use both:

Bill has travelled *farther* than anyone he knows. (*farther = a longer distance*)

Mortimer thinks *further* attempts may upset Lucinda, so he's avoiding her. (*further = more*)

Almost begins the comparison. Lulu *almost wrote*, but she didn't. Or Lulu wrote for *almost an hour*, but not for a *whole hour*. In deciding where to put these words, add the missing words and see whether the position of the word makes sense. (There's more on comparisons in Chapter 17.)

Placing only

If only the word *only* were simpler to understand! Like the other tricky words in this section, *only* changes the meaning of the sentence every time its position is altered. For example:

Only Bill went to Iceland last summer. (No one else went.)

Bill *only* went to Iceland last summer. (He went, but he didn't do anything else.)

Bill went *only* to Iceland last summer. (He skipped Antarctica.)

Bill went to Iceland *only* last summer. (Two possible meanings: *either* he didn't go three years ago or at any other time, but he did go last summer *or* the word *only* means *just*, as in *recently.*)

Chapter 9

Prepositions, Interjections and Articles

*H*ow does the proverb go? Little things mean a lot? Whoever said that was probably talking about prepositions. Some of the shortest words in the language – at least most of them – these little guys pack a punch in your sentences. All the more reason to use them correctly. In this chapter, we explain everything you always wanted to know about prepositions but hoped you wouldn't have to ask. We also give you the basics on interjections (the rarest parts of speech) and articles (the most common words in the language).

Proposing Relationships: Prepositions

Imagine that you encounter two nouns: *aardvark* and *book*. (A *noun* is a word for a person, place, thing, or idea.) How many ways can you connect the two nouns to express different ideas?

the book *about* the aardvark

the book *by* the aardvark

the book *behind* the aardvark

the book *in front of* the aardvark

the book *near* the aardvark

the book *under* the aardvark

The italicised words relate two nouns to each other. These relationship words are called prepositions. *Prepositions* may be defined as any word or group of words that relates a noun or a pronoun to another word in the sentence.

Take a look at Table 9-1 for a list of some common prepositions.

Table 9-1	Common Prepositions		
about	above	according to	across
after	against	along	amid
among	around	at	before
behind	below	beside	besides
between	beyond	by	concerning
down	during	except	for
from	in	into	like
of	off	on	over
past	since	through	toward
underneath	until	up	upon
with	within	without	

The objects of my affection: prepositional phrases and their objects

Prepositions never travel alone; they're always with an object. In the examples in the previous section, the object of each preposition is *aardvark*. Just to get all the annoying terminology over with at once, a *prepositional phrase* consists of a preposition and its object. The object of a preposition is always a noun or a pronoun, or perhaps one or two of each. (A *pronoun* is a word that takes the place of a noun, like *he* for *Edgar* and so forth.)

Here's an example:

In the excitement, Edgar's snowball hit Clarence on his little bald head.

This sentence has two prepositions: *in* and *on*. *Excitement* is the object of the preposition *in*, and *head* is the object of the preposition *on*.

Why, you may ask, is the object *head* and not *little* or *bald*? Sigh. I was hoping you wouldn't notice. OK, here's the explanation. You can throw a few other things inside a prepositional phrase – mainly descriptive words. Check out these variations on the plain phrase *of the aardvark:*

> of the *apologetic* aardvark
>
> of the *always apoplectic* aardvark
>
> of the *antagonisingly argumentative* aardvark

Despite the different descriptions, each phrase is still basically talking about an *aardvark*. Also, *aardvark* is a noun, and only nouns and pronouns are allowed to be objects of the preposition. So you need to choose the most important word as the object of the preposition. Also, you need to choose a noun, not an adjective. Examine *his little bald head* (the words, not Clarence's actual head, which is better seen from a distance). *Head* is clearly the important concept, and *head* is a noun. Thus *head* is the object of the preposition.

Pop the question: questions that identify the objects of the prepositions

All objects – of a verb or of a preposition – answer the questions *whom?* or *what?* To find the object of a preposition, ask *whom?* or *what?* after the preposition.

In this sentence there are two prepositional phrases:

> Edgar suddenly realised that the book he usually kept beside his bed must be at Ms Stakes's house.

The first preposition is *beside. Beside* what? *Beside his bed. Bed* is the object of the preposition *beside.* The second preposition is *at. At* what? *At Ms Stakes's house. House* is the object of the preposition *at.*

What is the object of the preposition in this sentence?

> Nurse Oduwole knew that Inspector Barker was looking into her old English teacher's death.

Answer: *death* is the object of the preposition *into.* When you pop the question – *into* whom? or what? – the answer is *her old English teacher's death.* The most important word is *death*, which is a noun.

Why do I need to know this?

When you're checking subject–verb pairs, you need to identify and then ignore the prepositional phrases. Why? Because the prepositional phrases are distractions. If you don't ignore them, you may end up matching the verb to the wrong word. See Chapter 11 for more information on subject–verb agreement. You may also find it helpful to recognise prepositional phrases because sometimes, when you 'pop the question' to find an adjective or an adverb, the answer is a prepositional phrase. Don't panic. You haven't done anything wrong. Simply know that a prepositional phrase may do the same job as an adjective or adverb. (See Chapter 8 for more on adjectives and adverbs.)

Prepositional phrases fall into two large categories – *adjectival phrases* and *adverbial phrases.* You don't have any reason at all to know this fact, so forget it immediately unless you're set on being a grammarian yourself.

You should pay attention to prepositions because choosing the wrong one may be embarrassing:

> Person 1: May I sit *next* to you?
>
> Person 2: (smiling) Certainly.
>
> Person 1: May I sit *on* you?
>
> Person 2: (sound of slap) No! Help! Police!

Are you talking to I? Prepositions and pronouns

A big preposition pitfall is pronouns. A *pronoun* is a word that substitutes for a noun. The problem with pronouns is that only some pronouns are allowed to act as objects of prepositions; they're called *object pronouns.* (See Chapters 10 and 17 for details on pronoun rules.) Use the wrong pronoun – a non-object pronoun – and the grammar cops will be after you.

The object pronouns, cleared to act as objects of the preposition, are *me, you, him, her, it, us, them, whom* and *whomever.*

Take a look at some sentences with *pronouns* as objects of the prepositions:

> I have a theory about the murder, but I have to keep it between the inspector and *me.* (*Me* is one of the objects of the preposition *between.*)
>
> Without *them,* there will be 13 for dinner. (*Them* is the object of the preposition *without.*)

In the group: between/among

Between and *among* are two tricky prepositions that are often used incorrectly. Do you remember being taught that it's something to do with how many people or things you're talking about? The usual example is something to do with sharing sweets: we're supposed to share *between* two friends or *among* three or more. (Isn't the real problem to get people to share in the first place?) Well, here's the bad news. It's worse than that! You actually have to know the nature of the relationships between the people involved. Can you imagine that? Well, it's not that bad really. You don't have to know who's dating whom and who just split up. You just have to work out whether it's quite clear what the relationships are or whether the whole thing's a muddle. Look at these examples:

> When Damian was caught cheating, it altered forever the relationships between Damian, his father and his stepmother.

There are three people involved here (Damian, Damian's father and Damian's stepmother), but *between* is correct because we can list all the relationships: Damian has a relationship with his father and a relationship with his stepmother; Damian's father has a relationship with Damian and a relationship with Damian's stepmother; Damian's stepmother . . . Oh, who cares about Damian's stepmother! This is boring. But

you see what we mean. It's possible to work out all the relationships involved (if you can be bothered to do it). But that would be impossible for this sentence:

> Policing the city was made harder by the turf wars that were continually breaking out among the city's drug gangs.

Here, *among* is correct because it's not clear which gangs are at war with which other gangs, or even how many gangs there are at any given time. Alliances are formed and broken, truces are made and new disputes break out, and if we sat down to write a report on the situation it would probably be out of date by the time we'd finished it.

It's the fuzziness of the relationships that decides whether you should use *between* or *among*. Of course, not much fuzziness is possible if you're talking about two people or things, so you're safe using *between* if that's the case. The good news is that with the old rule we had to learn a list of exceptions – when you had to use *between* even though there were more than two things (for example, that treaties were always *between* countries, however many countries were signing up). The fuzziness rule includes all the exceptions, so there's less to remember.

The anonymous letter contains a paragraph about *us*, but no one will tell us what it says. (*Us* is the object of the preposition *about*.)

What is one of the most common errors in the use of object pronouns? Is the correct prepositional phrase *between you and I* or *between you and me?* Answer: the correct expression is *between you and me*. *Between* = the preposition. *You and me* = the objects of the preposition. *Me* is an object pronoun. (*I* is a subject pronoun, so it can't be used as the object of anything, including prepositions.) The next time you hear someone say *between you and I*, you'll be able to explain the rule to them.

Which sentence is correct?

A. I was talking to Lucinda, and according to Alice and she the police aren't getting anywhere.

B. I was talking to Lucinda, and according to Alice and her the police aren't getting anywhere.

Answer: Sentence B is correct. *According to* is the preposition. The object of the preposition is *Alice and her. Her* is an object pronoun. (*She* is a subject pronoun.)

Most of the tough pronoun choices come when the sentence has more than one object of the preposition (*Alice and her*, for example, in the pop quiz). Your ear for grammar will probably tell you the correct pronoun when the sentence has a single pronoun object. You probably wouldn't say *according to she* because it sounds funny (to use a technical term).

If the sentence has more than one object of the preposition, try this rule of thumb. Take your thumb and cover one of the objects. Say the sentence. Does it sound right?

> According to Alice

OK so far. Now take your thumb and cover the other object. Say the sentence. Does it sound right?

> According to she

Now do you hear the problem? Make the change:

> According to her

Now put the two back together:

> According to Alice and her

This method is not foolproof, but there's a good chance that you'll get a clue to the correct pronoun choices if you check the objects one by one.

A good part of speech to end a sentence with?

As you read this paragraph, it's probably safe to say that global warming is increasing, we're under attack by terrorists, and your team is losing. In the midst of all these earth-shattering events, some people still walk around worrying about where to put a preposition. Specifically, they worry about whether or not ending a sentence with a preposition is acceptable. Let me illustrate the problem:

> Tell me whom he spoke *about.*

> Tell me *about* whom he spoke.

Here's the verdict: Both sentences are correct, at least for most people and even for most grammarians. But not, we must warn you, for all. You know the kind of person who insisted on ignoring the celebrations at midnight on 1 January 2000, because technically the millennium didn't really start until 1 January 2001? The kind of person who is right, but completely out of step with the rest of the culture? Well, those people still tsk-tsk when they hear a sentence that ends with a preposition. The rest of us are over it. Unless you're writing something for that kind of person, put the preposition wherever you like, including at the end of a sentence.

Interjections Are Easy!

Yes! An English topic that is foolproof. *Interjections* are exclamations that often express intense emotion. These words or phrases aren't connected grammatically to the rest of the sentence. Check out these examples:

> Yasmin: *Ouch!* I pricked my finger on that rose.

> Edgar: *Oh no.* I'm sorry – the florist swore they were thornless.

> Yasmin (laughing): *Curses,* foiled again.

Interjections may be followed by exclamation marks or full stops, but sometimes they're followed by commas. The separation by punctuation shows the reader that the interjection is a comment on the sentence, not a part of it. (Of course, in the case of the exclamation mark or full stop, the punctuation mark also indicates that the interjection is not a part of the sentence at all.)

You can't do anything wrong with interjections, except perhaps overuse them. Interjections are like salt. A little salt perks up the taste buds; too much is bad for your blood pressure (and if you really go overboard with the salt the food will be inedible).

Articles: Not Just for Magazines Any More

Another topic, this time almost foolproof. Articles are those little words – *a, an, the* – that sit in front of nouns. In meaning, *the* is usually more specific than *an* or *a.*

The superintendent wants *the* answer, and soon.

Here, *the superintendent* means one superintendent in particular. (The police force has more than one, but the sentence is referring to the one we all know and love. Everyone knows who *the* super is.) And he wants *the* answer. Not any old answer, but the truth: the name of the person who killed Ms Stakes.

The super wants *an* answer, and you'd better be quick about it.

We're still talking about one particular superintendent, but this time we're told that he wants *an* answer. Was this a slip of the tongue? Does the Superintendent really not care if it's the right answer, so long as the case is closed? Let's hope not. Perhaps the messenger just made a slip in delivering the message.

To sum up: Use *the* when you're speaking specifically and *an* or *a* when you're speaking more generally.

The is called the definite article. *A* and *an* are called indefinite articles.

So what's the difference between *a* and *an*? *A apple*? *An book*? *A* precedes words that begin with consonant sounds (all the letters except *a, e, i, o* and *u*). *An* precedes words beginning with the vowel sounds *a, e, i* and *o*. The letter *u* is a special case. If the word sounds like *you*, choose *a* (it's *a university*, for example). If the word sounds like someone kicked you in the stomach – *uh* – choose *an* (as in *it was an understandable mistake*).

Another special case is the letter *h*. If the word starts with a hard *h* sound (as in *horse*) choose *a*. If the word starts with a silent letter *h* (as in *honorable*), choose *an*. Here are some examples:

a computer (c = consonant)

an egg (e = vowel)

a UFO (*U* sounds like *you*)

an unidentified flying object (*u* sounds like *uh*)

a helmet (hard *h*)

an hour (silent *h*)

Note particularly the UFO example. This is a special case as it's an abbreviation. These can be tricky, as sometimes people read out the letters and sometimes they say them like a word. How it sounds is what decides whether you put *a* or *an* in front of it. It doesn't make any difference in the case of UFO, as the first sound is the same either way: you-fo, you-eff-oh. Members of the

Science Fiction Club use both. But they abbreviate the name of their club to SFC. This is not something you can say as a word unless you think it's in some alien language . . . OK, they may. And the only way to know for sure is to ask them or to listen to what they say. But they'd probably go to *an* SFC meeting (pronounced ess-eff-see, which begins with a vowel), not *a Sfic* meeting.

Special note: Most of us say *a historic event* (and *a heroic act* and *a hotel*). Some sticklers prefer *an historic event* (and *an heroic* and *an hotel*).They're harmless. If they say *an 'istoric*, they're just pointing out that they know the word was originally French, and that back when it was new the *h* wasn't pronounced (which is why the word got *an* and not *a*). If they say *an* but then pronounce the *h* you have our permission to laugh at them (quietly and just to yourself, to avoid giving offence). If you hear anyone talking about *an hat*, they should probably be locked up.

Chapter 10

Everyone Brought Their Homework: Pronouns

*P*ronouns are words that substitute for nouns. Even though they're useful, pronouns can also be pesky. You see, English has many different types of pronoun, each governed by its own set of rules. (See Chapters 4 and 6 for information on subject and object pronouns.)

The whole topic of pronouns is enough to give you a headache, so get out the aspirins. In this chapter, we concentrate on how to avoid the most common errors associated with this part of speech.

Pairing Pronouns with Nouns

A pronoun's meaning can vary from sentence to sentence. Such versatility comes from the fact that pronouns don't have identities of their own; instead, they stand in for nouns. In a few very weird situations, pronouns stand in for other pronouns. (For more on pronoun–pronoun pairs, see the section 'More Pronoun Problems', later in this chapter.)

To choose the appropriate pronoun, you must consider the word that the pronoun is replacing. The word that the pronoun replaces is called the pronoun's *antecedent*.

Identifying the pronoun–antecedent pair is really a matter of reading comprehension. If the sentence (or the paragraph) doesn't make the pronoun–antecedent connection clear, the writing is faulty. Time to edit! But in most cases the meaning of the pronoun leaps off the page. Take a look at some examples:

Edgar, *who* types five or six words a minute, was hard at work writing a new novel when the police arrived to arrest *him* for the murder. (The pronouns *who* and *him* stand for the noun *Edgar*.)

Fortunately, the flight attendants gave *him* an alibi. *They* remembered *him* because *he* broke a glass vase as *he* boarded the plane. (The pronouns *he*, *him* and *he* stand for the noun *Edgar; they* stands for the noun *flight attendants*.)

The police were stumped. *Everybody* had an alibi. (The pronoun *everybody* stands for *the suspects* – they haven't been mentioned but they're understood.)

'Well, Sergeant, *we*'ve missed something,' said the inspector. '*Our* investigation isn't getting anywhere. Isn't the neighbour back from *her* holiday now? *I* don't suppose *she* knows anything, but let's go and talk to *her*.' (The pronoun *I* stands for the person who's speaking (the inspector); the pronouns *we* and *our* stand for the speaker and someone else – in this case the inspector and the person he's speaking to (the sergeant); *she* and *her* stand for the noun *neighbour*.)

Mildred wasn't surprised when the police knocked on *her* door. *She* offered *them* tea and biscuits, which *they* gratefully accepted, and told *them* what *she* had seen. (The pronouns *she* and *her* stand for the noun *Mildred;* the pronouns *they* and *them* stand for the noun *police*.)

When analysing a sentence, you seldom find a noun that's been replaced by the pronouns *I* and *we*. The pronoun *I* always refers to the speaker and *we* refers to the speaker and someone else.

The pronoun *it* sometimes has no antecedent:

It is raining heavily.

It was obvious that no cricket would be played that day.

In these sentences, *it* is just setting up the sentence for the true expression of meaning.

And sometimes the meaning of the pronoun is explained in a previous sentence:

Bibi's ice cream was melting. *She* dropped *it*. (The pronoun *she* refers to the noun *Bibi; it* refers to the noun *ice cream*.)

Identify the pronouns and their antecedents in this paragraph:

It was snowing as Mortimer arrived at his mother's charity ball. In the ballroom, he glimpsed Lucinda and her boyfriend dancing the tango. Suddenly, she tripped. She sailed across the floor and landed at Mortimer's feet. His mind went blank. He was frozen with joy at the sight of her – a purple heap with a stray strand of hair across her face.

He said the only four words he could think of. Even as he spoke them he knew he was making a terrible mistake.

Answer: *It* (no antecedent) was snowing as Mortimer arrived at *his* (*Mortimer's*) mother's charity ball. In the ballroom, *he* (*Mortimer*) glimpsed Lucinda and *her* (*Lucinda's*) boyfriend dancing the tango. Suddenly, she (*Lucinda*) tripped. *She* (*Lucinda*) sailed across the floor and landed at Mortimer's feet. *His* (*Mortimer's*) mind went blank. *He* (*Mortimer*) was frozen with joy at the sight of *her* (*Lucinda*) – a purple heap with a stray strand of hair across *her* (*Lucinda's*) face. *He* (*Mortimer*) said the only four words *he* (*Mortimer*) could think of. Even as *he* (*Mortimer*) spoke *them* (*the words*) *he* (*Mortimer*) knew *he* (*Mortimer*) was making a terrible mistake.

Deciding between Singular and Plural Pronouns

All pronouns are either singular or plural. Singular pronouns replace singular nouns, which are those that name one person, place, thing, or idea. Plural pronouns replace plural nouns – those that name more than one person, place, thing, or idea. A few pronouns replace other pronouns. When this happens, singular pronouns replace other singular pronouns, and plurals replace plurals. You need to understand pronoun number – singulars and plurals – before you place them in sentences. Take a look at Table 10-1 for a list of some common singular and plural pronouns.

Table 10-1	Common Singular and Plural Pronouns
Singular	*Plural*
I	we
me	us
myself	ourselves
you	you
yourself	yourselves
he/she/it	they/them
himself/herself/itself	themselves
who	who
which	which
that	that

Goldilocks and the three theres

They're putting *their* coats in that room over *there*. In other words, *they're* is short for *they are* (the apostrophe shows where the letter *a* has been left out), *their* shows ownership and *there* is a place. Some examples:

RIGHT: 'Look over *there*,' said Yasmin. 'Isn't that Martin? And Alice!'

WHY IT'S RIGHT: *There* is a place.

RIGHT: 'Edgar, what do you think *they're* doing in the travel agent's?'

WHY IT'S RIGHT: *They're* means *they are*.

RIGHT: 'We probably shouldn't speculate,' sighed Edgar. 'After all, that's *their* business.'

WHY IT IS RIGHT: *Their* means *belonging to them* (Martin and Alice).

Notice that some of the pronouns in Table 10-1 do double duty: they take the place of both singular and plural nouns or pronouns. Most of the time choosing between singular and plural pronouns is easy. You're not likely to say

Sandy tried to pick up the ski poles, but it was too heavy.

because *ski poles* (plural) and *it* (singular) don't match. Automatically you say

Sandy tried to pick up the ski poles, but *they* were too heavy.

If you're learning English as a second language, your ear for the language is still in training. Put it on an exercise regimen of at least an hour a day of careful listening. A radio station or a television programme in which reasonably educated people are speaking will help you to train your ear. You'll soon become comfortable hearing and choosing the proper pronouns.

Using Possessive Pronouns

Possessive pronouns – those all-important words that indicate who owns what – also have singular and plural forms. You need to keep them straight. Table 10-2 helps you identify each type.

Table 10-2	Singular and Plural Possessive Pronouns
Singular	*Plural*
my	our
mine	ours
your	your
yours	yours
his	their/theirs
her	their
hers	theirs
its	their
whose	whose

Do you have an *its* problem? We're not talking about a rash that you need to scratch all the time. We're talking about a possessive pronoun and a *contraction* (a shortened word in which an apostrophe substitutes for one or more letters). In other words, do you know the difference between *its* and *it's*?

Its shows possession:

> Sandy experimented with her new pressure cooker, unaware that *its* pressure valve was faulty.

It's means *it is* or *it has:*

> No one liked Mortimer's new play at first, but *it's* sold out now that Alice has taken over the lead role.

So *it's* nice to know that grammar has *its* own rules. By the way, one of those rules is that *no possessive pronoun ever has an apostrophe.* Ever. Never. Never ever. Remember: if it owns something, dump the apostrophe. Here are some additional examples:

> WRONG: *Its* a rainy day, and Bill's dog is tired of getting *it's* paws wet.

> WHY IT'S WRONG: The first *its* should be *it's* because *it is* a rainy day. The second *its* shouldn't have an apostrophe because no possessive pronoun ever has an apostrophe. (You can tell it's a possessive pronoun because it doesn't mean *it is*.)

RIGHT: *It's* a rainy day, and Bill's dog is tired of getting *its* paws wet.

ALSO RIGHT: *It's* a rainy day, and Bill's dog is getting tired of getting *his* paws wet.

WHY IT'S ALSO RIGHT: *It* and *its* may refer to animals, but many people prefer to use *he, she, his* and *her* for pets. Of course, Bill's dogs annoy just about everyone because they make so much noise. So, although Bill refers to Fido as *Fido* or *him*, everyone else calls Fido *Bill's dog* or *it*.

WRONG: *Its* paws wrapped in towels, Fido seems to be thinking that *its* time for a new bone.

WHY IT'S WRONG: The first *its* is OK because the paws belong to Fido. The second *its* needs an apostrophe because *it is* time.

RIGHT: *Its* paws wrapped in towels, Fido seems to be thinking that *it's* time for a new bone.

Positioning Pronoun–Antecedent Pairs

Keep the pronoun and its antecedent near each other. Often, but not always, they appear in the same sentence. Sometimes they're in different sentences. Either way, the idea is the same: if the antecedent of the pronoun is too far away, the reader or listener may become confused. Check out this example:

> Edgar picked up the discarded *wrapper*. There had been three bomb scares that week, and the rubbish bins had been removed as a security precaution. But that was no excuse for leaving litter all over the place, as far as Edgar was concerned. The real threat to civilisation wasn't bombs, but the little things that make everyday life miserable for so many people. *It* made the park look messy.

It? What's the meaning of *it?* You almost have to be psychic to figure out that *it* refers to *wrapper*. Try the paragraph again.

> There had been three bomb scares that week, and the rubbish bins had been removed as a security precaution. But that was no excuse for leaving litter all over the place, as far as Edgar was concerned. The real threat to civilisation wasn't bombs, but the little things that make everyday life miserable for so many people. The discarded wrapper made the park look messy, so Edgar picked it up.

Now the antecedent and pronoun are closer to each other. Much better!

Rewrite these sentences, moving the pronouns closer to their antecedents.

Edgar had hay fever. He pulled out his handkerchief. He blew his nose. Yasmin had given it to him – the love of his life. He was terrified of losing her. He sniffed. It was always worse when he walked through the park. She was a treasure.

There's more than one problem here. *Yasmin* is too far from *she*, and we have no idea what's worse when he walks through the park, his hay fever or his emotional state. (And did she really give him his *nose?*) This sort of thing is often done deliberately in fiction either to mislead the reader or for comic effect, but if you need to be clear what you mean, here's one possible answer:

Edgar had hay fever, and it was always worse when he walked through the park. He pulled out his handkerchief. Yasmin – the love of his life – had given it to him. She was a treasure. He was terrified of losing her. He sniffed and blew his nose.

Position alone is sometimes enough to indicate a pronoun–antecedent pairing. It's true that a pronoun is more likely to be understood if it's placed near the word it represents. In fact, you should form your sentences so that the pairs are neighbours. However, position isn't always enough, especially if there's more than one possible antecedent. Look at this sentence:

Lucinda told her mother that she was out of cash.

Who's out of cash? The sentence has one pronoun (*she*) and two nouns (*Lucinda* and *Lucinda's mother*). *She* could refer to either of them. The best way to clarify the meaning of a pronoun is to make sure that only one easily identifiable antecedent may be represented by each pronoun. If your sentence is about two women, don't use *she*. Provide an extra noun to clarify your meaning. If you can interpret the sentence in more than one way, rewrite it using one or more sentences until your meaning is clear:

Lucinda said, 'Mum, can I have a loan from the cookie jar? *I'm* out of cash.'

or

Lucinda saw that her mother was out of cash and told her so.

What does this sentence mean?

Sandy and her sister went to Lucinda's birthday party, but she didn't have a good time.

A. Sandy didn't have a good time.

B. Sandy's sister didn't have a good time.

C. Lucinda didn't have a good time.

Who knows? Rephrase the sentence, unless you're talking to someone who was at the party and knows that Sandy loved every minute of it and Sandy's sister left with a boy she's been keen on for weeks, but Lucinda spilled wine on her dress and broke a heel on her shoe, and that was before the cops arrived to arrest Mortimer. If your listener knows all that, the sentence is fine. If not, here are a few possible rewrites:

> Sandy and her sister went to Lucinda's party. Lucinda didn't have a good time.

or

> Lucinda didn't have a good time at her own birthday party, even though Sandy and Sandy's sister were there.

or

> Sandy and her sister went to Lucinda's party, but Lucinda didn't have a good time.

More Pronoun Problems

Most of the time, determining whether a pronoun should be singular or plural is easy. Just check the noun that acts as the antecedent, and bingo – you're done. But sometimes a pronoun takes the place of another pronoun. The pronouns being replaced can be confusing because they're singular, even though they look plural. In this section we'll look at these, and in particular how to avoid sexist pronoun usage.

Using troublesome singular pronouns properly

Everybody, *somebody* and *no one* (not to mention *nothing* and *everyone*) are pronouns that sometimes cause problems. All of these are singular:

- ✔ The 'ones': one, everyone, someone, anyone, no one.
- ✔ The 'things': everything, something, anything, nothing.
- ✔ The 'bodies': everybody, somebody, anybody, nobody.
- ✔ And a few more: each, either, neither.

These pronouns don't sound singular. *Everybody* and *everyone* sound like a crowd. If you didn't leave anyone out, if you included *everyone* or *everybody*, how can you be talking about a singular word? Well, you are. The logic (yes, logic applies, even though English grammar rules don't always bother with logic) is that *everyone* talks about the members of a group one by one. You follow this logic, probably unconsciously, when you choose a verb. You don't say

> Everyone *are* here. Let the party begin!

You say:

> Everyone *is* here. Let the party begin!

But a problem crops up with sentences that talk about people. Look at these:

1. It will be simpler if everyone brings *their* own lunch.
2. It will be simpler if everyone brings *his* own lunch.
3. It will be simpler if everyone brings *his or her* own lunch.

Are they all correct? Some people insist that only 2 and 3 can be grammatically correct. (And some say that sentence 2 isn't allowed because it's sexist – see more on this in the section 'Sexist language', later in this chapter.) But let's think about sentence 1 for a minute or two.

For centuries the words *they*, *them* and *their* were used to refer to both singular and plural words. Such usage meant that the writer or speaker didn't have to make a gender choice because *their* didn't refer specifically to either men or women. This was very useful. But then grammarians decided that this was wrong. They proclaimed that from then on we were only allowed to use these words in their plural sense. So sentence 1 was outlawed. What about sentence 3, then? Well, they decided that wasn't necessary. After all, in the world they were writing about, women weren't allowed to do much. So they decided that the word *man* should henceforth be taken to include women as well, and that we should say *his* (not *their*) when what we're talking about is singular *regardless of gender*. And it worked, because most of the time when they said they were talking about *everyone* what they really mean was *all the men*.

The interesting thing is that use of *they*, *them* and *their* in a singular sense never came close to disappearing. You can see examples everywhere. There may be a notice in the kitchen where you work, saying:

> *Everyone* is expected to do *their* own washing up.

Most people don't think there's anything wrong with this because it sounds right. (It also makes sense, as it's simpler than using *his or her*.) Grammar books are divided on the issue. Some insist that it's wrong to use *their* like this. Others don't see any problem (or give in reluctantly). There's likely to be argument about this issue for a long time to come. But there's one reason why using *they*, *them* and *their* to refer to something singular is likely to become accepted again. That's the issue of *sexist language*. (We'll come back to that in the next section.)

For now, just remember that the pronouns *everyone*, *everything*, *everybody* and so on (as listed above) are *always* singular and any pronoun referring to one of them must be singular too. Here are some examples:

> As they took Mortimer in, Inspector Barker and the Sergeant *each* ran through in *his* mind what Mildred had told them. (*His* refers to *each*; *each* is singular – it refers to the inspector and the sergeant separately.)

> *Neither* had quite believed *his* ears. (*His* refers to the singular pronoun *neither*.)

> 'Emmeline always liked *everything* in *its* place,' Mildred had said. '*Anything* out of *its* place used to drive her crazy.' (The first *its* refers to *everything*; the second refers to *anything*; *everything* and *anything* are singular.)

> 'So I noticed that the gnome was missing. She'd thrown another one away the week before. *Neither* was looking *its* best. Frost damage. And then there was that flashy car.' (*Its* refers to *neither* – each gnome considered individually.)

Sexist language

One very important principle of Western liberal democracy is that all human beings are fundamentally equal. We should all be respected as individuals. So no one should be refused a place to train as a doctor or an engineer on the grounds that they're female. Or denied the right to travel by bus on the grounds that they're in a wheelchair. Or turned down as a tenant because of their skin colour or religion or because they're gay.

To avoid reinforcing a lot of bad ideas, publishers of books like *English Grammar For Dummies* edit the books they publish to make sure they don't use any language that's racist, sexist, ageist or any other –ist. (Authors often forget about this in the excitement of writing the book!) This is a good thing. It's sometimes called *political correctness*, but this is not a neutral term: it's often used as a sort of insult when people don't agree with the changes.

Whatever you think about this, it's an important issue. And it affects pronouns. Look at this sentence:

> A doctor is no longer expected to visit *his* patients at home.

We aren't talking about any particular doctor here. This is any doctor – or a *typical* doctor, if you like – and he's male. He visits *his* patients (or not). How can we avoid suggesting that no doctors are women? Simply declaring to the world that words mean what we say they mean (that *his* is meant to include women) doesn't really work. Everyone really thinks that this sentence is saying that the typical doctor is (or even should be) male.

So how are we to include women? Perhaps we should just say *or her* every time *him* crops up:

> A doctor is no longer expected to visit *his or her* patients at home.

That's clumsy, isn't it? And it makes *her* sound like an afterthought (which she was if she wasn't thought of until the editing stage). Can we use *their* in its old singular sense here? Let's try it:

> A doctor is no longer expected to visit *their* patients at home.

Well, no, we haven't quite come to that. Very few people would feel happy with that sentence because we're using *their* to refer to a singular *noun* (not a pronoun). Although some people are encouraging this sort of thing, we don't think it's a good idea for you to try it. Fortunately there are other ways to avoid using *his:*

> *Doctors* are no longer expected to visit *their* patients at home. (Put the whole thing into the plural, then the gender-neutral *their* is correct because it's also plural.)

> A doctor is no longer expected to visit *patients* at home. (Leave the pronoun out.)

But when it comes to the pronouns we've been talking about, it's very useful to allow *their* to be used:

> *No one* should have to feel that *their* life is at risk. (*no one* = singular, *life* = singular, *their* = singular)

We can't see any reason why something as useful and natural-sounding as this (and with such a long unbroken history of use in the language) shouldn't be allowed, so you have our permission to use it.

The issue here is not whether pronouns like *everyone* and *anybody* are singular or plural. They're singular. No problem. It's whether *they*, *them* and *their* can be singular. We've decided they can, but only when referring to pronouns, not when referring to nouns.

Sex or gender?

The word *gender* used to refer only to words. For example, the gender of *his* is masculine, and the gender of *her* is feminine. The word that describes male or female genetic identity – the *It's a boy! It's a girl!* birth announcement sort of identity – is *sex*. Also, as everyone eventually finds out, *sex* refers to the activity that perpetuates the human race.

In the late twentieth century, people began to analyse the way men and women were treated by society, the way men and women related to each other, and many similar topics. To speak of *sex* in reference to these topics was correct according to the dictionary definition of *sex*, but it was becoming clear that our genetic sex didn't determine our behaviour (in everything from what clothes we like to wear to whom we are likely to fall in love with). If we were going to be quite clear what we were talking about,

we needed two words. Luckily, we already had the word *gender*, so it wasn't necessary to invent a completely new word. It took a while for this new use of *gender* (outside the subject of grammar) to catch on. For a few years, every article advocating gender equality seemed to be followed by a letter from an outraged grammarian complaining about the new term. But, as usually happens when grammarians object to a helpful change in the use of a word, the language carried on regardless. Despite all those outraged grammarians, the word *gender* settled comfortably into its new meaning. *Gender* still has its old use in grammar to describe masculine and feminine words, but it's also accepted as a term to sort people, societal roles and anything else into male and female categories when you're not just talking about genetics (which is still *sex*).

Which sentence is correct?

A. Sandy says that no one should wear their earplugs in the pool in case she needs to shout at them (the people, not the earplugs).

B. Sandy says that no one should wear his or her earplugs in the pool in case she needs to shout at him or her.

Answer: Grammatically speaking, they're both correct. In sentence A, *them* is being used in a singular sense (which we've said is allowed) to refer to the singular pronoun *no one*. Unfortunately, *them* could also refer to *earplugs*, so the speaker has had to clarify this (making it either funny or a bad sentence, depending on your point of view). Sentence B avoids this confusion, and opts for the ultra-correct singular *his or her*, but has had to use this twice, which makes it clumsy. So A and B are both correct but both horrible.

Now write a sentence that says the came thing and avoids the problems.

One answer: As she sometimes needs people to be able to hear her, Sandy says that no one should wear earplugs in the pool.

Chapter 11

Just Nod Your Head: About Agreement

*H*ollywood filmmakers and about a million songwriters have tried to convince the public that opposites attract. Grammarians have clearly not heard about this! Instead of opposites, the English language prefers matching pairs. Matching, in grammar terminology, is called *agreement*. In this chapter, we'll explain agreement in *number* – the singular or plural quality of a word. Here's the rule: you must match singular elements with other singular elements, and you must pair plurals with other plurals. In this chapter, we'll show you how to make subjects and verbs agree. Then we'll show you some special cases – treacherous nouns and pronouns that are often mismatched.

Writing Singular and Plural Verbs

If you're a native speaker of English, you correctly match singular and plural subjects and verbs most of the time. Your ear for proper language effortlessly creates these subject–verb pairs. Helping you along with this task is the fact that, in most tenses, you use exactly the same form for both singular and plural verbs. In this section we'll show you the forms that don't change and the ones that do.

The unchangeables

When you're writing or speaking regular verbs in the simple past, simple future, past perfect and future perfect tenses, agreement is easy. (Some of the progressive forms change; see the next section for more detail.) The non-progressive forms of these verbs don't change. Here are some samples, all with the regular verb *to snore*, of tenses that use the same form for both singular and plural subjects.

> Lucinda *snored* constantly, but her cousins *snored* only on bank holidays. (The simple past tense verb *snored* matches both the singular subject *Lucinda* and the plural subject *cousins*.)

> Bill *will snore* if he eats cheese before bed, but his dogs *will snore* whenever they fall asleep. (The simple future tense verb *will snore* matches both the singular subject *Bill* and the plural subject *dogs*.)

> Edgar *had snored* before his tonsils were removed, but on sleepovers all his school friends *had snored* too. (The past perfect verb *had snored* matches both the singular subject *Edgar* and the plural subject *school friends*.)

> By the time the tutorial is over, the professor *will have snored* for at least ten minutes, and his students *will have snored* for even longer. (The future perfect verb *will have snored* matches both the singular subject *professor* and the plural subject *students*.) For more information on verb tenses, see Chapter 3.

The changeables

Have you just resolved to speak only in those unchanging tenses? Sorry! You won't be able to keep to that resolution. The other tenses are crucial to your communication skills. But take heart. You need to know only a few principles to identify singular and plural verbs.

Simple present tenses

In the simple present tense, nearly all the regular verb forms are the same for both singular and plural. If the subject of the sentence is *I*, *we* or *you*, don't worry. They all use the same verb, and number isn't an issue (*I snore*, *we snore*, *you snore*).

In choosing simple present tense verbs, you do have to be careful when the subject is a singular noun (*Lucinda*, *tribe*, *motorcycle*, *loyalty* and so on) or a plural noun (*planes*, *trains*, *automobiles* and so on). You also have to be on your toes when the subject is a pronoun that replaces a singular noun (*he*, *she*, *it*, *another*, *someone* and so on). Finally, you have to take care when the subject is a pronoun that replaces a plural noun (*they*, *both*, *several* and so on). To boil all this down to a simpler rule: be careful when your sentence is talking *about* someone or something. You don't need to worry about subject–verb agreement in sentences in which the subject is *I*, *you* or *we*.

For sentences that talk about someone or something, here's how to tell the difference between the singular and plural forms of a regular verb: the singular verb ends in *s* and the plural form doesn't. Here are some examples of simple present tense regular verbs:

Singular	*Plural*
the dog *bites*	the dogs *bite*
Lucinda *rides*	they *ride*
she *screams*	the girls *scream*
Bibi *burps*	both *burp*

When in Rome and Greece: classical plurals

Granted, the Colosseum is a magnificent sight and the Greek myths are fun. But those languages! Thanks to the ancient Romans and Greeks, a number of English words form their plurals in a strange way. Here are some singular/plural pairs:

✔ **Analysis/analyses:** *Analysis* is the singular, meaning 'a course of psychological therapy' or, more generally, 'a serious investigation or examination'. The plural changes the *i* to *e*.

✔ **Parenthesis/parentheses:** This paragraph has a section in *parenthesis* (which means an aside or interruption) and *the parenthesis* or interruption is also in *parentheses* – two round brackets. We try not to write with too many parentheses because they can be confusing.

✔ **Datum/data:** Technically, *data* is the plural of *datum* and takes a plural verb (*the data are clear*). However, more and more people are matching *data* with a singular verb (*the data is clear*), and this is so common when anyone's talking about computer data that it's now considered incorrect to do anything else. In other contexts, it's still correct to match *data* with a plural verb.

✔ **Phenomenon/phenomena:** The singular term is *phenomenon*, a noun meaning 'a marvel, a special occurrence or event'. The plural term is *phenomena*. Something odd seems to be happening to these words. In the UK, *phenomenon* seems to be disappearing: everyone seems to want *phenomena* to be both singular and plural. In the US, it's the other way round: they like *phenomenon* and are losing *phenomena*. So I guess we'll just have to wait and see what happens next – over the next 20 or 50 years or so. Oh, this is so exciting! We can't wait to see who wins!

You understand, don't you?

You may have noticed that the word *you* is both singular and plural. We can say

> You are crazy.

to Alice when she says that she's not sure she wants a career on the stage. We can also say

> You are crazy.

to all the people who think that they've been abducted by aliens. In either case, we use the plural form of the verb (*are*). The fact that *you* is both singular and plural may be responsible for the popularity of such terms as *you guys* and *you people*. These terms are colourful but not correct in formal English. Use *you* for both singular and plural subjects and, if you care enough, make the meaning clear with context clues:

> Today you must all wear clothes to the Introduction to Nudism class because the central heating is broken.

> 'I must have you and only you!' cried Damian to his soon-to-be-ex girlfriend.

Progressive tenses

Progressive tenses – those that contain an *–ing* verb form – may also cause singular/plural problems. These tenses rely on the verb *to be*, a grammatical weirdo that changes drastically depending on its subject. Just be sure to match the subject to the correct form of the verb *to be*. (See Chapter 3 for all the forms of *to be*.) Check out these examples of progressive verbs:

- ✔ **Singular present progressive:** I *am biting*, you *are biting*, Bibi *is biting*, no one *is biting*.

- ✔ **Plural present progressive:** we *are biting*, you *are biting*, the dogs *are biting*, they *are biting*.

- ✔ **Singular past progressive:** I *was biting*, you *were biting*, Bibi *was biting*, no one *was biting*.

- ✔ **Plural past progressive:** we *were biting*, you *were biting*, the dogs *were biting*, both *were biting*.

In case you're wondering about the future progressive, I'll mention the good news: this one never changes! Singular and plural forms are the same (I*'ll be biting*, you*'ll be biting* and so on). No problems here. (For information on the use of *shall* and *will* – so that you know what *'ll* stands for – see Chapter 3.)

Present perfect and future perfect tenses

The present perfect and future perfect tenses (both progressive and non-progressive) contain forms of the verb *to have*. Use *have* when the subject is *I*, *you* or a plural noun or pronoun. Use *has* when you're talking about a singular noun or pronoun. Some examples:

✔ **Singular present perfect:** I *have bitten*, I *have been biting*, you *have bitten*, you *have been biting*, Damian *has bitten*, Bibi *has been biting*, she *has bitten*, everyone *has been biting*.

✔ **Plural present perfect:** we *have bitten*, we *have been biting*, you *have bitten*, you *have been biting*, the dogs *have bitten*, the dogs *have been biting*, several *have bitten*, they *have been biting*.

Easier Than Marriage Counselling: Making Subjects and Verbs Agree

Once you're able to tell a singular from a plural verb (see the previous section), you can concentrate on matchmaking. Remember that you must always pair singular subjects with singular verbs, and plural subjects with plural verbs. No mixing allowed.

Notice how, in these sample sentences, singular subjects are matched with singular verbs, and plural subjects are matched with plural verbs:

Mortimer is miserable when he is recovering from an illness. (*Mortimer* = singular subject, *is* = singular verb; *he* = singular subject, *is recovering* = singular verb)

His friends keep him company. (*friends* = plural subject, *keep* = plural verb)

They entertain him for hours. (*they* = plural subject, *entertain* = plural verb)

Deborah cooks for him when his appetite recovers. (*Deborah* = singular subject, *cooks* = singular verb; *appetite* = singular subject, *recovers* = singular verb)

How did we know that the subject–verb pairs were either singular or plural? We determined the number of subjects performing the action and then matched the verbs.

Here are some steps to take to make sure that your subjects and verbs agree:

1. Pop the question to find the verb. (See Chapter 2.)

2. Pop the question to find the subject. (See Chapter 4.)

3. Determine whether the subject is singular or plural.

4. Match the appropriate verb: singular verb to singular subject, plural verb to plural subject.

Time isn't money, but in grammar they're both singular

Time and money are the same, at least in grammar. In grammar, treat them as singular whenever we think of them as a lump. Thus,

> Fifty minutes *is* not enough for a television documentary about Mortimer.

> A thousand pounds *was* a powerful temptation to Edgar, and he decided to allow Mortimer's company to use his latest computer program.

But money is plural when you talk about it as a physical thing — separate pieces of paper or metal. For example,

> Two five-pound notes *are* taped inside Damian's 'casino' jacket because he thinks that they bring him luck.

> One hundred pennies *were* dropped, one by one and with great ceremony, into the Bibi's piggybank.

Choosing Verbs for Two Subjects

Sentences with two subjects joined by *and* usually take a plural verb, even if each of the two subjects is singular. (Think of maths: one + one = two. One subject + one subject = plural subject.)

Here are some sample sentences with subjects joined by the word *and:*

> Mortimer and Deborah drink an expensive bottle of wine with dinner. (*Mortimer + Deborah* = plural subject, *drink* = plural verb)

> Mortimer and his butler give each other an alibi. (*Mortimer + butler* = plural subject, *give* = plural verb)

> Inspector Barker and the Sergeant plan to interview everyone again when they can spare the time from their other cases. (*Inspector Barker + Sergeant* = plural subject, *plan* = plural verb)

Subjects joined by *or*, like subjects joined by *either/or*, may take either a singular or a plural verb. See Chapter 21.

Which sentence is correct?

   A. Rashid and Alice plan to speak to Mortimer.

   B. Rashid and Alice plans to speak to Mortimer.

Answer: Sentence A is correct. The subject is *Rashid and Alice*, a plural subject. The plural verb *plan* is needed.

Try one more. Which sentence is correct?

A. Rashid and his neighbour have had enough of Mortimer's noisy clock.

B. Rashid and his neighbour has had enough of Mortimer's noisy clock.

Answer: Sentence A is correct. The subject is still plural (*Rashid and his neighbour*), so it needs a plural verb. The verb in sentence A is *have had*, which is also plural. In sentence B the verb (*has had*) is singular.

The Question of Questions

Just to make subject–verb agreement even more complicated, English grammar shuffles a sentence around to form questions and often throws in an auxiliary verb or two. (See Chapter 2 for more information on auxiliary verbs.) Adding insult to injury, questions are formed differently in different tenses. In this section, we show you how to form singular and plural questions in each tense.

Present tense questions

Check out the italicised subjects and verbs in these questions:

Do the *nurses enjoy* their work? (*nurses* = plural subject, *enjoy* = plural verb)

Does the *restaurant* on the corner *serve* a decent curry? (*restaurant* = singular subject, *does serve* = singular verb)

Do Damian and *Deborah need* a good divorce lawyer? (*Damian + Deborah* = plural subject, *do need* = plural verb)

Does Alice like jazz? (*Alice* = singular subject, *does like* = singular verb)

You've probably figured out that the verbs are formed by adding *do* or *does* to the main verb. *Do* matches all plurals as well as the singular subjects *I* and *you*. *Does* is for all other singular subjects. That's the system for most present tense questions. (Questions formed with the verb *to be* don't need *do* or *does*.) When *do* or *does* is used to form a question, the main verb doesn't change. So, when checking subject–verb agreement in present tense questions, be sure to note the auxiliary verb – *do* or *does*.

Just for comparison, here are a couple of questions with the verb *to be:*

> *Is Bermuda* a fashionable holiday destination right now? (*Bermuda* = singular subject, *is* = singular verb)

> *Am I* a good person? (*I* = singular subject, *am* = singular verb)

> *Are* the *neighbours complaining* again? (*neighbours* = plural subject, *are complaining* = plural verb)

> *Is Lucinda shopping* again? (*Lucinda* = singular subject, *is shopping* = singular verb)

Change this statement into a question:

> Edgar meets Yasmin's parents today.

Answer: *Does* Edgar *meet* Yasmin's parents today? To form the question, add the auxiliary verb *does.*

Past tense questions

Past tense questions make use of the auxiliary verb *did.* You'll probably cheer when you hear that *did* forms both singular and plural questions. Questions with the verb *to be* (always a maverick) don't need auxiliary verbs, but the order changes. Here are some examples of past tense questions:

> *Did Sandy run* in the marathon? (*Sandy* = singular subject, *did run* = singular past tense verb)

> *Did* the *students complain* about the course? (*students* = plural subject, *did complain* = plural past tense verb)

> *Was Mrs Edwards* on the Committee of the Noise Abatement Society? (*Mrs Edwards* = singular subject, *was* = singular past tense verb)

> *Were the nurses* angry about their pay? (*nurses* = plural subject, *were* = plural verb)

> *Was I talking* too fast? (*I* = singular subject, *was talking* = singular verb)

> *Were the dogs* barking? (*dogs* = plural subject, *were barking* = plural verb)

Change this statement into a question.

> Yasmin and Ellie *had* the invitations.

Answer: *Did* Yasmin and Ellie *have* the invitations? To form the past tense question, add the auxiliary verb *did.*

Future tense questions

Once again, the future tense is easy when it comes to singular and plural questions. The future tenses already have auxiliary verbs, so no additions are necessary. Here's the best part: the auxiliary verbs are the same for both singular and plural subjects. Read these future tense questions:

> *Will Lucinda* and *Damian go* to the races together? (*Lucinda* + *Damian* = plural subject, *will go* = plural future tense verb)

> *Will Damian* ever *see* the error of his ways? (*Damian* = singular subject, *will see* = singular future tense verb)

> *Will Mortimer be screening* his new movie tonight? (*Mortimer* = singular subject, *will be screening* = singular future tense verb)

> *Will both* of you *be ordering* another dessert? (*both* = plural subject, *will be ordering* = plural future tense verb)

Negative Statements and Subject–Verb Agreement

Some present tense negative statements are also formed by adding *do* or *does*, along with the word *not*, to a main verb. Remember that *does* is always singular. The auxiliary verb *do* may be paired with the singular subjects *I* and *you*. *Do* is also used with all plural subjects. Here are some examples:

> *Dr Mackenzie does* not *drive* a sports car because she wants to project a wholesome image. (*Dr Mackenzie* = singular subject, *does drive* = singular present tense verb)

> *Wasps do* not *bother* Damian, because they are afraid of him. (*wasps* = plural subject, *do bother* = plural present tense verb)

> *I do* not *want* to learn anything else about verbs ever again. (*I* = singular subject, *do want* = singular present tense verb)

> *You do* not *seem* to be enjoying yourself! (*You* = singular or plural subject, *do seem* = singular or plural present tense verb)

One more joyous thought: to form past and future tense questions, you don't need additional auxiliary verbs, and the auxiliary verbs are the same for both singular and plural. Don't worry about these tenses!

Change this statement into a negative (its opposite).

> Mortimer gave me tickets for the musical.

Answer: Mortimer *did not give* me tickets for the musical. You form the negative with the auxiliary verb *did*.

Questions and negative statements in many foreign languages are formed in a different way. In Spanish, for example, all you have to do is raise the tone of your voice or add question marks to statements to indicate that you're asking a question. A Spanish-speaking questioner need only say the equivalent of *He sings?* or *He not sings*. In English, however, an auxiliary verb is necessary for these statements.

The Distractions: Prepositional Phrases and Other Irrelevant Words

Subjects and their verbs are like nannies and babies on a stroll through the park: they always travel together. From time to time, a passer-by comes along and interrupts their quiet afternoon, leaning into the buggy and making funny faces or talking baby talk. The passer-by is a distraction, irrelevant to the nanny and – after a few moments of wriggling and cooing – to the baby as well.

The sentence world has lots of distractions. These show up, slip between a subject and its verb, and distract you from the important stuff. The best strategy is to ignore them. Identify them and then cross them out (at least mentally) to get to the bare bones of the sentence (the subject–verb pair).

Common distractions are prepositional phrases, clauses and participles. A *prepositional phrase* contains a preposition (*on*, *to*, *for*, *by* and so on) and an object of the preposition (a noun or pronoun). These phrases may contain some descriptive words as well. For a full discussion of prepositional phrases, see Chapter 9. For more information on clauses and participles, see Chapter 24.

The following sentences contain distractions. They're not all prepositional phrases, and to help you identify them they are italicised.

The dress *with the bows and sequins* was one of Lucinda's favourites. (*dress* = subject, *was* = verb)

In this sentence, the subject (*dress*) is singular. If you pay attention to the prepositional phrase, you may incorrectly focus on *bows* and *sequins* as the subject – both plural words.

The new secretary, *fascinated with folktales*, keeps a furry plastic troll on her desk. (*secretary* = subject, *keeps* = verb)

By ignoring the distracting phrase in this sentence, you can easily pick out the subject–verb pair (*secretary–keeps*).

> The penguins, *not the rabbit in the children's corner or the elephant ride*, were Bibi's favourite. (*penguins* = subject, *were* = verb)

In this sentence, *penguins* is the subject. If you go for the distraction, you may incorrectly match your verb to *ride* or *rabbit* (or even *corner* or *elephant*), all of which are singular.

So remember: ignore all distracting phrases and find the true subject–verb pair.

Which sentence is correct?

A. The boy in the first row, along with most of the critics, was bored by the play.

B. The boy in the first row, along with most of the critics, were bored by the play.

Answer: Sentence A is correct. The subject is *boy*. The boy *was bored. Along with most of the critics* is a distraction (in this case, a prepositional phrase).

Another: which sentence is correct?

A. The girl in the bikini, but not the boys leaning on the wall, are here on holiday.

B. The girl in the bikini, but not the boys leaning on the wall, is here on holiday.

Answer: Sentence B is correct. The subject is *girl*. The verb must therefore be singular (*is*). The distraction (a prepositional phrase) is *but not the boys leaning on the wall.*

Sentences with unusual word order or with the words *here* and *there* often cause confusion. See Chapter 4 for tips on matching subjects and verbs in these cases.

Can't We All Just Get Along? Agreement with Difficult Subjects

Every family has a problem child, or at least a problem cousin. Every topic in English grammar has at least one problem child, including the topic of subject–verb agreement. In this section, we look at some difficult subjects.

Five puzzling pronouns as subjects

Earlier in this chapter, we told you to ignore prepositional phrases. Now we must confess that this rule has one small exception . . . well, five small exceptions. Five pronouns – five little words that just have to stir up trouble – change from singular to plural because of the prepositional phrases that follow them. Here they are:

- ✔ all
- ✔ any
- ✔ most
- ✔ none
- ✔ some

Here they are with some prepositional phrases and verbs. Notice how the prepositional phrase affects the verb number.

Singular	*Plural*
any of the book is	*any* of the magazines are
all of the pie is	*all* of the shoes are
most of the city is	*most* of the pencils are
none of the pollution is	*none* of the animals are
some of the speech is	*some* of the politicians are

See the pattern? For these five words, the prepositional phrase is the determining factor. If the phrase refers to a plural idea, the verb is plural. If the phrase refers to a singular idea, the verb is singular.

Whenever you come across one of these (or a word that you think may be one), try putting the word in the phrases '. . . of it' and '. . . of them'. If the word fits in these phrases (*some of it*, *all of them* and so on), remember that if it's '. . . of it' the verb has to be singular. If it's '. . . of them', the verb has to be plural.

Here and there you find problems

A variation on unusual word order is a sentence beginning with *here* or *there*. In the examples below, the subject–verb pairs are italicised:

Here *is* the *university* with its award-winning new building.

There *are* many *students* beginning university next week.

Here, for example, *are Yasmin and Edgar.*

There *is* very little *space* in the halls of residence.

As you see, the words *here* and *there* aren't italicised. These words are never subjects! The true subject in this type of sentence comes after the verb, not before. For more examples of *here* and *there* sentences, see Chapter 4.

The Ones, the Things and the Bodies

You won't find the *Ones*, the *Things* and the *Bodies* in the phone book (unless the people in your town have really weird names), but they are families. The *Ones*, the *Things* and the *Bodies* are families of pronouns, and they delight in mischief-making. Here's the family tree:

The Ones: *one, everyone, someone, anyone, no one*

The Things: *everything, something, anything, nothing*

The Bodies: *everybody, somebody, anybody, nobody*

These pronouns are always singular, even if they're surrounded by prepositional phrases that express plurals. These pronouns must be matched with singular verbs. Take a look at these examples:

Everybody *is* happy because *no one has caused* any trouble.

Anything goes.

Anyone in her circle of friends *dances* better than Lucinda.

One of the million reasons why I hate you *is* your tendency to use bad language.

Not *one* in a million customers *creates* as much trouble as Damian.

Each and every mistake is painful

Each and *every* are very powerful words: they're strong enough to change whatever follows them in the sentence – no matter what – into a singular idea. Look at these examples:

Each boy and girl *was given* a chocolate rabbit.

Every skirt and top in that shop *is* in the sale, and Lucinda's in a spending mood.

Each of the pistachios *was* still in its shell, but Bibi ate them anyway.

Every one of the girls *had been auditioned* by Mortimer in an attempt to find someone to star in his new film.

Do these sentences look wrong to you? Each has some expression of a plural in it: two things (*boy and girl*) in sentence one, another two things (*skirt and top*) in sentence two, *pistachios* in sentence three, and *girls* in sentence four. Because the sentences are about groups, they call for plural verbs. Right?

Wrong. When *each* or *every* is placed in front of a group, you take the items in the group one at a time. In the first sample sentence, the subject consists of one boy, one girl, another boy, another girl and so on. Therefore, the sentence needs a singular verb to match the singular subject. So, in the sample sentences, singular verbs match with the subjects that are made singular by the magic words, *each* and *every*:

Each boy and girl was given

Every skirt and top is

Each of the pistachios was

Every one of the girls had been auditioned

Remember: *each* mistaken subject and verb *is* a problem, and *every* grammar rule and example *is* important.

I want to be alone: either and neither without their partners

Either often hangs out with its partner *or*, just as *neither* spends a lot of time with *nor*. (For information on matching verbs to subjects in sentences with *either–or* and *neither–nor* pairs, see Chapter 21.) But each of these words does a Garbo from time to time, saying, 'I want to be alone.' When they're alone, *either* and *neither* are always singular, even if you insert a huge group (or just a group of two) between them and their verbs. Hence

Either of the two armies *is* strong enough to take over the entire planet.

Neither of the football teams *has* any chance of winning against Bill's team.

Either of the swarms of locusts *was* capable of consuming all the country's vegetation.

Neither of the lawyers *does* anything without invoicing me.

Because the sample sentences are about armies, teams, swarms and lawyers (all plural), you may be tempted to choose plural verbs. Resist the temptation! No matter what the sentence says, if the subject is *either* or *neither*, singular is the way to go.

Final answer: *either* and *neither*, without their partners *or* and *nor*, always indicate singular subjects and always take singular verbs.

Politics, statistics and other irregular subjects

Besides dirty tricks and spin masters, the problem with politics is number. Specifically, is the word *politics* singular or plural? Surprise! *Politics* is singular and you must match it with a singular verb. And while we're at it, what about *mathematics*, *news*, *economics*, *measles*, *mumps* and *analysis*? These nouns are all singular as well, even though they end with the letter *s*. Thus, these nouns are paired with singular verbs:

> Lucinda thinks that *politics* (or *mathematics* or *economics*) *is* overrated. She'd like to see the subject dropped from the school curriculum.

> The *news* about the war *is* not encouraging.

> 'Do you think that *measles is* a serious disease?' asked Bill. 'No, *mumps is* a lot worse,' replied Mortimer, speaking from personal experience.

> 'Your troubles are all in your mind,' said Dr Mackenzie. '*Analysis is* the answer.'

Some words – *statistics* and *acoustics*, for example – may be either singular or plural depending on what you're saying. If you're talking about numbers, you may have two or more *statistics*. For example:

> *Statistics show* that knowledge of grammar is declining.

You may also have one *statistic* when you're using the word to refer to a number:

> I don't want to become a motorway-fatality *statistic.*

And if you're talking about the sound properties of an auditorium *acoustics* is plural. For example:

> The *acoustics* have improved since we removed all the seats.

But if you're talking about a course or a field of study, *statistics* and *acoustics* are always singular. For example:

Acoustics is a difficult subject. *Statistics is* easier.

The English language also has words that are always *plural*. Here are a few of them: *pants, trousers* and *scissors*. (You can't put on *a pant* or *a trouser*, and you can't cut with *a scissor.*) Other common plural-only words are *credentials, earnings, headquarters* and *ceramics.* When in doubt, check your dictionary and remember to match singular nouns with singular verbs and plural nouns with plural verbs.

Part III
No Garage, but Plenty of Mechanics

'This is a more upmarket product for the brighter child – It contains punctuation.'

In this part . . .

Passed any building sites lately? If so, you've probably noticed giant piles of timber, steel or bricks – all very useful and very noticeable parts of the new building. Off to the side, you've probably seen some of the little things that also make the building possible – the nails, the nuts, the bolts.

In this part, we explain the nails, nuts and bolts of writing: apostrophes, quotation marks and other punctuation, as well as the rules for capitalisation. By the time you finish reading this part, you'll understand why those little things are an essential part of the package that carries your meaning to the reader.

Chapter 12

Apostrophes

. . . .

. . . .

*1*t happens every time we take a walk. We're strolling along, thinking all kinds of perfectly grammatical thoughts, when a sign catches our eye.

> Stamp's Sold Here
>
> Smiths Furniture – the Best Deals in Town!

We hear a thud as the apostrophe rule bites the dust yet again. Apostrophes are those little curved marks you see hanging from certain letters – as in the *stamps* sign example. Why do those signs upset us? Because, in both signs, the apostrophe (or lack thereof) is a problem. The signs should read:

> Stamps Sold Here
>
> Smith's Furniture – the Best Deals in Town!

Why don't they? We don't know. We do know that even very well educated people throw those little squiggles where they don't belong and leave them out where they're needed. In this chapter, we explain how to use apostrophes to show ownership, how to shorten words with apostrophes, and how to form some plurals.

The Pen of My Aunt or My Aunt's Pen? Using Apostrophes to Show Possession

English is a little unusual in that it gives us two ways of indicating possession. We can do it the French way, for example:

the pen of my aunt

the letters of the lovers

the fine wines of that corner bar

Or we can say the same thing using the apostrophe. Take a look at these same phrases – with the same meanings – using apostrophes:

my *aunt's* pen

the *lovers'* letters

that corner *bar's* fine wines

All these phrases include nouns that express ownership. You can think of the apostrophe as a little hand, holding on to an *s* to indicate ownership or possession. In two of these examples, you'll notice that the apostrophe is used to show that a singular noun owns something (*aunt's pen, bar's fine wines*). In the third, the apostrophe indicates that a plural noun owns something (*lovers' letters*).

Ownership for singles

No, we're not talking about property deals for unmarried people. We're talking about using apostrophes to show ownership with singular nouns. Here's the bottom line: to show possession by one owner, add an apostrophe and the letter *s* to the owner:

The *dragon's* treasure hoard (The treasure hoard belongs to the dragon.)

Lucinda's diary (The diary belongs to Lucinda.)

Damian's gold-filled tooth (The gold-filled tooth belongs to Damian.)

Another way to think about this rule is to see whether the word *of* expresses what you're trying to say. With the *of* method, note that

the tears *of* the crocodile = the *crocodile's* tears

the long memory *of* the elephant = the *elephant's* long memory

and so on.

Sometimes, no clear owner seems present in the phrase. These cases arise mostly when you're talking about time. If you can insert *of* into the sentence, you may need an apostrophe. To give you an idea of how to run this *of* test, here are some phrases that express time:

one week *of* homework = one week's homework

one year *of* free dental care = a year's free dental care

Who's, whose

Whose shows ownership. It seldom causes any problems, except when it's confused with another word: *who's*. *Who's* is a contraction that is short for *who is*. In other words:

> Sandy, *whose* cooking leaves a lot to be desired, wonders who's going to accept her dinner invitation.

and

> *Whose* bar of chocolate is on the radiator? *Who's* stupid enough to put chocolate on a radiator?

Here are more correct examples for your consideration:

> *Whose* review will Mortimer read first?

> *Who's* going to tell Mortimer that his star has the measles?

Here's the bottom line: when you're talking about time, give your sentence an *of* test. If it passes, insert an apostrophe.

Which sentence is correct?

A. Sandy's tennis coach told her that she needed a years work on her backhand.

B. Sandy's tennis coach told her that she needed a year's work on her backhand.

Answer. Sentence B is correct because Sandy (not her tennis coach) needs *a year of work* on her backhand. (Actually, her forehand needs work too, but the year's work on her backhand is a start.)

Because Bill Gates doesn't own everything: plural possessives

You'd be finished figuring out apostrophes now if everything belonged to only one owner. Bill Gates is close, but even he hasn't taken over everything yet. You still need to deal with plural owners. The plurals of most English nouns – anything greater than one – already end in *s*. To show ownership, all you do is add an apostrophe after the *s*. Take a look at these examples:

> four *dogs'* muddy paws (The muddy paws belong to the four dogs.)

the *dinosaurs'* petrified eggs (The petrified eggs belong to the dinosaurs.)

the twelve *roses'* fading petals (The fading petals belong to the twelve roses.)

If you grew up speaking English you already know all this, because you'd never think of saying *dogs's* or *dinosaurs's* or *roses's*. But you may have problems when you're writing because you may expect to see the apostrophe *before* the *s*. The *of* test is useful here (yes, it works for plurals too) because it will help you to identify the word you're starting with. Then you just have to remember to add the apostrophe on the end.

three *days'* building work on Mortimer's new house = three days *of* building work (*Days* has an *s* to begin with, so just add the apostrophe.)

two *years'* neglect of the garden = two years *of* neglect (*Years* has an *s* to begin with, so just add an apostrophe.)

Which is correct?

A. Dr Mackenzie was worried about her son's behaviour.

B. Dr Mackenzie was worried about her sons' behaviour.

Answer: Sentence A is correct if you're talking about one son. Sentence B is correct if you're talking about more than one.

Try another. Which sentence is correct?

A. The Halloween pumpkins carved faces frightened Bibi. Susie was disappointed, as carving all the pumpkins had taken her a long time.

B. The Halloween pumpkins' carved faces frightened Bibi. Susie was disappointed, as carving all the pumpkins had taken her a long time.

C. The Halloween pumpkin's carved faces frightened Bibi. Susie was disappointed, as carving all the pumpkins had taken her a long time.

Answer: Sentence B is correct. The context of the sentence (*all the pumpkins*) makes it clear that there's more than one pumpkin, and *pumpkins'* is a plural possessive. In sentence A, *pumpkins* has no apostrophe, although it should show possession of the carved faces. In sentence C, the apostrophe is placed before the *s*, so the sentence is talking about a single pumpkin (which is clearly not the case).

Irregular plural possessives

That would be all you needed to know if all plural English words ended in *s*. But they don't. Some of them are irregular. For example, you don't have *tooths*, you have *teeth* (unless you're down to your last one). English has lots of words like this. To show ownership for an irregular plural (one that doesn't end in *s* before you start), add an apostrophe and then the letter *s* (*teeth's*). Check out these examples:

the *women's* children (The children belong to the women.)

the *children's* pet mice (The mice belong to the children.)

the *mice's* cage (The cage belongs to the mice.)

Compound plural possessives

What happens when two people own something? (We're talking about grammar.) The *grammatical* answer is one apostrophe because we're usually talking about something being owned collectively and an apostrophe can apply to a whole group of words (not just the one it's connected to):

Susie and Bibi's house. (The house is home to both of them.)

George and Vicky's daughter Lucinda (Lucinda claims both of them as her parents.)

George and Vicky's wedding anniversary (The wedding anniversary will be for both of Lucinda's parents.)

If two people own things separately, as individuals, you can use two apostrophes to make this clearer (you'll see this more often in American writing):

Edgar's and Lucinda's attitudes towards dieting (Edgar doesn't need to diet because he's skinny. He eats like a horse and he's still skinny. There should be a law against it. Lucinda carries around a nutrition chart and checks the calories in every scrap of food she eats. She's skinny too, but she thinks that three peas make a portion and wouldn't dream of eating a chip.)

Lucinda's and Damian's sleeping habits (It's not what you think. Damian sleeps all day because he spends all night gambling in his local casino. Lucinda wouldn't think of sleeping when the shops are open, but insists she needs ten hours' beauty sleep every night.)

But it's OK to manage with one apostrophe, especially where the context makes it impossible to understand the sentence in any other way:

Edgar and Lucinda's attitudes towards dieting are so different! (They obviously don't share ownership of the attitudes because they're *different*.)

Lucinda and Damian's sleeping habits are abnormal. (OK, that's a tricky one. But if you really need to be quite clear what you mean it's better not to lump people together like this in the first place. You could start rumours!)

Not every plural noun has an apostrophe

Remember that an apostrophe shows ownership. Don't use an apostrophe when you just have a plural (a word that's *not* expressing ownership). Here are some examples:

> RIGHT: Habits are hard to break.
>
> WRONG: Habit's are hard to break.
>
> ALSO WRONG: Habits' are hard to break.

Look at another set:

> RIGHT: Garden gnomes aren't to everyone's taste.
>
> WRONG: Garden gnome's aren't to everyone's taste.
>
> ALSO WRONG: Garden gnomes' aren't to everyone's taste.

To sum up the rule on plurals and apostrophes: if the plural noun is not showing ownership, *don't* use an apostrophe. If the plural noun shows ownership, *do* add an apostrophe after the *s* (for regular plurals). For irregular plurals showing ownership, add *'s*.

Possession with Company Names

Companies, shops and other organisations also own things, so these proper nouns also get apostrophes. Put the apostrophe at the end of the name:

> *Marks & Spencer's* finest foods
>
> *Microsoft's* latest software
>
> *BT's* pricing policy
>
> *Hodges Figgis's* wide range of books
>
> *Jones plc's* contract

Some companies (often shops) have apostrophes in their names, even without a sense of possession. For example, *Foyle's* is a bookshop in London. In the preceding sentence, *Foyle's* is written with an apostrophe, but there's no noun after the shop's name. Nevertheless, everyone calls it *Foyle's*, including the shop itself. Such names are probably shortened versions of a longer name (perhaps *Foyle's Book Shop*).

Don't get too happy with this. Shops call themselves whatever they like. You may expect Bettys (a wonderful tea shop in Yorkshire) to have an apostrophe, but it doesn't. And, even as these words are being written, Harrod's in London has decided to call itself Harrods. (Grammarians are, of course, up in arms.) This shouldn't shock you too much – it's quite common for proper nouns to do odd things. Here are some examples: Barclays Bank, Booksellers Association. The moral is, if it's a proper noun you can't guess whether there's an apostrophe (any more than someone can guess how you spell your name).

You can sometimes avoid the whole problem of the apostrophe by thinking of the owner as a sort of adjective instead: *Marks & Spencer* foods, *Microsoft* software, *BT* pricing policy, the *Hodges Figgis* range of books, the Jones plc contract. This doesn't always work, but it can get you out of some tricky situations:

Marks & Spencer (M&S)'s lingerie range? Try *the Marks & Spencer (M&S) lingerie range.*

British Telecommunications' (BT's) customers? Try *British Telecommunications (BT) customers* – or, of course, *customers of British Telecommunications (BT).*

Place apostrophes where they're needed in this paragraph.

Bills offer to go to Bettys to collect the cake for George and Vickys party was gratefully accepted. He had to go shopping anyway because he needed food for the puppies dinner and a card for his brothers birthday. Lucinda would have gone, but she had a lot to do to prepare for her parents party. She wasn't sure that candles were required for an anniversary cake, so she asked Bill to get some and made a note to ask her friends what they thought.

Answer: Bill's offer to go to Bettys to collect the cake for George and Vicky's party was gratefully accepted. He had to go shopping anyway because he needed food for the puppies' dinner and a card for his brother's birthday. Lucinda would have gone, but she had a lot to do to prepare for her parents' party. She wasn't sure that candles were required for an anniversary cake, so she asked Bill to get some and made a note to ask her friends what they thought.

Ownership with Hyphenated Words

Other special cases of possession involve compound words – son-in-law, mother-of-pearl and all the other words with *hyphens* (those little horizontal lines). The rule is simple: put the apostrophe at the end of the word. Never put an apostrophe inside one of these. Here are some examples of singular compound nouns:

> the *secretary-treasurer's* report (The report belongs to the secretary-treasurer.)
>
> the *editor-in-chief's* office (The office belongs to the editor-in-chief.)
>
> my *mother-in-law's* best vase (The vase belongs to my mother-in-law.)

The same rule applies to plural compound nouns that are hyphenated. Take a look at these examples:

> the *doctors-of-philosophy's* common room (The room is for the use of all the doctors-of–philosophy.)
>
> Damian's *sisters-in-law's* wedding present (The wedding present was from all his sisters-in-law.)

Possessives of Nouns that End in s

Singular nouns that end in *s* present special problems. Charles Dickens wrote a lot of books. The name *Dickens* is singular, because he was only one person. When people talk about his books, they may say

> I love Charles Dickens' books.

or

> Charles Dickens's books are so long and boring!

Both of these sentences are grammatically correct (whether or not you agree with the opinions they express). Why are there two options – *Dickens'* and *Dickens's*? The answer has to do with sound. If the letter *s* crops up too many times, the words can be hard to say (and you can find yourself hissing and spitting all over your listener – not a good idea). The second sentence sounds better to a lot of people. So, if the name of a singular owner ends in the letter *s*, you may add only an apostrophe, or you may add an apostrophe and another *s*. Not everyone will agree with your choice, but grammarians will respect your right to choose.

There *is* general agreement on names like these:

> RIGHT: Ms Bridges' new novel
>
> ALSO RIGHT: Mrs Humphreys' home-made chutney
>
> WRONG: Ms Bridges's new novel
>
> ALSO WRONG: Mrs Humphreys's home-made chutney.

Why? Because, in addition to all the hissing and spitting, both these names end with the sound *iz*. This is also the sound of the *'s*, and everyone agrees that putting two of them together just sounds silly. (Mrs Bridgiziz? Ms Humphriziz? No, they just won't do.)

Which sentence is correct?

A. Edgar Edwards' first novel shot into the bestseller list.

B. Edgar Edwards's first novel shot into the bestseller list.

Answer: Both are correct. (Yes, it was a trick question. You know how teachers are.) Sentence B uses a little more saliva and follows the rule that says you add an apostrophe and an *s*. Sentence A breaks this rule, but follows the one that says you should add an apostrophe but forget the *s* if it makes the word hard to say.

Try another set. Which sentence is correct?

A. The whole Edwards family got together at Christmas. The Edwards' make quite a houseful!

B. The whole Edwards family got together at Christmas. The Edwardses make quite a houseful!

Answer: Sentence B is correct because *Edwardses* is a plural, not a possessive. In sentence A, the apostrophe is incorrect because plurals shouldn't have apostrophes unless they are owning something. (Incidentally, you're right that *Edwardses* is horrible. Most people try to avoid plurals like this if they can. They say things like *the Edwards family* instead.)

Common Apostrophe Errors with Pronouns

English also supplies pronouns – words that take the place of a noun – for ownership. Here are some possessive pronouns: _mine, yours, his, hers, its, ours_ and _theirs_. No possessive pronoun ever has an apostrophe.

Here are some more possessive pronouns: _my, your, his, her, its, our, their_. The words in this group are also adjectives: they combine with nouns in phrases like _my hat, our cat_ and so on. They can be called _possessive adjectives_ if you want to give them a name of their own. And they don't have apostrophes either. Not ever.

Here are some examples of possessive pronouns in action:

WRONG: That unruly child of your's has been arrested by the police.

ALSO WRONG: That unruly child of yours' has been arrested by the police.

RIGHT: That unruly child of yours has been arrested by the police.

WHY IT'S RIGHT: Possessive pronouns don't have apostrophes. _Your's_ and _yours'_ don't exist.

WRONG: I'm proud of that daughter of our's.

RIGHT: I'm proud of that daughter of ours.

WHY IT'S RIGHT: Possessive pronouns never have apostrophes. _Our's_ and _ours'_ don't exist.

WRONG: The new gift shop has sections called His and Her's.

RIGHT: The new gift shop has sections called His and Hers.

WHY IT'S RIGHT: Possessive pronouns never ever have apostrophes. _Her's_ and _hers'_ (and _his'_) don't exist.

WRONG: Each dog has it's own favourite chair.

RIGHT: Each dog has its own favourite chair.

WHY IT'S RIGHT: Possessive pronouns never under any circumstances have apostrophes. _It's_ only gets an apostrophe when it's short for _it is_.

Which sentence is correct?

A. Lucinda's parents are telling everyone that Edgar is a friend of their's.

B. Lucinda's parents are telling everyone that Edgar is a friend of theirs.

C. Lucindas parents are telling everyone that Edgar is a friend of theirs.

Answer: Sentence B is correct. In sentence A, the apostrophe is needed in *Lucinda's* because the parents belong to Lucinda. However, *their's* should not have an apostrophe because no possessive pronoun ever has an apostrophe. In sentence C, *their* is written correctly, but *Lucindas* needs an apostrophe.

Just one more. Which sentence is correct?

A. A weeks book signing has made Edgar suddenly popular with girl's, but he assures Yasmin that he is hers and hers alone.

B. A week's book signing has made Edgar suddenly popular with girls, but he assures Yasmin that he is her's and her's alone.

C. A week's book signing has made Edgar suddenly popular with girls, but he assures Yasmin that he is hers and hers alone.

Answer: Sentence C is correct. In sentence A, *a weeks* needs an apostrophe because the phrase means *a week of*, and *girl's* shouldn't have an apostrophe because it's only a plural. In sentence B, neither *her's* should have an apostrophe because (shout it out loud) no possessive pronoun ever has an apostrophe.

For more information on possessive pronouns, see Chapter 10.

Shortened Words for Busy People: Contractions

Like just about everyone in our society, you probably use contractions when you speak. A *contraction* shortens a word by removing one letter or more and substituting an apostrophe in the same spot. For example, chop *wi* out of *I will*, throw in an apostrophe, and you have *I'll*. The resulting word is shorter and faster to say, with only one syllable (sound) instead of two.

Take a look at Table 12-1 for a list of common contractions. Note that some are irregular. (*Won't*, for example, is short for *will not.*)

Table 12-1		Contractions	
Phrase	*Contraction*	*Phrase*	*Contraction*
are not	aren't	she is	she's
cannot	can't	that is	that's
could not	couldn't	they are	they're
do not	don't	they will	they'll
does not	doesn't	they would	they'd
did not	didn't	we are	we're
he had	he'd	we had	we'd
he will	he'll	we will or we shall	we'll
he would	he'd	we would	we'd
he is	he's	we have	we've
is not	isn't	what is	what's
it is	it's	what has	what's
it has	it's	who is	who's
I am	I'm	who has	who's
I had	I'd	will not	won't
I will or I shall	I'll	would not	wouldn't
I would	I'd	you are	you're
I have	I've	you have	you've
she will	she'll	you will	you'll
she would	she'd	you would	you'd

If you'd like to make a contraction that isn't in Table 12-1, check your dictionary to make sure it's legal! There's no real reason why *amn't* shouldn't be an allowable contraction of *am not*, but it isn't. The irregular version *ain't* is in common use, but isn't allowed in polite speech and writing.

There are also a few very odd contractions floating around. *O'clock*, for example (for *of the clock*) and *fo'c's'le* (for *forecastle* – a part of a ship that's sometimes written *fo'c's'le* because it's pronounced *fo'c's'le*).

Your right to use apostrophes

You're in trouble if *your* apostrophes are in the wrong place, especially when you're writing in the second person. (The second person is the form that uses *you, your* and *yours*, both singular and plural.) *You're* means *you are*. *Your* shows possession. These two words are not interchangeable. Some examples:

'*You're* going to wear that trifle if you don't stop following me around,' threatened Lucinda. (*You are* going to wear)

'I just want to be your friend,' said Damian. (*Your* indicates possession. It doesn't mean *you are*, so it doesn't need an apostrophe.)

'*You're* not going to drink that,' declared Susie, as she moved the champagne out of Bibi's reach. (*You are* not going to drink)

'*Your* refusal to eat my trifle used to upset me,' sighed Vicky. (*Your* indicates possession. It doesn't mean *you are*, so it doesn't need an apostrophe.)

Common contraction mistakes

Chances are you've seen a sign like this:

Rings 'n Things

or

Rings n' Things

We know we're fighting a losing battle here, and we know we should be worried about much more important issues, such as the environment. But we also care about the grammatical environment, and thus we make a plea to shop owners and sign painters of the English-speaking world. Please don't put *'n* or *n'* in anything. To be a legal – though totally undesirable – contraction of *and* it would have to be *'n'*. We rest our case. Thank you.

Woulda, coulda, shoulda. These three 'verbs' are potholes on the road to better grammar. Why? Because they don't exist. Here's the recipe for a grammatical crime. Start with three real verb phrases:

would have   could have   should have

And turn them into contractions:

would've   could've   should've

Now turn them back into words. But don't turn them back into the words they actually represent. Instead, let your ears be your guide. Now you say the following:

would of   could of   should of

Now say them quickly and drop the ends of the words so that they become:

would o'   could o'   should o'

(woulda)   (coulda)   (shoulda)

Would of, *could of* and *should of*, and *woulda*, *coulda* and *shoulda* are **never** correct. Don't use them! Take a look at these examples:

> WRONG: If you'd asked me whether Edgar would one day be a famous author, I would of said 'No way'.

> RIGHT: If you'd asked me whether Edgar would one day be a famous author, I would have said 'No way'.

> ALSO RIGHT: If you'd asked me whether Edgar would one day be a famous author, I would've said 'No way'.

An extra *of* sometimes crops up in other places too:

> WRONG: I could've told the inspector that I was with Mortimer all day if he'd *of* asked.

> RIGHT: I could've told the inspector that I was with Mortimer all day if he'd asked.

Which is correct?

A. Edgar could'nt go on a book-signing tour of America because his course had started.

B. Edgar couldn't go on a book-signing tour of America because his course had started.

Answer: Sentence B is correct. *Couldn't* is short for *could not*. (The *o* is missing.)

The questions never stop, do they? Try again. Which is correct?

A. It would of been nice to see the States, but he still wants to study mathematics.

B. It would have been nice to see the States, but he still wants to study mathematics

C. It wouldve been nice to see the States, but he still wants to study mathematics

Answer: Sentence B is correct. Sentence A contains an incorrect verb form (*would of*). The verb in sentence C lacks an apostrophe (*wouldve*).

Contractions you ne'er use except in poetry and novels

Poets often create unusual contractions when they need a certain number of syllables in a line. In real life, no one ever says

o'er (over)	o' (of)	'gainst (against)
ne'er (never)	wi' (with)	ta'en (taken)
e'en (evening)	'twas (it was)	ow'st (owest)

and so forth. But, in poems, these and other unusual contractions aren't uncommon. Poets writing in a strict format throw in an apostrophe when they need to drop a syllable from the line. (The reverse is also true. To add an extra syllable, poets place an accent mark above a normally silent letter – *markéd*, for example, is pronounced *mark-éd.*) They're cheating, but poetry is hard to write.

Authors of prose may also have to use unusual contractions to indicate how their characters are pronouncing words (*mornin'* instead of *morning*, for example) or to write down dialect (English that's very different from standard English) – here the possibilities are endless.

Using Apostrophes with Symbols, Abbreviations and Numbers

The rules for symbols, abbreviations and numbers are exactly the same as the rules for words. An apostrophe indicates possession:

M&S's new range is selling well.

I think 1963's pop hits have always been my favourites.

To make a plural, just add *s:*

Rashid was dismayed when the new PCs arrived because he didn't have time to worry about installing a new computer.

Sandy thinks photographs of her parents in the 1960s are hilarious.

However, sometimes a plural *s* added to a lower case letter makes it hard to read:

> Edgar's gs look just like his qs.

So it's OK to break the rules occasionally to help your readers:

> Edgar's g's look just like his q's.

Just try to be consistent when you make an exception like this. (Don't mix your *g's* and *qs*.)

Symbols and numbers rarely need apostrophes to indicate that we've shortened them because they're already about as short as they can get. But we do sometimes write *the 60s* instead of *the 1960s*, and some people prefer to make it *the '60s* (presumably so that we're all clear we're not talking about the first century AD).

Chapter 13

Quotations: More Rules than Revenue & Customs

*I*n this chapter, we'll explain how to use 'scare quotes' correctly (that was a pair of them round the words *scare quotes*) and how to get the punctuation right with scare quotes and brackets. Then we'll tell you how to handle quotations and how to punctuate speech. There's often more than one way to do things, so we'll explain where you have a choice because how you do things is not a matter of grammar but of style.

Scare Quotes

One of the most annoying grammatical errors is unnecessary use of *scare quotes*. These are quotation marks used to highlight a word or a phrase. Properly used, they are useful. They can tell the reader what you're talking about when it wouldn't be clear otherwise:

> The word processor is about a hundred years old. (We're talking about machines called *word processors*.)

> The word 'processor' is about a hundred years old. (We're talking about a word – the word *processor*.)

We use scare quotes like this in *English Grammar For Dummies*. (We also put words in italics to do the same thing.)

Scare quotes can also indicate that you're using a word in an unusual sense or that you're suspicious about its use:

> Damian phoned in sick. He's got the 'flu' again. (Everyone knows he's got a hangover.)

> This 'antique' table has woodworm holes that appear to have been made with a drill. (It isn't an antique at all.)

Slang often uses words in unusual senses. (For more information on slang, see Chapter 1.) Quote marks with slang are used to show that the writer knows that it's slang or that a speaker isn't comfortable using the word:

> 'Is that what you'd call "cool"?' asked Clarence.

> 'Not unless I wanted to sound like a wrinkly,' said Rob. 'It's "evil".'

But scare quotes are often used when they have no meaning at all, and then they're irritating – or misleading. Look at these examples:

> George uses 'scare quotes' a lot. They aren't usually 'necessary', but he likes the way they 'look' and thinks that they 'spice up' his writing. (If you took the scare quotes away, the sentence would say the same thing and be more readable.)

> We sell 'stamps'. (Are the people who wrote this sign selling postage stamps or something else that they're calling stamps? Are they using the word 'stamps' in some special sense that we're unaware of?)

A useful test is to take the scare quotes away and see whether you're still saying what you mean. If the sentence says the same thing without the scare quotes, leave the scare quotes out.

Punctuating scare quotes is straightforward. When you put quotes round a word or phrase, the quotes belong to the word or phrase. The full stop at the end of the sentence and any other punctuation along the way belong to the whole sentence. So the punctuation goes outside the quotes:

> Susie really likes Vicky's 'antiques'.

> Vicky is proud of her 'antiques', even though she knows that they're phony.

Brackets

It's sometimes useful to put words in round brackets (also called *parentheses*). Like that. As you know, these come in pairs. It's a good idea to check anything you've written to make sure that both halves of the pair are there every time you've used brackets.

If you need to put brackets inside brackets, you can use parentheses (round brackets) for both sets (but some people prefer to use square brackets [also called just *brackets*] for the inside pair). See? It used to be a general rule that you used round brackets first and square ones inside if an inner set was needed, but increasingly people are deciding that they don't like the look of square brackets here (so they use parentheses for both (inner and outer)). Like that. So this is a style choice. Just be consistent, and make sure that you have the right number of brackets: it's even easier to leave out a bracket by mistake if there are two sets and they're both the same.

Square brackets are also used when you're quoting something and adding words of your own in the middle, to let the reader know that these words weren't part of the original. These brackets do have to be square brackets or we wouldn't know whose brackets were whose. For example:

> Yasmin wrote in her essay that 'the twentieth century (as we know it) began with the five papers that [Einstein] wrote in 1905'.

Yasmin wrote *(as we know it)*, including its parentheses, but she didn't write the word *Einstein;* she wrote *he*. We had to add *[Einstein]* so that you'd know who she was talking about.

Some people are quite happy with what we did here, replacing *he* with *[Einstein]*, but sticklers may insist that you leave all the original words, like this:

> Yasmin wrote in her essay that 'the twentieth century (as we know it) began with the five papers that he [Einstein] wrote in 1905'.

The word most commonly added to quotations in this way is *sic.* This is Latin for *thus* (or *Don't blame us for this mistake – it's in the original*). For example:

> Lucinda wrote in her history essay that 'Mary Queen of Scots went to her cousin Elizabeth for refuse [*sic*]'.

Lucinda meant *refuge*, but that's not what she wrote. We put the *[sic]* in so that you'd know it was her mistake, not a spelling mistake in *English Grammar For Dummies*.

These brackets are always square, and *sic* is in italics to show that it isn't English.

Text in round brackets is *in parentheses* because round brackets are called *parentheses* (by printers, at least) and the text is surrounded by (and therefore 'in') the parentheses. (One bracket is a *parenthesis*.) But this text can also be described as being *in parenthesis* (a Latin expression meaning that the text is set off from the main sentence as an aside – any interruption to the sentence). And it can be referred to as *a parenthesis*, which just means it's 'an aside'.

The rules for punctuation with brackets (round and square) are the same as for punctuation with scare quotes. A full stop belongs to the sentence, not to the bracketed bit. Look at this example:

WRONG: Bill took all the dogs on holiday with him (including the five puppies.)

RIGHT: Bill took all the dogs on holiday with him (including the five puppies).

WHY IT'S RIGHT: The full stop belongs to the whole sentence, not just the phrase in the parentheses.

This goes for commas too:

WRONG: Deborah received a lot of support from her friends (especially Bill and Susie,) when she got divorced.

RIGHT: Deborah received a lot of support from her friends (especially Bill and Susie), when she got divorced.

WHY IT'S RIGHT: The comma is part of the sentence structure. It doesn't belong to the words in parentheses.

The full stop only goes inside brackets if the whole of the sentence is inside the brackets. Here are some examples:

WRONG: Susie loves Christmas, especially now that Bibi is old enough to enjoy it. (She particularly misses her husband at Christmas, though).

WHY IT'S WRONG: The full stop at the end has been separated from the sentence it belongs to.

RIGHT: Susie loves Christmas, especially now that Bibi is old enough to enjoy it. (She particularly misses her husband at Christmas, though.)

And you should never put a comma *before* an opening bracket. Look at this sentence:

WRONG: All year round, but especially in the summer, (when the nights are hot), Mortimer suffers from insomnia.

WHY IT'S WRONG: There's a comma before an opening bracket. And putting a pair of commas and a pair of brackets is like putting two sets of brackets.

ALSO WRONG: All year round, but especially in the summer, (when the nights are hot) Mortimer suffers from insomnia.

WHY IT'S WRONG: There's a comma before an opening bracket.

RIGHT: All year round, but especially in the summer (when the nights are hot), Mortimer suffers from insomnia.

EVEN BETTER: All year round, but especially in the summer when the nights are hot, Mortimer suffers from insomnia. (Don't over-use brackets.)

Which is correct?

A. Edgar said that the latest nutritional research was, 'suspect' because the laboratory was 'unfair.'

B. Edgar said that the latest nutritional research was 'suspect' because the laboratory was 'unfair'.

Sentence B is correct. In sentence A, the full stop doesn't belong to *unfair*, so it should be outside the quotes. And the comma before *'suspect'* is wrong. You wouldn't put a comma there if the scare quotes weren't there, so you shouldn't put one if they are.

Quotations

A *quotation* is a repetition of someone else's written or spoken words – just one word or a whole statement or passage. You see quotations in almost all writing: newspapers, magazines, novels, essays, letters and so on. We'll deal with speech in the next section, but in this section we tell you the general rules.

Quotations great and small

When a quotation consists of a few words but not a complete sentence, follow the rules for scare quotes (see the first section of this chapter). If you're quoting whole sentences, it's a bit more complicated. Here are the rules.

When you write an essay, you may put some short quotations (up to about three lines) into the text in quote marks. However, you shouldn't place longer quotations in the text. Instead, you should indent and single-space the quoted material, with space above and below it, so that it looks like a separate block of print. Such quotations are called *displayed* quotations. Here's an example from Dr Jones's latest book:

Witherby, in his paper 'Why homework is useless', makes the following point:

Studies show that students who have no time to rest are not as efficient as those who do. When 1,000 teens were surveyed, they all indicated that sleeping, listening to music, talking on the phone and watching television were more valuable than schoolwork.

If you're writing about poetry, you may use the same format. Here's a quote from another book by Jones:

The postmodern imagery of this stanza is in stark contrast to the imagery of the Romantic period:

Roses are red,

Violets are blue,

Edgar is sweet,

And clever too.

Punctuating quotations

The simplest way to punctuate a displayed quotation is to introduce each one with a colon (as we have in each of the examples above). You're allowed to do this whether the text before the quotation is a complete sentence or not, so you don't have to think about it.

Some people prefer to vary the punctuation though, treating the whole quotation as though it's part of the paragraph and displaying it as an afterthought. That's a style choice. The punctuation rules are then the same as for punctuating text that isn't a quotation. But there's no reason to complicate things if you're just getting the hang of punctuation.

Never ever ever put a dash after the colon:

WRONG: Witherby says that:–

WHY IT'S WRONG: You should never put a dash after a colon.

Note that we didn't give the displayed material any quotation marks in the displayed examples above. That's because the space around the quotation shows that you're quoting, so quote marks are unnecessary. You can add them if you prefer (this is just a style choice), but they serve no useful purpose and may make your writing look a little cluttered and old-fashioned. If you like them, just add one set – the opening quote before the quotation starts and the closing quote at the end after the punctuation – however many paragraphs there are. Like this:

'Studies show that students who have no time to rest are not as efficient as those who do.

When 1,000 teens were surveyed, they all indicated that sleeping, listening to music, talking on the phone and watching television were more valuable than schoolwork.'

And yes, of course, you can use double quotes if you prefer – that's also just a style choice.

When a quotation is not displayed, you can't leave the quotes out because you need to show where the quotation begins and ends:

Jones says that 'The postmodern imagery of this stanza is in stark contrast to the imagery of the Romantic period'.

There are two interesting things to note here. One is the capital T in the middle of our sentence. The other is that we've left out the professor's colon.

Most people don't mind that capital letter at the start of the quotation because they know that it's part of the quotation. (Others will insist on changing the T to t – or to [t], which we don't think is an improvement!) Because the omitted word, *the*, doesn't belong solely to the professor, you can also get round this problem by starting the quotation a little later, like this:

Jones says that the 'postmodern imagery of this stanza is in stark contrast to the imagery of the Romantic period'.

Leaving out the colon is doing the same thing at the other end of the quotation: stopping a little early. We're allowed to do this because the colon doesn't alter the sense of the professor's words and would look silly, as we still need a full stop to end our sentence:

WRONG: Jones says that 'The postmodern imagery of this stanza is in stark contrast to the imagery of the Romantic period:'.

Careful decisions about where to start and stop the quotation can solve most problems like this.

A couple of other points. Look at this:

Witherby goes on to say that 'When 1,000 teens were surveyed, they all indicated that . . . listening to music . . . and watching television were more valuable than schoolwork.'

The first thing to note is that we haven't quoted all the words in the professor's sentence. For the purpose of what we're talking about, some words are not relevant, so we've put three dots where we've left something out. The dots tell our readers that we've done this, and they can check the professor's book if they want to see what we've left out. You don't need to put the dots in square brackets (as you would if you were adding words of your own – see the section on Brackets earlier in this chapter) unless the professor writes with dots of his own and the two may be confused.

The other important thing about this last example is that we don't seem to have a full stop for our own sentence. That because there's no need for two. We have to make a choice. These are both correct:

> He goes on to say that 'When 1,000 teens were surveyed, they all indicated that . . . listening to music . . . and watching television were more valuable than schoolwork.' (We've given Professor Wetherby's full stop and let it end our sentence as well.)

> He goes on to say that 'When 1,000 teens were surveyed, they all indicated that . . . listening to music . . . and watching television were more valuable than schoolwork'. (We've left out the professor's full stop – ending the quotation a little early – and kept our own one to end the whole sentence.)

But it would be wrong to do this:

> Jones says that the 'postmodern imagery of this stanza is in stark contrast to the imagery of the Romantic period.'

because we've said that there's a full stop in Dr Jones's book but there wasn't – there was a colon.

You aren't required to be consistent about placement of these full stops (because it's practically impossible), but it's nice if you can be.

Which are correct?

A. Professor Witherby says in his letter that 'Dr Jones raises some interesting issues in his kind review of [the] book.'

B. Professor Witherby says in his letter that 'Dr Jones raises some interesting issues in his . . . review.'

C. Professor Witherby says in his letter that Dr Jones's review raises some 'interesting issues.'

D. Professor Witherby says in his letter that 'Dr Jones raises some interesting issues in his kind review of my book.'.

Only sentence A is correct. It quotes a complete sentence from the letter and puts the full stop inside the quotes. (It's the full stop that the sentence has in the original letter, but it also stands for the full stop at the end of our sentence.) We can also put the full stop outside the quotes. The writer feels that replacing *my* with *the* makes the sentence more readable. The square brackets tell us that a change has been made, so this is allowed.

Sentence B is wrong. The ellipsis dots are fine: the writer doesn't want to include the flattery, and has put ellipsis dots to show that something has been left out. But the end of the sentence is also missing and the full stop is *inside the quotes*, suggesting that this was the end of the sentence. The full stop must go outside the quotes.

Sentence C is also wrong. It's OK to pick out the significant words and put them in scare quotes. (This avoids all sorts of problems that the other sentences have to use ellipsis dots and square brackets to get around.) But you must then follow the rules for punctuating scare quotes: the full stop must go outside the quotes.

Sentence D is wrong too. You can't have the full stop in the quotation and another one to end our sentence. It looks silly. Choose one.

Speech

Indirect speech

Indirect speech tells you about a conversation, but it doesn't give people's exact words. It's a report of their ideas, but not a record of the words actually spoken or written, and it needn't use any of their own words. The rules for punctuation are the same as the rules for text in general:

> Mrs Robinson, who had tea with the deceased shortly before the murder, spoke to our reporter this morning. She is still shocked by events, and expressed her disappointment at the lack of progress by the police. She says that the whole community has been greatly upset by the loss of Ms Stakes.

You can slip in the occasional word or two from the conversation as a direct quote. Punctuate these following the rules for scare quotes (see the first section in this chapter):

> Mrs Edwards said that she was 'too horrified to think about it'. She insists that it's a 'disgrace' that the police haven't caught the killer yet.

Direct speech

> 'It'll be lonely for you when Edgar goes to university.'
>
> 'Yes, I expect it will.'

'But it'll be a relief knowing that he's not going to blow something up with one of his experiments.'

'That's true. I always feel safer when he's in one of his writing phases.'

This is *direct speech*. We are quoting everyone's exact words. The first thing to note here is that the full stop always (*always*) goes *inside* the quotation marks. If the speech ends with an exclamation mark or a question mark instead, this also goes inside the quotes. Like this:

'What will you do when Edgar's gone?'

'I'll be able to go to night classes!'

So that's simple. Note how helpful the question mark and exclamation mark are in telling us how the speakers are saying the words.

In fact, punctuation is so helpful that (especially in fiction) it's used to tell us about how the speaker sounds rather than whether the sentence is in the *form* of a sentence or a question. So these are also considered correct *in speech*:

'It'll be strange with Edgar gone?'

Here, a sentence that would usually be considered a statement has been given a question mark to show that it's being said as though it's a question. Perhaps this character always forms questions like this, or perhaps he/she thinks that the house is very quiet but isn't sure whether Edgar's mother would agree, as Edgar strikes the speaker as a quiet sort of person to begin with.

'Won't it be quiet when Edgar's away at university!'

This looks as though it should be a question (*Will it be quiet?*), but the exclamation mark tells us that the speaker isn't saying it like that. They're saying *It'll be very quiet!*

Putting the speaker first

The second thing you'll have realised about the conversation at the beginning of this section is that we have no idea who's saying anything. Obviously there's more than one person, but there may be two or three and we don't know who they are. We need more information. Try this:

Annie Edwards stopped knitting for a moment and said, 'I expect the term will go very quickly.'

Now we know that it's Edgar's mother speaking. We've put that information first.

Note that we've put a comma before the opening quote. There's general agreement that when you're punctuating speech you must have some punctuation here. Sadly, there's not much agreement on what it should be. Lots of people like commas. But some people like colons instead. And some people like to vary the punctuation, using a mixture of commas, colons and even – sometimes – full stops!

If you want to keep life simple, use commas (as we did in the example above) and stick to them. If you want to be more flexible there are more rules. Sorry.

Rule 1 is that you can only use a full stop with a complete sentence.

> WRONG: Annie said. 'I'll miss him.'

> WHY IT'S WRONG: Although *Annie said* has a subject and a verb (and is therefore technically a complete sentence), it doesn't express a complete idea. We wouldn't expect the sentence to stop there. We are going on to say what she said, and this needs to be included in the sentence. So the full stop is wrong.

> RIGHT: Annie stopped knitting for a moment and then spoke a little sadly. 'He does so much to help me around the house.'

> WHY IT'S RIGHT: *Annie stopped knitting for a moment and then spoke a little sadly* is complete in itself.

Rule 2 is that a colon should be used with long or dramatic speeches and commas with short simple ones.

> RIGHT: He shouted: 'Help!'

> WHY IT'S RIGHT: *Help!* is very dramatic. A colon emphasises this.

> ALSO RIGHT: Mortimer explained: 'As you know, Alice stepped in at short notice when Gloria was taken ill. Now that we know Gloria won't be able to return to the role, we have to think long term. I'd be delighted for Alice to stay on, but she has plans of her own – she's engaged to be married and doesn't want to continue with her acting career.'

> WHY IT'S RIGHT: The speech is a long one, and the colon prepares us for this.

> WRONG: He said: 'Only last Wednesday.'

> WHY IT'S WRONG: The speech is trivial (it's not even a complete sentence). There's no reason to start with a colon (unless, of course, you've decided to follow the all-colons rule).

This let's-go-for-variety rule can be applied very subjectively because you get to decide how dramatic a speech is.

A simpler way of applying it is to use a colon only with long speeches (more than one sentence) and a comma otherwise.

Decide which rules you're following and then use them correctly.

Putting the speaker last

If we put the information about who's speaking after the speech instead, we move the full stop to the end of our whole sentence (which will, of course, be outside the quotes) and replace it with some other punctuation: a comma, question mark, or exclamation mark. Everything else remains unchanged.

'Yes,' said her husband without looking up from his book.

'Yes?' asked her husband without looking up from his book.

'Yes!' agreed her husband without looking up from his book.

Note especially that there's no capital letter after the comma (as you'd expect), but there's also no capital letter after the question mark or exclamation mark. You may think that this is odd. Exclamation marks and question marks end sentences, so there should be a capital letter, right? Wrong! This is just one of the peculiarities of the rules with speech. These punctuation marks are regarded as indicating tone of voice rather than the end of the sentence (which comes where the full stop is). Clearly, George has mastered the art of holding up his end of a conversation with Vicky without having to stop reading. Varying his tone of voice convinces her (for a little while at least) that he is actually listening to what she's saying.

Which sentence is correct?

A. Rob muttered, 'I really want to watch that X-rated film on TV'.

B. Rob muttered, 'I really want to watch that X-rated film on TV.'

Answer: Sentence B is correct, because the full stop is inside the quotation marks.

Here's another pair. Which sentence is correct?

A. 'I wonder if Uncle Mike will let me watch it at his house,' he thought.

B. 'I wonder if Uncle Mike will let me watch it at his house', he thought.

Answer: Sentence A is correct, because the comma is inside the quotation marks.

Interruptions: putting the speaker in the middle

Sometimes the information about who's speaking lands in the middle of a sentence:

> 'It's a great relief,' Alice said, 'that I don't have to go on stage tonight.'

In this sentence, the speech is interrupted to tell us who's speaking. Right there in the middle, we've added

> , Alice said,

Here are the rules for interruptions.

Rule 1: Nothing about the original speech changes. There's no capital letter at the start of the second half. But there must be two more quote marks so that we still know which words are being spoken and which are just telling us who's speaking.

Rule 2: The interruption has to have a pair of commas, and the second goes at the end of the interruption.

Rule 3: The first comma goes *inside* the quotes as though it's part of the first half of the speech.

Some people disagree with Rule 3. Remember how we punctuated our example?

> 'It's a great relief,' Alice said, 'that I don't have to go on stage tonight.'

These people say that you shouldn't do this because if the words weren't a speech it would be wrong to put a comma here:

> It's a great relief, that I don't have to go on stage tonight.

They're right. If you look at the speech on its own, that comma would break the rules for the use of commas. So they insist that the speech should be:

> 'It's a great relief', Alice said, 'that I don't have to go on stage tonight.'

They'd put the first comma of our pair *outside* the quotes.

So there are two possible rules. In one, you have to think about how to punctuate the words of the speech in their own right and not get it wrong. And in the other you don't have to think at all – you can just follow the rule and put the comma inside the quotes.

Choose which rule you want to follow and stick to it. We're going with the simple rules and putting the comma inside every time!

Which sentence is correct?

A. 'After the film', begged Rob, 'I promise I'll go straight to bed and not have any nightmares.'

B. 'After the film,' begged Rob, 'I promise I'll go straight to bed and not have any nightmares.'

Answer: Sentence B is correct. In sentence A, whichever rule you're following, the comma after *film* is in the wrong place. It should be inside the quotes. (Even if you sometimes like to put the first comma outside the quotes, it's wrong to put it outside if it's possible to put it inside.)

Try another. Which sentence is correct?

A. 'Although I'm only a humble policeman, said Mike, 'even I am not going to fall for that one.'

B. 'Although I'm only a humble policeman,' said Mike 'Even I am not going to fall for that one.'

C. 'Although I'm only a humble policeman,' said Mike, even I am not going to fall for that one'.

D. 'Although I'm only a humble policeman,' said Mike, 'even I am not going to fall for that one.'

Answer: Sentence D is correct. In sentence A, there should be a closing quotation mark *before said*. In sentence B, there should be a comma after *Mike*, and *Even* should not have a capital letter. In sentence C, a quotation mark is needed before *even I*, and the full stop should be inside the quotes. (Annoying rules, aren't they? So many things can go wrong with this type of sentence!)

Note that, in all the interrupted quotations in this section, the quoted material adds up to only one sentence even though it's written in two separate parts.

Avoiding run-on sentences with interrupted speech

When you interrupt someone's conversation, make sure that you don't create a run-on sentence. A *run-on sentence* is actually two sentences that have been stuck together (that is, *run* together) with nothing to join them. (For more information on run-on sentences, see Chapter 7.) Just because it's speech is no reason to ignore the rules about joining sentences. Check out these examples:

WRONG: 'I don't understand why you're so soft on Damian,' complained Ellie, 'he'll ruin you if you're not careful.'

RIGHT: 'I don't understand why you're so soft on Damian,' complained Ellie. 'He'll ruin you if you're not careful.'

The spoken material forms two complete sentences:

SENTENCE 1: I don't understand why you're so soft on Damian.

SENTENCE 2: He'll ruin you if you're not careful.

Because the spoken material forms two complete sentences, you must write two separate sentences. If you cram this quoted material into one sentence, you've got a run-on sentence. Here's another set:

WRONG: 'We were at school together,' explained Mortimer, 'I suppose I just feel sorry for him.'

RIGHT: 'We were at school together,' explained Mortimer. 'I suppose I just feel sorry for him.'

WHY IT'S RIGHT: There are two complete sentences, so you can't run them together into one sentence. (Sentence 1 = *We were at school together*. Sentence 2 = *I suppose I just feel sorry for him*.) Both start with a capital because *I* has to have a capital letter whatever happens. But only here is the punctuation right as well.

Remove the information about who's speaking and check the spoken material. What's left? Enough for half a sentence? That's OK. A speech doesn't need to express a complete thought. Enough material for one sentence? Also OK. Enough material for two sentences? Not OK, unless you write two sentences.

Which is correct?

A. 'You are grounded until I say otherwise,' said Dr Mackenzie to her son, Angus. 'I'm sorry it's come to this, but it's for your own good.'

B. 'You are grounded until I say otherwise,' said Dr Mackenzie to her son, Angus, 'I'm sorry it's come to this, but it's for your own good.'

Answer: Sentence A is correct. The quoted material forms two complete sentences and you must quote it that way. Sentence 1 = *You are grounded until I say otherwise*. Sentence 2 = *I'm sorry it's come to this, but it's for your own good*.

Speech within speech

Bill said, 'Mildred had the nerve to say I should have replaced the fence.'

Well, that's OK, but what if Bill wants to tell us Mildred's exact words? We need some more quotation marks:

Bill said, 'Mildred had the nerve to say, "I'm surprised you haven't replaced this fence with a wall."'

A sentence like this has to be sorted out.

The first rule is that you use the other kind of quotation marks for the inner speech. So, if you used double quotes to start with, you use single quotes when you get to the inner speech; if you used single quotes first, switch to double ones.

Another example. Lucinda was thinking of piercing her tongue, but she discussed it with Mortimer, who wasn't too happy. He said:

'I don't like the sound of that. It gives me cold shivers up my spine just to think about it.'

Here's what Lucinda told Alice:

Lucinda said, 'I was thinking of piercing my tongue, but Mortimer said, "It gives me cold shivers up my spine just to think about it."'

Lucinda's words are in double quotation marks and Mortimer's complete statement is in single quotation marks.

Commas and full stops follow the same rules in both double and single quotations. Look at the sentence in layers, working from the inside out, then get rid of any duplicated full stops:

Layer 1: *Mortimer said, 'It gives me cold shivers up my spine just to think about it.'*

Layer 2: Lucinda said, 'I was thinking of piercing my tongue.'

The layers combined: Lucinda said, 'I was thinking of piercing my tongue, **but** *Mortimer said, "It gives me cold shivers up my spine just to think about it."'.*

Then you just need to remove the extra full stop. Follow the usual rules: the full stop goes inside the speech (in this case inside the whole cluster of speech marks). So delete the second one.

Questions within questions

If a sentence includes quoted words and the whole sentence is a question but the quoted words aren't, the question mark goes outside the quotes. (Imagine giving both their punctuation and then deciding which to keep. A question mark or exclamation mark is more informative than a full stop, so that's the one we keep.) The same goes for exclamation marks:

Step 1 (WRONG): Did I hear that right? Did Bibi say, 'Good morning, Grandma.'?

Step 2 (Lose the full stop): Did I hear that right? Did Bibi say 'Good morning, Grandma'?

Step 1 (WRONG): Yes. Bibi said, 'Good morning, Grandma.'!

Step 2 (Lose the full stop): Yes. Bibi said, 'Good morning, Grandma'!

But, for those rare occasions when both the quoted words and the sentence are questions or exclamations, put the question mark or exclamation mark *inside* the quotation marks. (Imagine giving both their punctuation to start with and then keeping one. One placed outside the quotes will stand for the whole sentence only, as in the examples above. But one placed inside will do double duty for both – just as a full stop in speech always does. So that's the one we keep.) Here's an example:

Step 1 (WRONG): Did Damian really ask Alice, 'Why do you eat that stuff?'?

Step 2 (Lose the spare *outside* question mark): Did Damian really ask Alice, 'Why do you eat that stuff?' (RIGHT)

Step 1: Yes! And when she tried to defend her choice to be a vegetarian, he said, 'Oh, get a life!'! (WRONG)

Step 2 (Lose the spare *outside* exclamation mark): Yes! And when she tried to defend her choice to be a vegetarian, he said, 'Oh, get a life!' (RIGHT)

No matter what, don't use two question marks because they look silly:

WRONG: Why didn't she think to say, 'When are you going to learn some manners?'?

RIGHT: Why didn't she think to say, 'When are you going to learn some manners?'

Which sentence is correct?

A. Can Bibi say, 'My name is Barbara?'

B. Can Bibi say, 'My name is Barbara'?

Answer: Sentence B is correct. Because the quoted words are not a question and the entire sentence is a question, the question mark goes outside the quotation marks.

Joining sentences together when one contains speech

Every hundred years or so you may write a sentence that has both a quotation and a semicolon. (In Chapter 15, we explain the semicolon rules in detail.) When you need to combine semicolons and quotations, here's the rule. Put the semicolon *outside* the quotation marks.

Look at this example:

> Gloria said, 'I can't imagine eating anything but chocolate'; she thinks chocolate is a food group!

Which sentence is correct?

A. He complained, "She said to me, 'You're fat!'"

B. He complained, 'She said to me, "You're fat!"'

C. He complained, "She said to me, "You're fat""!

Answer: Sentences A and B are both correct. You must enclose *You're fat* in a different style of quotation marks from the larger statement *He said to me you're fat*, but it doesn't matter what style you choose as long as you're consistent throughout your work. The exclamation mark at the end of the sentence goes inside both marks because it can apply to both.

Quote or *quotation?* In conversational English, *quote* and *quotation* are interchangeable. Strictly speaking, however, *quote* is what you do (in other words, it's the verb *to quote*), a *quotation* is the text you're quoting, and the marks used to identify it are *quotation marks*. See Chapter 1 for more information on when conversational English is acceptable.

Who said that? Identifying speaker changes

In a conversation, people take turns speaking. Take a look at this extremely mature discussion:

> 'You sat on my tuna sandwich,' Lucinda said.
>
> 'No, I didn't,' Martin said.
>
> 'Yes, you did,' Lucinda said.
>
> 'Did not!' Martin said.
>
> 'Did too!' Lucinda said.

Note that, every time the speaker changes, we start a new paragraph. By starting a new paragraph every time the speaker changes, the conversation is easy to follow; the reader always knows who is talking.

Here's another version of the tuna fight:

'You sat on my tuna sandwich,' Lucinda said.

'No, I didn't,' Martin replied.

'Yes, you did.'

'Did not!'

'Did too!'

Sounds better, doesn't it? You can figure out who is speaking because of the paragraph breaks, so we can leave out a lot of boring repeated information about who's speaking. (By the way, Martin *did* sit on Lucinda's tuna sandwich, but it was her fault for leaving it on his chair.)

So the rule is this: every change of speaker is signalled by a new paragraph.

This rule applies even if the argument deteriorates into single-word statements such as

'Yes!'

'No!'

or some other single-word statements. A new paragraph signals each speaker change, no matter how short the speeches.

This rule also applies if a speech is interrupted:

'No, I didn't,' Martin said. He paused to think for a moment. No, he had no recollection of sitting on a sandwich. 'No, I'm sure I didn't.'

We didn't start a new paragraph for *'No, I'm sure I didn't'* because a reader might have thought it was Lucinda speaking and lost track of who was saying what. Remember that the rule is: every change of speaker is signaled by a new paragraph. Don't start a new paragraph in short speeches if there's not a change of speaker.

In novels, you may have a speech from one speaker that's several paragraphs long. Budding novelists who are reading this book, please take note: the speech begins with an opening quotation mark. **Don't** put a closing quotation mark at the end of any paragraph within the speech. (The reader will think it's a different person speaking.) Whenever you begin a new paragraph, **do** put an opening quotation mark (to remind the reader that it's still part of the speech). When the quotation is completely finished (at the end of the last paragraph), put the closing quotation mark.

Who said what? Add quotation marks, information about who's speaking and paragraphs to make sense of this conversation between Alice and Rashid.

> Martin doesn't get on with the new conductor at all, said Alice. Whyever not? He says he objects to his choice of tempo. But if he gives it a chance maybe they can come to some compromise. I think it's too late for that. He told him to his face yesterday that he dislikes his 'sentimental' style of conducting! Ah! What do you think Mortimer will do about it?

Answer: Here's the passage again. (Note the punctuation.)

> 'Martin doesn't get on with the new conductor at all,' said Alice.
>
> 'Whyever not?' asked Rashid.
>
> 'He says he objects to his choice of tempo,' replied Alice.
>
> 'But if he gives it a chance maybe they can come to some compromise,' suggested Rashid.
>
> Alice thought for a moment. 'I think it's too late for that. He told him to his face yesterday that he dislikes his "sentimental" style of conducting!'
>
> 'Ah! What do you think Mortimer will do about it?' asked Rashid.

The last two sentences could also be read like this:

> 'Ah!' said Rashid, understanding at last.
>
> 'What do you think Mortimer will do about it?' said Alice in worried tones.

Punctuating Titles: When to Use Quotation Marks

In your writing, sometimes you may need to include the name of a magazine, the headline of a newspaper article, the title of a song or film and so on. It's important to show the reader which words are part of the title, so they need to be separated from the text in some way. There are two ways to do this:

1. Put the title in quotation marks. This is the usual way to indicate titles of smaller works or parts of a whole.

2. Set the title off from the rest of the writing with italics (or underlining, but italics is usual now – underlining was used when most people only had a typewriter). Titles of larger works or complete works are treated in this way.

These options aren't interchangeable. Each option has a different use.

Use quotation marks for the titles of

- Poems
- Short stories
- Essays
- Songs
- Chapters
- Magazine and newspaper articles
- Individual episodes of a television series

Use italics (or underlining if you can't do italics) for the titles of

- Collections of poetry, stories and essays
- Books
- CDs and DVDs
- Magazines and newspapers
- Television programmes
- Plays and films

Here are some examples:

- 'A thousand excuses for missing the deadline' (a newspaper article) in *Revenue News* (a newspaper)
- 'Ode to the tax man' (a poem) in *Tax Poems* (a book of poetry)
- 'I got the self-assessment blues' (a song title) on *Me and My Taxes* (a CD containing many songs)
- 'On the art of deductions' (an essay) in *Getting Rich and Staying Rich* (a magazine)
- 'Small business expenses' (an individual episode) on *The Tax Report* (a television series)
- *April 6th* (a play)

You may be wondering which letters you should capitalise in a title. A useful general rule is that anything that's in italics (or underlined) can have a capital letter on every important word. Anything in quotes usually has only one capital letter, at the start of the title. For more information on capitalisation, see Chapter 16.

Add quotation marks and italics to the following paragraph.

Rob slumped slowly into his chair as the teacher read The homework manifesto aloud in class. Rob's essay, expressing his heartfelt dislike of any and all assignments, was never intended for his teacher's eyes. Rob had hidden the essay inside the cover of his textbook, The Land and People of Continents You Never Heard Of. Sadly, the textbook company, which also publishes The Most Boring Mathematics Possible, had recently switched to thinner paper, and the essay was clearly visible. The teacher ripped the essay from Rob's desperate hands. He hadn't been so embarrassed since the publication of his poem I hate homework in the school magazine, Happy Thoughts.

Answer: Put 'The homework manifesto' and 'I hate homework' in quotation marks because they're titles of an essay and a poem. Italicise *The Land and People of Continents You Never Heard Of* and *The Most Boring Mathematics Possible* and *Happy Thoughts* because they're titles of books and a magazine.

Chapter 14

The Pause That Refreshes: Commas

· ·

In This Chapter

▶ Understanding why commas are important

▶ Using commas in a list

▶ Separating adjectives with commas

▶ Using a comma to indicate the person you're addressing

▶ Punctuating addresses and dates correctly

· ·

Commas are the sounds of silence – short pauses that contrast with the longer pauses at the end of each sentence. Commas are really signals for your reader. Stop here, they say, but not for too long.

Commas also cut parts of your sentence away from the whole, separating something from everything around it in order to change the meaning of the sentence. When you're speaking, you do the same thing with your tone of voice and the timing of your breaths.

So why do so many commas land in the wrong place? Perhaps because some writers throw them in wherever the writer needs to stop and think. The key is to put the commas where they help the reader to see the structure of the sentence. The rules concerning commas aren't very hard. In fact, they actually have a logic to them. In this chapter, we guide you through the logic so you know where to put these punctuation marks in several common situations. For more information on comma use, see Chapters 13 and 25.

Distinguishing Items: Commas in Lists

Imagine that Susie asks you to buy some things for her while you're shopping. She has only a small scrap of paper, so she writes everything on one line:

torch batteries butter biscuits ice-cream cake

How many things do you have to buy? Perhaps only three:

    torch batteries

    butter biscuits

    ice-cream cake

Or six:

    torch

    batteries

    butter

    biscuits

    ice-cream

    cake

How do you know? You don't, unless she uses commas. Here's what she actually needs (four items):

    torch batteries, butter biscuits, ice-cream, cake

To put it in a sentence:

    Susie needs you to buy torch batteries, butter biscuits, ice-cream and cake.

The commas between these items are signals. When you read the list aloud, the commas become short pauses. (Try reading the list out loud and you'll see what we mean.)

You need commas between the items in the list, with one important exception: you don't need one between the last two items. Why? Because, once you say *and*, you've already separated the last two items. But if you want to throw in an extra comma there, you're welcome to do so. It's your choice. If you add these commas in every list, the comma has a name. It's called the *serial comma* or the *Oxford comma*.

Susie's list is a list of nouns. Lists can be lists of other things – phrases or sentences, for example. The rules for the commas are the same.

 Never put a comma in a list of two things. This is always wrong. And if you're at school and have been taught never to put a comma before *and*, remember never to put a comma before *and* in your coursework or exams. (This will upset your teachers.)

If you decide **not** to add the extra comma before the *and* joining the last two items, you will sometimes find that your list needs one. Look at this sentence:

> You can buy good cakes at Harrods, Marks and Spencer and Bettys.

You probably know that Marks and Spencer is one shop and Bettys is another, but if you didn't you might be confused. This would be much better as

> You can buy good cakes at Harrods, Marks and Spencer, and Bettys.

or, of course, as

> You can buy good cakes at Harrods, Marks & Spencer and Bettys.

So the general rule here is this: if there's an item in the list that already has an *and*, put a comma before the *and* between the last two items.

You don't have to put a comma before the *and* in every list just because an occasional one is needed.

Punctuate the following sentence.

> Yasmin and Edgar wrote their Christmas present list early and decided that they needed a food hamper a weekend for two in Paris silk pyjamas a gold pendant and a pair of leather gloves.

Answer: Yasmin and Edgar wrote their Christmas present list together and decided that they needed a food hamper, a weekend for two in Paris, silk pyjamas, a gold pendant and a pair of leather gloves. You can also put a comma after *pendant* if you like.

Separating Adjectives

Your writing relies on nouns and verbs to get your point across. But, if you're like most people, you also enrich your sentences with descriptions. In grammar terminology, you add *adjectives* and *adverbs*. (For more information on adjectives and adverbs, see Chapter 8.) Look at the descriptions in the following sentence:

> When Susie dressed Bibi in the dress her grandparents had given her, she looked like a cuddly frilly pink cushion.

There are three descriptive words: cuddly, frilly and pink. You'll notice that we didn't put any commas in the list of descriptive words. Lots of people now prefer not to separate adjectives with commas, but if you like commas this would also be legal:

> When Susie dressed Bibi in the dress her grandparents had given her, she looked like a cuddly, frilly, pink cushion.

Here, a comma separates each of the descriptions from the next, but there is no comma between the last description (*pink*) and the word that it's describing (*cushion*).

The three descriptions in the previous example are adjectives. All these adjectives describe the noun *cushion*.

Here's a little more about Susie's Christmas preparations:

> 'I've got two big presents to save up for,' said Susie.

Now look closely at what Susie said. There are no commas in *two big presents*. Would it be legal to write *two, big presents*? No. Why not? There's no comma after *two* because numbers are in a different category. They count how many things you're talking about, but they don't count as adjectives. They give you different information (how many presents, not what sort).

Numbers aren't separated from other descriptions or from the word(s) that they describe. Don't put a comma after a number.

> RIGHT: Mortimer bought two large, glass-fronted, mahogany bookcases for his new home.

> WRONG: Mortimer bought two, large, glass-fronted, mahogany bookcases for his new home.

Also, don't use commas to separate other descriptions from words that indicate number or amount – *many*, *more*, *few*, *less* and so forth.

> RIGHT: He owned many expensive rare books.

> ALSO RIGHT: He owned many expensive, rare books.

> WRONG: He owned many, expensive, rare books.

More descriptive words that you shouldn't separate from other descriptions or from the words that they describe include *other*, *another*, *this*, *that*, *these* and *those*.

> RIGHT: Those comfy, little, brown chairs are to go in the library.

> WRONG: Those, comfy, little, brown chairs are to go in the library.

Punctuate this sentence.

> Ellie was worried about the musical number in which she had to sing while running down 14 steep dark slippery steps.

Answer: It's correct as it is, but if you like commas between adjectives you can punctuate it like this:

> Ellie was worried about the musical number in which she had to sing while running down 14 steep, dark, slippery steps.

Note: Don't put a comma after a number (*14*) or after the last description (*slippery*).

Sometimes, words that look like adjectives shouldn't have commas. Look at this sentence:

> 'I'd need a large crystal ball to figure out what my mother-in-law would like for Christmas,' sighed Susie.

There are no commas in *large crystal ball*. Is this just because we decided we didn't like commas? No. There's no comma between *large* and *crystal* because they're not both adjectives. We're not talking about a ball that's large and crystal, but a crystal ball that's large. *Crystal ball* is a compound word, so *crystal* doesn't count as an adjective.

And sometimes one word is clearly more important than the rest. Technically the list of descriptions may provide two or three separate facts about the word that you're describing, but in practice they don't deserve equal attention. Take a look at this example:

> Lucinda just bought that funny little French hat.

You already know that you should not separate *that* from *funny* with a comma. But what about *funny*, *little* and *French*? If you write

> Lucinda just bought that funny, little, French hat.

you're giving equal weight to each of the three descriptions. Do you really want to emphasise all three qualities? Probably not. In fact, you're probably not making a big deal out of the fact that the hat is *funny* and *little*. Instead, you're emphasising that the hat is *French*. You don't need to put commas between the other descriptions.

So you can put commas between adjectives but you have to be sure that they're really adjectives and that they deserve equal emphasis. If in doubt, it's probably safer to leave them out (the commas, not the adjectives).

Sentences like the last example require judgment calls. Use this rule as a guide: if the items in a description are not of equal importance, don't separate them with commas. And think about how the sentence sounds: if pauses sound wrong, don't put commas in.

You Talkin' to Me? Direct Address

When writing a message to someone, you need to separate the person's name from the rest of the sentence with a comma. Otherwise, your reader may misread the intention of the message. Take a look at the following sentence, which Susie wrote at the end of a letter:

'Bibi is crying because it's time to eat Grandma.'

You may be thinking that there's nothing odd about that: little children want to eat all sorts of things and often try to taste people! However, Susie isn't really saying that it's time for Bibi to eat her grandmother. Here's what she meant:

'Bibi is crying because it's time to eat, Grandma.'

In grammarspeak, *Grandma* is called a *vocative* or is said to be in the *vocative case*. (All this means is that it's the person – or thing, if you want to talk to the trees – being spoken to.) You can put these vocatives anywhere in the sentence:

'Grandma, would you pass me the salt please?'

'I was thinking, Grandma, that you should stay with us at Christmas.'

'Could you stay until New Year, Grandma?'

Just remember that they have to be separated off by a comma (or a pair of commas if they're in the middle of the sentence).

Which sentence is correct?

A. The professor called, Edgar, but I took a message.

B. The professor called Edgar, but I took a message.

Answer: It depends. If you're talking to Edgar, telling him that the professor phoned him, sentence A is correct. However, if you're explaining to Yasmin that the professor phoned to speak to Edgar but got you instead and you have a message for her to give to Edgar, sentence B is correct.

Using Commas in Addresses and Dates

Commas are good, all-purpose separators. They won't keep you and your worst enemy apart, but they do a fine job on addresses and dates – especially when items that are usually placed on individual lines are put next to each other on the same line.

Addressing addresses

Edgar has to write to his publisher. That means typing their address at the top of the letter and putting it on the envelope. It will look like this in both places:

Bestseller Publishers Ltd

223 River Street

London

WC3 2BU

Each item has a line of its own if there's room. If there isn't, put a comma between any items you're combining except the post code and whatever's in front of it. Edgar also has to write to his grandmother:

Mrs A. Edwards

'Apple Tree Cottage', Station Road

Barndale LB1 9JA

If you put the address into a sentence, you have to separate each item of the address:

Edgar's publisher has an office at 223 River Street, London WC3 2BU.

Mortimer just built a house in Barton-on-the-Marsh, Oxfordshire.

Notice that the house number and street are not separated by a comma (but a house *name* and the street are), nor are the town (or city) and the post code.

If the sentence continues, you should separate the last item in the address from the rest of the sentence with another comma:

Edgar's publisher has an office at 223 River Street, London WC3 2BU, but the company is moving to Cardiff next month.

Sandy's sister lives in Strathkirk, Scotland, on the shores of a loch.

Punctuate the following sentence.

> Police want to talk to anyone who was in the vicinity of 14 Hill Lane Hilbrough Road Dunford on the afternoon of the 19th.

Answer: Police want to talk to anyone who was in the vicinity of 14 Hill Lane, Hilbrough Road, Dunford, on the afternoon of the 19th.

Here's another sentence that needs additional punctuation:

> Responding to an alarm, police proceeded to offices at 2/4 The Passage River Walk in the City of London where a burglary had taken place.

Answer: Responding to an alarm, police proceeded to offices at 2/4 The Passage, River Walk, in the City of London, where a burglary had taken place. (This one's particularly sneaky, as it contains an extra bit of information that's not part of the address – *in the City of London*. It also contains a peculiar number – 2/4. The offices occupy numbers 2 and 4 but not number 3, which is a newsagent's on the other side of the road. There is also an office at number 7–9, where for some reason no one can remember the numbers 7, 8 and 9 are on the *same* side of the road!)

Punctuating dates

There are lots of ways to write the date. Here are four:

> 28 September 2006
>
> 28/9/06
>
> Sept. 28th, 2006
>
> 28.09.06

You only need a comma where you put two numbers next to each other without any other sort of punctuation, but you can separate the year with a comma if you like. Don't put a comma between the date and the name of the month.

You can put a comma after the day of the week, but you don't have to (*Wednesday 28 September* and *Wednesday, 28 September* are both correct).

Months can be abbreviated in some contexts, but look better in full on a letter. If you abbreviate the months, be consistent. The ones with short names (May, June, July) aren't usually abbreviated, and September is usually shortened to Sept., but you can choose to abbreviate all of them to three letters, and on graphs and charts it's common to use just their initial letters (J F M A M J J A S O N D) to save space.

If you're sending letters all over the world, remember that they put the information in a different order in other countries, which can lead to confusion. In the USA, for example, 6/10 means the 10th of June, but in the UK it means the 6th of October. And in Japan 06.09.05 means the 5th of September 2006. So it's a good idea to write the month and year in full whatever order you put the day, month and year in.

To insert a date into a sentence, you may need one more comma:

> On 28 September 2006, Bibi ate three boxes of chocolates.

or

> Bibi was especially quiet for an hour on 28 September 2006, when she ate three boxes of chocolates.

Which of these sentences are correct?

A. Lucinda's grandmother was born on Monday September 28th 1938.

B. Lucinda's grandmother was born on 28 Sept., 1938.

C. Lucinda's grandmother was born on Monday 28 September 1938.

D. Lucinda's grandmother was born on Monday, 28 September 1938.

Answer: Sentences B, C and D are all correct. Sentence A (which shows the date in a form often used by Americans) isn't, because you need a comma between *28th* and *1938*

Flying Solo: Introductory Words

When a sentence begins with an introductory word such as *yes, no, well, oh* or *OK*, you must separate it from the rest of the sentence with a comma. If you omit these words, the sentence still means the same thing. Read these examples twice, once with the introductory words and once without. See how the meaning stays the same?

> Yes, you are allowed to eat as much as you like at the party, but don't complain to me if you're sick.

> No, you can't have the day off – half the staff have got the flu.

Well, maybe you should take a holiday.

Oh, I didn't know that you needed the report today.

OK, I'll get it done by lunchtime.

To sum up the rule on introductory words: use commas to separate them from the rest of the sentence, or omit them entirely.

Which sentence is correct?

A. Well Edgar plays the piano well when he's in the mood.

B. Well, Edgar plays the piano, well, when he's in the mood.

C. Well, Edgar plays the piano well when he's in the mood.

Answer: Sentence C is correct. If you omit the first word, the sentence means exactly the same thing. *Well* is an introductory word that a comma should separate from the rest of the sentence. In sentence A, there is no comma after *well*. In sentence B, the first comma is correct, but the second *well* shouldn't be separated from the rest of the sentence because it's not an introductory word.

Chapter 15

Adding Information: Semicolons, Dashes and Colons

*I*n a classic episode of *The Rockford Files*, the hero's sidekick writes a book. He hands a thick pile of paper to Jim Rockford and waits for his reader's reaction. Jim studies the manuscript for a moment and points out that the entire thing is written as one sentence. There is no punctuation whatsoever. Nowadays, novel-writers do this sort of thing deliberately, but Jim's friend just finds it too difficult to think about the punctuation at the same time as the words. He explains that he's going to put 'all that stuff' in later.

Many writers sympathise with the hero's sidekick. 'All that stuff' is a real pain. Who has time to worry about punctuation when the fire of creativity burns? But the truth is that, without punctuation, you may not get your point across. In this chapter, we explain three useful little items – semicolons, colons and dashes.

Gluing Complete Thoughts Together: Semicolons

A semicolons (;) can glue one complete sentence to another. An example:

Sentence 1: Edgar broke a shoelace.

Sentence 2: He went out to buy a new pair.

You can glue these two sentences together with a semicolon:

Edgar broke a shoelace; he went out to buy a new pair.

You can also join sentences together with words such as *and*, *but*, *or*, *nor*, *since*, *because*, *so* and so forth. In general, semicolons attach sentences to each other without joining words. The sentences that semicolons attach should have a logical relation to each other. For more information on joining sentences and a complete discussion of how to do so with semicolons, see Chapter 7.

Joining words are called conjunctions. *And*, *or*, *but*, *yet*, *nor*, *so* and *for* are co-ordinating conjunctions. *Because*, *since*, *after*, *although*, *where*, *when* and so forth are subordinating conjunctions. For more information on conjunctions, see Chapter 7.

Using semicolons with false joiners

It's almost time for the marathon. As you stretch your muscles and focus your mind, you notice that the sole of your running shoe is loose. A gaping hole gives you a fine view of your sweat socks. What to do? You run into a nearby store and grab a stapler. Five quick clicks and you're on your way to glory.

Or not! The stapler looks like a solution to your problem, but in reality it was never intended to attach soles to shoes. (What really happens? Your shoe falls apart, a staple sticks in your foot, and you drop out about 26 miles too soon. Then you get arrested for shoplifting the stapler.)

Some words are like a stapler at a marathon. Think of them as *false joiners*. At first glance they look like conjunctions: analyse the meaning of each, and you see that they relate one idea to another. But grammatically they aren't conjunctions, and they were never intended to attach one sentence to another. These false joiners don't do the job. If you use them improperly, your sentence loses the race. Here's an example:

Mortimer ran into the house to get his briefcase, however, the butler couldn't find it.

Why is the sentence incorrect? You've got two complete sentences:

SENTENCE 1: Mortimer ran into the house to get his briefcase.

SENTENCE 2: The butler couldn't find it.

However is not a joining word, even though it looks like one. So the two complete sentences are jammed into one long sentence with nothing holding them together. In grammarspeak, they've become a *run-on sentence*. (For more information on run-on sentences, see Chapter 7.) If you want to keep the *however*, add a semicolon. Here's a legal combination:

> Mortimer ran into the house to get his briefcase; however, the butler couldn't find it.

Alternatively, you can make it two sentences:

> Mortimer ran into the house to get his briefcase. However, the butler couldn't find it.

The most common false joiners are *however*, *consequently*, *also*, *moreover*, *therefore*, *nevertheless*, *besides*, *thus*, *indeed* and *then* (which are adverbs, if you're interested – you don't need to know what they're called to get the punctuation right) and *for example* and *for instance* (which are prepositional phrases). Don't put these words on your no-no list, because they add lots of meaning to a sentence. Here, for instance:

> When the theatre caught fire just before the performance, Mike and Lucinda made sure that everyone was kept outside. Mortimer, however, rushed into the burning building to rescue his briefcase.

That *however* is perfectly correct with two commas because it isn't trying to join two sentences together. Just make sure that you use these false joiners with semicolons or with a single idea. Never use them to combine sentences.

It may help to tell whether one of these words has developed delusions of grandeur and is trying to join two sentences all on its own if you ask yourself which bit of the whole sentence it belongs to. If it clearly belongs to the whole thing, it's OK without a semicolon. You can tell that it refers to the whole sentence by moving it around and seeing whether the meaning changes. Look at these:

> Mortimer, however, rushed into the burning building to rescue his briefcase.

> However, Mortimer rushed into the burning building to rescue his briefcase.

> Mortimer rushed into the burning building to rescue his briefcase, however.

The sense is the same in each case (only the emphasis has changed). Now look at these:

> Mortimer ran into the theatre to get his briefcase, however, he couldn't find it and accidentally rescued the ice cream lady.

> However, Mortimer ran into the theatre to get his briefcase, he couldn't find it and accidentally rescued the ice cream lady.

> Mortimer ran into the theatre to get his briefcase, he couldn't find it and accidentally rescued the ice cream lady, however.

Because we started with two commas, we're really not sure which half the *however* belongs to. There are three things that it could refer to: *Mortimer ran into the theatre*, *he couldn't find his briefcase*, and *he rescued the ice cream lady*. This is a good indication that commas won't do. This should be:

> Mortimer ran into the theatre to get his briefcase; however, he couldn't find it and accidentally rescued the ice cream lady.

or

> Mortimer ran into the theatre to get his briefcase. However, he couldn't find it and accidentally rescued the ice cream lady.

Correct or incorrect?

   A. Ellie sang with all her heart; however, the glass in the recording booth didn't shatter.

   B. Ellie sang with all her heart, however, the glass in the recording booth didn't shatter.

   C. Ellie sang with all her heart. However, the glass in the recording booth didn't shatter.

Answer: Sentences A and C are correct, but sentence B is incorrect. *However* is a false joiner. If you want to use it, add a semicolon or start a new sentence.

Here's the bottom line: in combining two complete sentences, be sure to use a semicolon or a conjunction. Don't use a comma, an adverb, or a prepositional phrase.

Separating items in a list with semicolons

Mortimer is writing his guest list for his annual New Year Ball. He plans to invite quite a few important people. Here, without punctuation, are some of the lucky guests:

Oscar Smith the nation's leading composer his piano tuner Leo Biddle a musicologist from the local university the movie star Gloria Griddle Bert Witherby-Jones his member of parliament and of course all his friends.

Confusing, isn't it? Perhaps commas will help:

Oscar Smith, the nation's leading composer, his piano tuner, Leo Biddle, a musicologist from the local university, the movie star Gloria Griddle, Bert Witherby-Jones, his member of parliament, and, of course, all his friends.

The caterer wants to know how many people to cater for, but the list has some names and some titles and descriptions. A few of the names and titles are paired, indicating one person. A few are not paired, indicating two people. Excluding his friends, is that eight people or only five? How can you tell?

If the list isn't punctuated or is punctuated only with commas, you can't tell the difference. All those names and titles are jumbled together. You need something stronger than a comma to separate the elements of the list. You need – super comma! Well, actually you need semicolons. Here's the correct version:

Mortimer is writing his guest list for his annual New Year Ball. He plans to invite Oscar Smith, the nation's leading composer; his piano tuner; Leo Biddle, a musicologist from the local university; the movie star Gloria Griddle; Bert Witherby-Jones, his member of parliament; and, of course, all his friends.

The rule for semicolons in lists is very simple:

- ✔ When any items in a list include commas, separate all the items with semicolons.

- ✔ Put a semicolon between the last two items on the list (before the conjunction). Note that a comma here is optional if you separate items with a comma (see Chapter 14 for more information on commas in lists). But there must be a semicolon if you're using semicolons (leaving it out isn't an option).

Which is correct?

A. While she watched the football match with Bill, Deborah thought of all the things she had to do: wash up the dishes, which had been piling up since last time she visited, sell the house, decide how to talk Damian into letting her keep the dog, which she was very fond of, and arrange a day at the spa to cheer herself up.

B. While she watched the football match with Bill, Deborah thought of all the things she had to do: wash up the dishes, which had been piling up since last time she visited; sell the house; decide how to talk Damian into letting her keep the dog, which she was very fond of; and arrange a day at the spa to cheer herself up.

Answer: The punctuation of sentence B is correct. Two of the items in the list have commas in them:

wash up the dishes, which had been piling up since last time she visited

decide how to talk Damian into letting her keep the dog, which she was very fond of

so you must separate the items on the list by semicolons. Notice that you need a semicolon before the word *and*.

Creating a Stopping Point: Colons

A colon (:) shows up when a simple comma isn't strong enough. The colon shows more intensity. (It also shows up in those smiley faces – *emoticons* – that people write in their e-mails.) In this section, we'll look at the colon in its natural habitats: lists and sentences.

Introducing lists

When you insert a list of items into a sentence, you may not need a colon. It depends how you lead up to the list. Think of the colon as a wake-up nudge telling the reader that you haven't got to the end of the sentence yet. The colon precedes the first item. Here are two sentences that use colons at the beginning of lists:

Sandy needed quite a few things for her round-the-world trip: a boat, a satellite phone, food, water and suitable clothing, for a start.

Lucinda thought her list of things to do in her life was quite ambitious. It included the following: work for a major fashion designer in Paris, buy a Rolex, have a big white wedding, honeymoon in Hawaii, and see a diamond being cut.

If you put a colon in front of a list, check the beginning of the sentence – the part before the colon. Does it make sense? Can it stand alone? If so, no problem. The words before the colon should form a complete thought. If not, you don't need a colon. Here are some examples:

WRONG: The problems with Lucinda's life plan are: she doesn't speak French, she hasn't got a job, she's broken up with Damian and she doesn't know where diamonds are cut.

WHY IT'S WRONG: The words before the colon (*The problems with Lucinda's life plan are*) can't stand alone. They form an incomplete thought.

RIGHT: The problems with Lucinda's life plan are numerous: she doesn't speak French, she hasn't got a job, she's broken up with Damian and she doesn't know where diamonds are cut.

WHY IT'S RIGHT: The words before the colon (*The problems with Lucinda's life plan are numerous*) can stand alone. They form a complete thought. To add the list on the end you need something to connect it to the sentence, and that something is the colon.

ALSO RIGHT: The problems with Lucinda's life plan are that she doesn't speak French, she hasn't got a job, she's broken up with Damian and she doesn't know where diamonds are cut.

WHY IT'S RIGHT: We added *that* and then we didn't need a colon.

AND ANOTHER RIGHT ONE: The problems with Lucinda's life plan are:

> She doesn't speak French
>
> She hasn't got a job
>
> She's broken up with Damian
>
> She doesn't know where diamonds are cut

WHY IT'S RIGHT: We cheated. We 'displayed' the list, using bullets. When you do that, you can have a colon every time if you like (or you can follow the rules – this is a style choice). It's the *look* of the list that counts most when you display it. (That's why we can get away with the capital letters and having no punctuation.)

Here's another set:

WRONG: You should: build a fire, toast marshmallows, drink cocoa and sing campfire songs.

WHY IT'S WRONG: The words before the colon (*You should*) don't form a complete thought.

RIGHT: You should do the following: build a fire, toast marshmallows, drink cocoa and sing campfire songs.

WHY IT'S RIGHT: The words before the colon are a complete sentence. (Yes, we know. When you say *the following* you're waiting for more information. However, grammatically they form a complete sentence. For more information on complete sentences, see Chapter 5.)

ALSO RIGHT: You should build a fire, toast marshmallows, drink cocoa and sing campfire songs

WHY IT'S RIGHT: We didn't use a colon.

Joining explanations

Colons sometimes show up inside sentences, joining one complete sentence to another (and occasionally joining a complete sentence to a sentence fragment – we'll get to those at the end of this section). Usually joining words such as *and*, *but* and so on glue one sentence to another, or a semicolon does the job. (See 'Gluing Complete Thoughts Together: Semicolons', earlier in this chapter.) But there's one special circumstance in which a colon may take over.

When the second sentence explains the meaning of the first sentence, you may join them with a colon.

Mortimer has a problem: he wants to help Lucinda, but she won't let him.

The first sentence tells you that Mortimer has a problem. The second sentence tells you the problem.

Note that there's not a capital letter after the colon. You may see capitals here occasionally (especially if you read American fiction, as some Americans like these), and typists used to be trained to put a capital letter after a colon. However, it's wrong in British English. Only give the word a capital letter if it needs one anyway. (Words like English and Monday, for example.)

Here's one more example:

Lucinda has refused to take the job that Mortimer offered her: she believes he's just being kind and she doesn't want to abuse their friendship.

The second half of the sentence explains why Lucinda doesn't want to take the job. (You can think of the colon as replacing the word *because* or sometimes the words *that is to say*.)

Which sentence is correct?

A. Rashid wants to play the part of the monster in the Dramatic Society's new production of *Frankenstein*, he wants to try a part that requires a lot of make-up.

B. Rashid wants to play the part of the monster in the Dramatic Society's new production of *Frankenstein;* he wants to try a part that requires a lot of make-up.

C. Rashid wants to play the part of the monster in the Dramatic Society's new production of *Frankenstein:* he wants to try a part that requires a lot of make-up.

Answer: Both B and C are correct. Sentence A is a run-on sentence, with two complete thoughts joined only by a comma. Not allowed! Sentence B has a semicolon, and sentence C has a colon. Both are acceptable. (You can also write the same thing as two sentences or join the two halves with the word *because*.)

You are also allowed to do this:

There's just one problem: Lucinda.

Rashid wants to play the part of the monster in *Frankenstein:* a part that requires a lot of make-up.

The words after the colon here aren't sentences. That's OK as long as the bit before the colon is a complete sentence.

Giving Additional Information – Dashes

Dashes tell the reader that you've jumped tracks onto a new subject for a moment. They can add extra information in the middle of a sentence (in which case you need a pair of dashes, just as you would need a pair of brackets) or they can add something on the end (in which case, you need only one). Here are some examples:

After we take the dogs for a good long run – I didn't manage to take them out yesterday – we'll stop at the doughnut shop.

Vicky was crossing the road at the pedestrian crossing – she'd waited for the green man to light up before stepping into the road – when she was nearly hit by a speeding cyclist who went through the red light.

Susie was astonished that Lucinda couldn't name Bibi's dinosaur, as even Bibi knew that the soft toy was a stegosaurus – she calls it a 'stessassus'.

To test whether you've got the dashes right, take out the dashes and all the text between them (or, if there's only one dash, the dash and all the text after it) and see what happens. If you've got the dashes right, the sentence will still make sense (it will be a complete sentence). The material inside the dashes relates to the information in the rest of the sentence, but it acts as an interruption to the main point that you're making.

Dashes can look like this (—) or like this (–). Which you choose is simply a matter of style. Printers call the long dash an *em rule*. *(Rule* is just printer-speak for *line.)* The short one is called an *en rule*. That's *M rule* and *N rule* (they're named after the letters on the principle – a principle often ignored by the people who design the em and en rules in different typefaces – that the em rule is as wide as a capital M and the en rule is as wide as an N). The em rule can be set with or without space on each side, but the en rule must have spaces. Look at these examples:

> Fido is surprisingly intelligent — for a dog.

> It was the same car — George noted with mild curiosity — that he'd seen on the day of the murder.

> Natasha nearly hit a pedestrian – again!

> The anonymous letter claimed that Alice – a committed vegetarian – regularly bought chicken and chips late at night at a chip shop near the theatre.

Choose which one you like the look of and stick to it. Don't mix them!

You may find that if you type a hyphen with spaces on both sides your computer will change the hyphen to '–' automatically. (You may choose this style for dashes for this reason.) If so, you can type an en rule deliberately by typing Ctrl and the hyphen on the number keypad. (An em rule is Ctrl Alt and the hyphen on the number keypad.)

Which of these are correct?

A. Everyone who saw the accident – even Dr Jones, who's a keen cyclist himself, agreed that Natasha was at fault.

B. Everyone who saw the accident – even Dr Jones, who's a keen cyclist himself – agreed that Natasha was at fault.

C. Everyone who saw the accident agreed that Natasha was at fault – even Dr Jones, who's a keen cyclist himself.

D. Everyone who saw the accident (even Dr Jones, who's a keen cyclist himself) agreed that Natasha was at fault.

Answer: Sentence A is wrong. If you stop the sentence at the dash, you lose the end of the sentence. *Everyone who saw the accident* on its own isn't complete. Sentence B is correct: we have the end of the sentence back (*agreed that Natasha was at fault*) after the second dash. So are sentence C, where we've reassembled the main idea of the sentence before the dash, and sentence D, where we've used brackets instead.

Dashes may be fun to write, but they're not always fun to read. Used sparingly (and legally – according to the laws of grammar), dashes are fine. For a little change of pace dash a new idea into your sentence. But too many dashes can make your writing choppy and disconnected – or just totally incomprehensible. Just don't dash in too often! Look at this paragraph, for example:

> The inspector saw that George was walking through the door and – because he knew that George had come to complain about Vicky's near-accident – he hurried away to his office. However, he ran straight into the sergeant and Dr Mackenzie – who had come to collect her son – he'd been caught shoplifting – and the doctor – seeing George – immediately began to talk about the accident. It could have been serious – Vicky has osteoporosis – even a small fall could have broken a bone – and the police should do something about these dangerous cyclists.

It's not easy to follow, is it? It would be very tiring reading a whole book written like this.

Rewrite the paragraph above.

Answer: There's more than one way to do this. Here's one possibility:

> The inspector saw that George was walking through the door. Because he knew that George had come to complain about Vicky's near-accident, he hurried away to his office. However, he ran straight into the sergeant and Dr Mackenzie. The doctor had come to collect her son – he'd been caught shoplifting. When she saw George, she immediately began to talk about the accident. It could have been serious, she said. Vicky has osteoporosis, so even a small fall could have broken a bone. The police should do something about these dangerous cyclists.

As you can see, we've shortened a lot of the sentences. A lot of dashes is often a sign that your sentences are too long for readers to understand them easily.

You're probably wondering why you're not allowed to use an en rule (–) without spaces as a dash. There is a good reason. The closed-up en is used for something else: it's used instead of hyphens if the two words joined together are of equal importance. Look at these examples:

Mortimer's long-term plans (*Long-term* has a hyphen to show that *long* is describing *term*, not *plans*.)

Lucinda's light-brown handbag (*Light-brown* has a hyphen because *light* is describing *brown*, not *handbag*.)

Damian's new import–export company (*Import–export* has an en rule because *import* is not describing *export*: the two are of equal importance.)

Rashid's cost–benefit analysis (*Cost–benefit* has an en rule because *cost* is not describing *benefit*: the two are of equal importance.)

An en rule (–) is also used with names to indicate that you're talking about more than one person:

Bert Witherby–Jones is Mortimer's MP.

The Witherby–Jones theory (that bread lands sticky side down when you drop it only if it's buttered *and* marmaladed) was invented by Professor Witherby and Dr Jones.

And you can use an em rule instead of quotation marks to indicate speech if you don't mind your novels being labelled 'experimental':

— Natasha gets over-excited when she's cycling and doesn't see the red lights, explained Mortimer.

— She should be more careful. She nearly hit my wife, said George.

— I know, but she gets distracted by creative thoughts about interior decorating.

— Well, that's no excuse!

This is **not** something to do outside a novel.

Chapter 16

CAPITAL LETTERS

. . . .

In This Chapter

▶ Referring to titles of people, family members and the deity

▶ Giving directions and naming areas of the country, seasons of the year and other times

▶ Capitalising school courses and subjects and the titles of creative works

▶ Writing eras and events

▶ Capitalising abbreviations and acronyms

▶ Capitalising lines of poetry

. . . .

*F*ortunately, the basic rules for capital letters are easy:

    ✔ Begin every sentence with a capital letter.

    ✔ Capitalise *I*.

    ✔ Begin quotations with a capital letter unless you're jumping to the middle of a quotation. (See Chapter 13.)

The rest of this chapter covers a few of the stickier points of capitalisation.

Capital letters (the ones you may have called *big* letters when you started school) are also called upper case letters. That's because, when printing was first invented, the individual letters that the typesetter used to assemble the printing plates were kept in wooden cases. The *lower case* was for the little letters and the *upper case* was for the big ones. (This makes sense. They wouldn't have used as many capitals as little letters, so they put them in the case they had to reach for. Less stretching!) So, of course, they referred to them as the upper case letters and the lower case letters, and the words stuck.

Capitalising (or Not) References to People

If human beings were content to be called only by their names, life would be much simpler, at least in terms of capital letters. Unfortunately, most people pick up a few titles as they journey through life. Even more unfortunately, along with the titles come rules for capitalisation. In this section we'll tell you what's up (*up* as in *upper case*, or capital letters) when you refer to people.

Addressing the chief dogcatcher and other officials

Allow us to introduce our friend. He's *Mr* George Robinson, a *director* of a small local printing firm. Next year, the *Managing Director* plans to run for the local council. His wife is pleased that he will be a *councillor*, but hopes he will one day run for *mayor*. She'd like to be Lady Mayoress.

Now what's going on with the capitals? Here are some general rules:

- ✔ Abbreviated titles (*Mr*, *Mrs*, *Miss* and *Ms*, but also *Dr*, *Prof.*, *Rev.* and so on) are always capitalised because they're attached to names. They aren't used alone. (If they are, they're usually written out as, for example, *mister* and *missus*.)

- ✔ Titles like *director* and *councillor*, which refer to lots of people (there's more than one director and more than one councillor), may be capitalised if associated with a name but not on their own. (So we'd write *Lieutenant* Jones but He's been promoted to *lieutenant*.)

  Titles that belong to only one person at a time (for example, the Secretary-General of the United Nations, the President of the United States and the Prime Minister) are capitalised when you're referring to one particular holder of the title. You can also choose to capitalise them however they're used.

These rules are flexible in application. To some extent, capitalisation is a style choice. You can write *the queens of England* (because there have been quite a lot of them) or *the Queens of England* (because it's the title of one person at a time), but it would be wrong to write *queen Elizabeth II* (as there's only one). You can write *when Elizabeth became queen* or *when Elizabeth became Queen*. When in doubt, check with your boss, teacher or whoever gets to make these decisions. Just make sure that you know what rules you're supposed to be following.

Writing about family relationships

It's not true that Susie's *husband* is in prison. I know for a fact that he died. However, her *Uncle* Cyril was (it was a case of mistaken identity) and Lucinda's *grandmother* was arrested for shoplifting once. "Oh dear," said *Grandma*. "I just wasn't thinking. I'm so sorry." And she looked such a sweet old lady that Bill's *brother* let her go with a warning.

What do you notice about the family titles in the preceding paragraph? Some of them are capitalised and some are not. The rules for capitalising the titles of family members are simple. If you're labelling a relative, don't capitalise. (We're talking about kinship – aunt, sister, son and so on – not appearance or personality flaws – *tubby*, *sweet-faced*, *dishonest* and so on.) If the titles take the place of names (as in *Uncle Cyril*), capitalise them.

Bill's brother Mike took their cousin's son to the zoo on his day off. (*Brother* and *cousin* are labels, not names, in this sentence.)

His motivation became clear when Grandma Robinson saw him chatting to Susie and Bibi by the penguin pool. (*Grandma Robinson* is a name, not a label.)

She went at once to tell her daughter-in-law what she'd seen. 'Oh, good!' said Vicky. 'I told Father I thought the Inspector liked Susie.' (*Daughter-in-law* is a label. *Father* is a title – in this case of her husband, not her father, because Lucinda's parents address each other as *Father* and *Mother*. When Vicky refers to George as *your father* they know that one of them's in trouble. When they think of the *Inspector* they think of him with a capital letter because he's the only one they know.)

If you can substitute a real name – Vicky or Robinson, for example – in the sentence, you probably need a capital letter:

I told *Father* that he needed to fix the cat-flap.

I told *George* that he needed to fix the cat-flap. (The substitution sounds fine, so capitalise *Father*.)

If the substitution sounds strange, you probably need lower case:

'I told my *brother* that he should ask Susie out,' said Bill.

'I told my *Mike* that he should ask Susie out,' said Bill. (The substitution doesn't work because you don't say *my Mike*. Use lower case for *brother*.)

This test won't be infallible because we do say *our Mike* (to distinguish the Mike in our family from the Mike that one of us married), but the word *my* and other possessive pronouns (*your, his, her, our, their*) often indicate that you should lower-case the title. (For more information on possessive pronouns, see Chapter 17.)

Which sentence is correct?

A. 'Tell mother I won't be home for dinner tonight,' said Rashid.

B. 'Tell Mother I won't be home for dinner tonight,' said Rashid.

Answer: Sentence B is correct. *Mother* is used as a name, not a label, so you must capitalise it. (The test works!)

Now try these:

A. Now that he's engaged to Alice, Rashid is helping his mother to fix things around the house as much as possible because he knows he'll be moving out soon.

B. Now that he's engaged to Alice, Rashid is helping his Mother to fix things around the house as much as possible because he knows he'll be moving out soon.

Answer: Sentence A is correct. *Mother* is used as a label, not a name, so you must lower-case it. (The test works here too.)

Capitalising the deity

Words referring to God require a special capitalisation rule. Traditionally, believers may capitalise all words that refer to the being they worship, including pronouns. Look at this line from a famous hymn:

> *God* works in a mysterious way *His* wonders to perform.

Some churches don't capitalise the pronouns, but if in doubt you should capitalise the pronouns too, to avoid giving offence.

On the other hand, we capitalise mythological gods only when giving their names:

> The Greeks offered tributes of wine to their *gods*, but the most lasting tribute is the collection of stories immortalising their names. Who is not familiar with the stories of *Zeus, Hermes, Hera* and other deities?

Capitalising Geography: Directions, Places and Languages

If you are a world traveller, you deal with capitalisation and geography every day. But, even if nothing more than your imagination leaves the living room, you still need to know the rules for capitalising the names of places, languages, geographical features, regions and directions. Here's a complete guide to capitalising geography.

Directions and areas of a country

Do swallows fly south or South for the winter? The *direction* of flight is south (lower case). But a fixed part of a country may be referred to as *the South*. So a rough guide is that if we are talking about a specific part of the world we capitalise the words *North*, *South*, *East* and *West* (a clue is that the word will probably have *the* in front of it if it's used on its own), but we lower-case them when we're just talking about a direction.

Another general rule is that, if one of these words is used as an adjective, sometimes the phrase becomes recognised as a geographical entity (West Sussex or West Africa, for example) and then the adjective is capitalised. Otherwise, it isn't (west Surrey, western Spain).

The names of other, smaller areas are often capitalised too. London has an East End and a West End; the Thames has a South Bank. These have capital letters because they're the names of specific parts of the city.

Now it gets tricky. Capitalisation is agreed for a number of words, but not for everything, and the rules have a tendency to change when you're not looking. In a lot of cases capitalisation is a matter of style. Should we refer to *south London* or *South London*? People will disagree. (People who live there may think of it as South London, but people who live in Glasgow may not.) If you're not sure, check a dictionary or a map, or decide on a sensible policy for yourself. Just be consistent.

Capitalising geographic features

Capitalise locations within a country when the proper name is given (the name of a city or region, for example). Be sure to capitalise the entire name. Here are some examples:

- ✔ the Pyrenees
- ✔ Greater Manchester
- ✔ the Congo

Is *the* part of the name? Usually not, even when it's hard to imagine the name without it. In general, don't capitalise *the*.

When the name doesn't appear, lower-case geographical features:

- ✔ mountain
- ✔ valley
- ✔ gorge
- ✔ beach

A few countries have kindly lent their names to common objects: *French bread*, *Scotch whisky*, *Venetian blinds* and so forth. Most people (and dictionaries) capitalise these too. For example:

The people of France speak French, but we all eat *French bread.*

The people of China have probably never heard of *Chinese checkers.*

Do Turks eat *Turkish delight?*

Tackling race and ethnicity

If you come from Manchester you're Mancunian (because when Manchester was part of the Roman Empire it was called *Mancunium*), and if you come from Liverpool you're a Liverpudlian (because someone once changed *pool* to *puddle* for a joke and it stuck). But if you come from London you're a Londoner. (Yes, we know, there's no logic to this. Sorry.)

At least capitalising these words is easy once you've found out what they are. But what about race and ethnicity? As the names change, so do the grammar books. But grammar authorities are always a little behind on this topic. Here are some guidelines concerning capitalisation and race:

- ✔ White and Black (or white and black) are acceptable, but be consistent. Don't capitalise one and not the other. Always capitalise *Asian* because the term is derived from the name of a continent.

- ✔ European, Asian, Australian and so on are all in capitals. So is Afro-American (a term that's now in disfavour – African-American is preferred). Other descriptions of national origin (Polish, Bulgarian) are written with capital letters because the terms are derived from country names.

Marking Seasons and Other Times

Sandie's sister hates the *summer* because of all the tourists who try to snap pictures of what she calls 'an imaginary monster'. She's been known to bemoan the loss of 'winter's peaceful *mornings*', even though she never wakes up before 1 *p.m.*

After reading the preceding example, you can probably figure out this rule without help. Write the seasons of the year in lower case, as well as the times of day. Poetry is an exception, but everyone knows that poets make up their own rules, so those exceptions don't count.

Here's the good news and bad news about the abbreviations for morning and afternoon – a.m. and p.m. Some people like full stops and some don't (preferring am and pm). So, no matter what you do, half your readers will think you're right (the good news) and half will think you're wrong (the bad news).

By the way, a.m. stands for *ante meridian*, when the sun hasn't yet reached its highest point (the *meridian*). *Ante* is Latin for *before*. The other term – p.m. – stands for *post meridian*, when the sun has passed its highest point in the sky. *Post* is Latin for *after*.

Schooling: Courses, Years and Subjects

As every student knows, school is complicated. So is the rule concerning the capitalisation of school-related words. Don't capitalise subjects (*history*, *mathematics*) unless the names refer to a language (*English*, *French*). On the other hand, capitalise the titles of courses. Here are some examples:

- Economics 101
- Mathematics for Poets
- Physics for Nuclear Terrorists
- Spanish Translation and You!
- The Meaning of the Paper Clip in Scandinavian History

Although interminable and incredibly important, the years in school and university are not capitalised: *our year* (in the sense of a group of students who started their studies together), *year 9*, *undergraduate*, *final year* and so on.

Correct the capitalisation in this paragraph.

> Hurrying to his Algebra class, Edgar slipped on the steps on the very first day of his First Year. He didn't really care what people thought, but he didn't want to embarrass Yasmin, the love of his life, who was standing nearby with a group of her Undergraduate friends who were early for the first lecture of their course on Lightwave Technology. They were all reading Physics and frighteningly intelligent. Their lecturers had already decided that they were the most impressive Year they'd seen in a long time.

Answer: Here's the correct version, with the reasons in parentheses:

> Hurrying to his algebra (don't capitalise subjects other than languages) class, Edgar slipped on the steps on the very first day of his first year (don't capitalise years). He didn't really care what people thought, but he didn't want to embarrass Yasmin, the love of his life, who was standing nearby with a group of her undergraduate (don't capitalise *undergraduate*) friends who were early for the first lecture of their course on Lightwave Technology (do capitalise course titles). They were all reading physics (don't capitalise subjects) and frighteningly intelligent. Their lecturers had already decided that they were the most impressive year (don't capitalise year) they'd seen in a long time.

Writing Capitals in Book and Other Titles

Mrs Edwards is planning a party to celebrate the success of Edgar's book, *I AM NOT A MONSTER: A TALE OF HORROR AND SELF-DECEPTION*. She has postponed the party three times because he can't decide how to capitalise the title on the invitations. What should she do? Here are some general principles:

- Capitalise the first word in the title.

- Capitalise important words (nouns and verbs, but also adjectives and adverbs).

- Lower-case unimportant words. This includes articles (*a*, *an* and *the*), conjunctions (*and*, *but*) and prepositions (*among*, *between* – see Chapter 9 for a list of common prepositions).

Unfortunately, these rules turn out to be quite tricky in practice. Let's try to apply these rules to the main title of Edgar's book:

> ✔ Capitalise *I*. No argument here: *I* is always upper case anyway and it's the first word of the title (which is always capitalised).
>
> ✔ Capitalise *Monster* because it's a noun. OK, everyone agrees with that.
>
> ✔ Capitalise *Am* because it's a verb, and verbs are at the heart of the title's meaning. But some people prefer not to capitalise the verb *to be*.
>
> ✔ Capitalise *Not* because it changes the meaning of the verb and thus has an important job to do in the sentence. But some people prefer not to capitalise it because it's a little word.
>
> ✔ Lowercase the only word left – *a*. Never capitalise articles (*a*, *an* and *the*) unless they're the first words in the title. No argument here.

Edgar's book doesn't have a preposition like *between*, so we don't have to decide whether we're lower-casing all prepositions or just short ones. But his book does have a subtitle. You have even more choice with a subtitle (sigh!):

> ✔ Lower case everything
>
> ✔ Capitalise only the first word after the colon
>
> ✔ Follow the same rules as for the main title.

The problem, as you can see, is deciding what is important and what isn't. Authorities vary. (See the sidebar on style manuals.) Check with your immediate authority (editor, boss, teacher and so on) to make sure that you write in the style they prefer. Above all, **be consistent.** Follow the same rules throughout your report or essay.

Mrs Edwards decided on *I Am Not a Monster:a tale of horror and self-deception*. The thing that finally helped her to decide about the subtitle is the fact that it has a hyphen. It took her hours to work out what to do with everything else, and she couldn't face deciding whether the word after a hyphen gets a capital or not.

You're probably waiting for us to tell you the answer. Unfortunately, there isn't one. Some people ignore the hyphen when deciding on the capitalisation (on the principle that no hyphen is going to tell them whether to capitalise a word), but most people lower case the word after a hyphen whatever it is. It's another style choice!

When writing the title of a magazine or newspaper, should you capitalise and italicise the word *the*? Yes, if *the* is part of the official name, as in *The Times*. No, if the publication doesn't include *the* in its official name, as in the *Daily Mail*.

Which words should you capitalise in these titles?

> the importance of being edgar
>
> romeo and lucinda
>
> slouching towards homework

Answers:

> *The Importance of Being Edgar* (*The* is the first word of the title. *Importance, Being* and *Edgar* are important words. Lower-case *of* because it's not an important word.)
>
> *Romeo and Lucinda* (*Romeo* is the first word of the title and is also a name. Similarly, *Lucinda* is a name. Lower-case *and* because it's not an important word.)
>
> *Slouching towards Homework* (*Slouching* is the first word of the title. *Homework* is important. *Towards* can go either way. It's a preposition – a relationship word – and thus may be lower case, at least according to some style guides. It's also a long word, which makes it suitable for capitalisation in the opinion of others.)

Concerning Historical Capitals: Events and Eras

If you had a time machine, where would you go? Would you set the dial for the *Middle Ages* or the middle of the *Industrial Revolution?* You should probably select a *period* that didn't involve a *war:* the *Civil War* may be interesting to historians, but it wasn't much fun to live through. How about the *nineteenth century?* Or the *Tudor period?* What do you mean, you're really only interested in the *Battle of the Bulge?* Oh, I see – you're talking about your diet!

This monologue should make the rules concerning the capitalisation of historical events and eras easy. Capitalise the names of specific time periods and events but not general words. Hence:

- ✔ Capitalised: Middle Ages, Industrial Revolution, Civil War, Battle of the Bulge (yes, it's a real battle – in the Second World War)
- ✔ Lower case: period, war

Some people capitalise *Nineteenth Century* and Tudor Period because they see them as specific (unique) time periods. Others say that you should lower-case numbered centuries and periods (but not *Tudor*, as it's the name of the dynasty of kings). We prefer lower case.

Everyone capitalises the Second World War, but some people (Americans in particular) call it World War II. Be consistent: don't use both.

Correct the capitalisation in this paragraph.

> Mozart once met Marie Antoinette, but it was before Bastille Day and the French revolution, when she was a child. The Eighteenth Century must have seemed to her to be a good time to be alive.

Answer, with explanations in parentheses:

> Mozart once met Marie Antoinette, but it was before Bastille Day (correct: capitalise the names of important days) and the French Revolution (the revolution was a unique event and should therefore be capitalised – we capitalise names of wars), when she was a child. The eighteenth century (a style choice, but we prefer to lower-case numbered centuries) must have seemed to her to be a good time to be alive.

If U Cn Rd Ths, U Cn Abbreviate

Faster! Faster! You're falling behind! Does that message sound familiar? Or are we the only ones who see life as an out-of-control train? We suspect that everyone occasionally feels the need to speed things up – when listening to a lecture on the joys of grammar, for example.

Abbreviations often arise from the need to get it over with quickly. Why write more than you have to? Why write *New York* when you can write *NY* or *New Zealand* when you can write *NZ?*

Why? Well, for several reasons. First of all, you want people to understand you. The first time you saw *e.g.*, did you know that it meant *for example?* If so, fine. If not, you probably didn't understand what the author was trying to say. Second, abbreviations clash with formal writing. Formal writing implies thought and care, not haste. So abbreviate text messages and e-mails to friends and family, but treat a business e-mail like a business letter. All the formal rules apply.

Now that you know why you shouldn't abbreviate, here's how to do it correctly:

✔ Put a full stop on the end of abbreviations formed by removing the end of the word. For example: Prof. Witherby, Rev. Archibald Thomson, Fig. 8, vol. 2.

✔ Don't put a full stop on the end of an abbreviation formed by removing the middle of the word but leaving both ends. (These special abbreviations are called contractions.) For example: Mrs Edwards (Mrs dates from a time when women were addressed as Mistress), Dr Jones, Jeremiah Jones Jr, St Francis, High St and Station Rd.

✔ Write abbreviations made from the initial letters of a number of words in capitals without full stops. For example: UK, USA, BBC. (Some people like to give them full stops – U.K. and so on – but most people don't now.) These are **not** *acronyms* (see below for more about them) because they're not pronounced as words. (Words abbreviated to one capital letter – such as R. for River – are usually given a full stop.)

✔ The United States Postal Service has devised a list of two-letter state abbreviations, for example *AZ* (Arizona), *CA* (California) and *WY* (Wyoming). However, there are other systems of abbreviations that are more informative for non-Americans. For example, California can be abbreviated Cal. or Calif. If you need to abbreviate states, decide which system you're using and stick to it. (You should find all the varieties in any large one-volume English dictionary, listed under the individual states.)

✔ Science uses SI units. Write them without full stops and never try to make them plural by adding an *s*. If you don't know the correct abbreviation, look it up in your English dictionary or in a science textbook. (The textbook will probably have a table of SI units, which makes it quicker to use if you have to check more than one.) For example:

• 30 s, 1 min, 2 h (the abbreviations for 30 seconds, 1 minute, 2 hours) – these are preferable to *sec*, *mins* and *hrs* in all contexts.

• m, km, cm (metre, kilometre, centimetre).

• K, N (kelvin, newton, named after Lord Kelvin and Sir Isaac Newton – note that the names of the units don't start with a capital letter, and that the symbol for kelvin is K, not °K).

Try not to use non-SI units if possible. If you have to use miles, inches, pounds and so on, don't abbreviate them.

Acronyms are new words made from the first letters of each word in a multi-word title. They usually start out as an abbreviation, but turn into acronyms when they become well known and people begin to say them as words. Some common acronyms include the following:

NATO: North Atlantic Treaty Organisation

OPEC: Organisation of Petroleum Exporting Countries

AIDS: Acquired Immune Deficiency Syndrome

Most people write all-capital abbreviations and acronyms without full stops. Some acronyms live long enough to turn into proper words and lose their capital letters. Probably the most famous of these are radar (RAdio Detecting And Ranging) and scuba (Self-Contained Underwater Breathing Apparatus). This is an ongoing process; for example, AIDS is becoming aids. If you're not sure what to do with one of these, check your dictionary.

Want to drive your teacher crazy? Write a formal essay with &, w/o and similar abbreviations. (For the abbreviation-challenged, & means *and*, and w/o means *without*.) These symbols are fine for your notes but not for your finished product.

See if you can decipher Yasmin's diary.

> Tues 9/11. Left B'ham early in the a.m. & arrived back at uni. in good time. Saw the prof., who introduced me to his cousin, Mr Witherby-Jones, who's an MP. Bought 2 vols of poetry for E.

Answer:

> Tuesday the 9th of November. I left Birmingham early in the morning and arrived back at the university in good time. I saw the professor, who introduced me to his cousin, Mr Witherby-Jones, who's a member of parliament. I bought two volumes of poetry for Edgar.

Did you have difficulty with any of the abbreviations? This is a common problem because people are always inventing new ones and don't always take the time to explain them.

The moral is: don't use abbreviations that won't be understood by your readers. In homework, don't use abbreviations except for ones that everyone understands (such as Mr and BBC) and easily understood acronyms. If this had been a note to a friend, however, the abbreviations would have been perfectly acceptable.

Giving the Last Word to the Poet

> One summer's morn
>
> Upon the lawn
>
> Did Clarence cry,
>
> 'Forlorn! Forlorn
>
> Am I and so shall sigh
>
> Until I die. Goodbye.'

What this year's comma is wearing: manuals of style

Not quite as exciting as a designer collection of clothes, but there are fashions in grammar. Yes, fashions. A comma here, a comma there. A full stop on one side of the Atlantic but not on the other. Capital letters for abbreviations and then lower case.

In this whirl of changing grammar rules, how can conscientious writers be sure that they're in style? Easy. Just check a manual. Many institutions publish manuals of style; each manual lists the institution's preferences for punctuation, capitalisation, citation, and lists of other *–ations* that you've never heard of. All you have to do is check the index to find the answer to your grammatical dilemma. (You'd have to be institutionalised if you sat down and read the whole thing. *Boring* doesn't even begin to describe them, but they're good for reference.)

Your teacher/boss/editor (whoever's judging your writing) will be able to tell you which manual of style they prefer. Then you know that your work will be in fashion, or at least in the fashion that your boss likes.

A few popular manuals of style are:

- *New Hart's Rules: the handbook of style for writers and editors* (possibly the one with the longest history, having reached its 39th edition before its title changed to include *New* in it) – published now by Oxford University Press

- *The Times Style and Usage Guide* (the style guide of *The Times*)

- *The Economist Style Guide* (the style guide of the *Economist*)

- *The Chicago Manual of Style* (the biggest style guide – suitable for use as a doorstop – and possibly the most famous of them all, but American) – published by the University of Chicago Press

One of the advantages of poetry is that you can usually convince people that your mistakes are artistic choices. (Try it on your teacher, but we offer no guarantees.) But poetry does have a system of rules for capital letters:

- In formal poems you usually capitalise the first word of each line, although some poets deliberately lower case everything.

- Regardless of where you are in the line, begin a new sentence with a capital letter.

- In quoting poetry, capitalise everything the poet capitalised. Put a slash (/) to show where a line ends if you're running lines together instead of laying them out as the poet did.

Part IV

Polishing without Wax – The Finer Points of Grammar

'To make sure he's going to a good home, I'm going to have to give you an English grammar test.'

In this part . . .

Think of this part of the book as sandpaper – a set of scratchy, annoying rules that rub the rough edges off of your writing. After you polish a paragraph according to the information in this part, the finished product will have the correct pronouns, the appropriate verb tense and no misplaced descriptions. All of your comparisons will be logical and complete, and none of your sentences will be unbalanced. For the finer points of grammar, read on.

Chapter 17

Pronouns and Their Cases

· ·

In This Chapter

▶ Choosing the correct pronoun as a subject and understanding compound subjects

▶ Selecting the right pronoun for a comparison

▶ Finishing linking-verb sentences with the correct pronoun (pronouns as complements)

▶ Using the proper object pronoun and showing possession with pronouns

▶ Choosing the correct pronoun for some nouns ending in –ing

· ·

Edgar Rice Burroughs' famous character Tarzan is a smart fellow. Not only can he survive in the jungle but he also teaches himself a fair-sized English vocabulary, saves his beloved Jane from quicksand, and – when he travels to England – learns how to tie his shoelaces. Despite all these accomplishments, one task trips him up. He never seems to grasp pronoun–verb pairs. 'Me Tarzan, you Jane,' he says over and over. 'I am Tarzan' is apparently beyond him.

Millions of suffering grammar students know exactly how Tarzan feels. Choosing the correct pronoun is enough to give even a 13-year-old a few grey hairs. But there's actually a logic to pronouns, and a few tips go a long way towards making your choices more obvious. In this chapter we cover the three sets, or cases, of pronouns – subject, object and possessive. So grab a vine and swing into the jungle of pronouns.

Me Like Tarzan: Choosing Subject Pronouns

The subject is the person or thing that is 'doing' the action of the verb (or 'being' the verb if it's a linking verb). (For more on locating the subject, see Chapter 4.) You can't do much wrong when you have the actual name of a person, place or thing as the subject – in other words, a noun – but pronouns are another story.

A subject pronoun is said to be in the *nominative case*.

Legal subject pronouns include *I, you, he, she, it, we, they, who* and *whoever*. If you want to avoid a grammatical sin, stay away from *me, him, her, us, them, whom* and *whomever* when you're selecting a subject.

Here are some examples of pronouns as the subject of a sentence:

> *I* didn't think her new dress suited her. (*I* is the subject of the verb *did think*.)

> *She* will bring the refreshments for this month's Science Fiction Club meeting. (*She* is the subject of the verb *will bring*.)

> *Whoever* marries Damian next should have her head examined. (*Whoever* is the subject of the verb *marries*.)

Compounding interest: pairs of subjects

Most people do OK with one subject, but sentences with two subjects are a different story. For example, we often hear otherwise grammatically correct friends say such things as

> Rashid and *me* are going to get some fish and chips. Do you want any?

> Damian and *me* hadn't met then.

See the problem? In the first example, the verb *are going* expresses the action. To find the subject, ask *who* or *what are going*. The answer right now is *Rashid and me are going*, but *me* isn't a subject pronoun. Here's the correct version:

> Rashid and *I* are going to the supermarket for some carrots and celery. (We couldn't resist correcting the nutritional content too.)

In the second example, the action – the verb – is *had met*. (*Not* isn't part of the verb.) *Who* or *what had met*? The answer, as it is now, is *Damian* and *me*. *Me* is not a legal subject pronoun. The correct version is as follows:

> Damian and *I* hadn't met then.

You may also hear children say things like this:

> *Him* and *me* have been invited to Susie's birthday party.

The verb is *have been invited*, and the subjects are *him* and *me*, but these aren't legal subject pronouns. They should say *he and I* or, better still,

Rob and *I* are going to Susie's birthday party.

Sometimes a sentence has more than one subject. For example, each of the preceding sample sentences in this section has more than one subject.

One good way to check your pronouns in sentences with more than one subject is to look at each one separately. If you've developed a fairly good ear for proper English, isolating the pronoun helps you decide whether you've chosen correctly. You may have to adjust the verb a bit when you're speaking about one subject instead of two, but the principle is the same. If the pronoun doesn't sound right as a solo subject, it isn't right as part of a pair either. Here is an example:

ORIGINAL SENTENCE: *Lucinda* and *me* went shopping in the sales yesterday.

CHECK: *Me* went shopping in the sales yesterday. Verdict: sounds terrible. Substitute *I.*

CHECK THE REVISED VERSION: *I* went shopping in the sales yesterday. Verdict: much better.

COMBINED, CORRECTED SENTENCE: *Lucinda* and *I* went shopping in the sales yesterday.

Which sentence is correct?

A. Mortimer, you and me appointed the judges for the beauty contest, so we have to live with their decisions, however wrong we think they are.

B. Mortimer, you and I appointed the judges for the beauty contest, so we have to live with their decisions, however wrong we think they are.

Answer: Sentence B is correct. *I* is a subject pronoun and *me* is not. If you take the subjects separately, you can hear the correct answer.

Attracting appositives

Do you want to say the same thing twice? Use an appositive. An *appositive* is a noun or a pronoun that is exactly the same as the noun or pronoun that precedes it in the sentence. Check out these examples:

Gloria, the TV Personality of the Year, will hold a press conference tomorrow at 10 a.m.

Natasha, a fan of bicycles, acknowledges that life on two wheels is sometimes hard on the complexion.

Do you see the pair of matching ideas in each sentence? In the first, *the TV Personality of the Year* is the same as *Gloria*. In the second, *Natasha* and *a fan of bicycles* are the same. The second half of each pair (*the TV Personality of the Year* and *a fan of bicycles*) is an *appositive*.

Appositives fall naturally into most people's speech and writing, perhaps because human beings feel a great need to explain themselves. You probably won't make a mistake with an appositive unless a pronoun or a comma is involved. (See Chapter 25 for more information on appositives and commas.)

Pronouns can serve as appositives, and they show up mostly when you have two or more people or things to talk about. Here are some sentences with appositives and pronouns:

> Vicky has won the raffle! The winners – George and she – will be flown to New York for a four-day luxury weekend. (appositive = *George and she*)

> We're embarrassed, Lucinda and I, to be so hopeless at dancing, so we've decided to take lessons. (appositive = *Lucinda and I*)

Why are *she* and *I* correct? In these sample sentences, the appositives are paired with the subjects of the sentence (*winners*, *we*). In a sense, the appositives are potential substitutes for the subject. Therefore, you must use a subject pronoun.

The appositive pronoun must always match its partner. If you pair it with a subject, the appositive must be a subject pronoun. If you pair it with an object, it must be an object pronoun.

You can confirm pronoun choice with the same method that we describe in the previous section. Examine each part separately. Adjust the verb if necessary, and then listen to the sentence. Here's the check for one of the sentences that we used earlier:

> CHECK 1: We're embarrassed to be so hopeless at dancing. Verdict: sounds OK.

> CHECK 2: Lucinda is embarrassed to be so hopeless at dancing. (You have to adjust the verb because *Lucinda* is singular, not plural, but the sentence sounds OK.)

> CHECK 3: I am embarrassed to be so hopeless at dancing. (Again, you have to adjust the verb, but the pronoun sounds OK.)

Bottom line: isolate the pronoun and listen. If it sounds fine, it probably is.

Picking pronouns for comparisons

Lazy people that we are, we all tend to take shortcuts, chopping words out of our sentences and racing to the finish. This practice is evident in comparisons. Read the following sample sentences:

Rob insisted that he had more problems than she.

That sentence really means

Rob insisted that he had more problems than she did.

If you say the entire comparison like this, the pronoun choice is easy. However, when you drop the verb (*had*), you may be tempted to use the wrong pronoun, as in this sentence:

Rob insisted that he had more problems than her.

Sounds right, doesn't it? But the sentence is wrong. The words you say must fit with the words you don't say. Obviously you aren't going to accept

Rob insisted that he had more problems than her did.

The technical reason? *Him* is an object pronoun, but you're using it as the subject of *did.*

Whenever you have an implied comparison – a comparison that the sentence suggests but doesn't state completely – finish the sentence in your head. The correct pronoun becomes obvious. Better still, finish it in your sentence as well – it will sound much more natural.

Implied comparisons often contain the word *than* (as in the preceding sample sentences). The words *so* and *as* are also frequently part of an implied comparison:

Irritated by Lucinda's boasting about the expensive tomatoes that Mortimer preferred, Vicky reminded her that the tomatoes that George grew tasted as good as they (did).

No one gave Mortimer so much trouble as she (did).

In some incomplete comparisons more than one word is missing. For example:

Grandma gives my sister more pocket money than me.

means

Grandma gives my sister more pocket money than Grandma gives me, because my sister is a spoiled brat and is always flattering the old bat.

and

> Grandma gives my nephew more pocket money than I.

means

> Grandma gives my nephew more pocket money than I do because Grandma has more money than I do.

Think before you make a decision, because the pronoun choice determines the meaning of the sentence. And be careful to say what you mean in such a way that no one can misunderstand you.

Which sentence is correct?

    A. Lucinda broke more nails than I when we weeded Grandma's garden.

    B. Lucinda broke more nails than me when we weeded Grandma's garden.

Answer: Sentence A is correct. Read the sentence this way: Lucinda broke more nails than I did when we weeded Grandma's garden. You can't say *me did.*

Last one! Which is correct?

    A. Edgar taught me more maths than she.

    B. Edgar taught me more maths than her.

Answer: Both are correct, depending on the situation. Sentence A means that Edgar taught me more maths than *she taught me.* Sentence B means that Edgar taught me more maths than *he taught her.* The problem is that people may not know which you meant. So it's better to add the missing words to make your meaning clear.

Connecting pronouns to linking verbs

Think of linking verbs as giant equals signs, equating two halves of the sentence. All forms of the verb *to be* are linking verbs, and other verbs (such as *seem*, *appear*, *smell*, *sound* and *taste*) can be linking verbs sometimes. The type of pronoun that begins the equation (the subject) must also be the type of pronoun that finishes the equation. (For more information on finding linking verbs and the pronouns that go with them, see Chapter 2.) In this section, we talk about pairs of subject pronouns with linking verbs. Check out this sentence:

> The new champions, who spelled 'sassafras' correctly for the first and only time, are Rob and me.

Correct or incorrect? Here's how to check. Think of the equal sign (the linking verb). If the pronoun is correct, you should be able to reverse the sentence. After all, 2 + 2 = 4 and 4 = 2 + 2.

If we reverse the sentence, we get

> Rob and me are the new champions who spelled 'sassafras' correctly for the first and only time.

Rob and me are? Not a good idea. What would you really say? *Rob and I are.* So go back to the original sentence. Change the pronoun. Now the sentence reads

> The new champions, who spelled 'sassafras' correctly for the first and only time, are Rob and I.

In conversation, many people ignore the reversibility rule and choose an object pronoun. In conversation you can get away with such a choice, but in formal writing the rules are tighter. If you have a linking verb followed by a pronoun, choose from the subject set.

Which sentence is correct?

A. The members proposed to replace Martin as Chairman when he stands down next month are Alice and I.

B. The members proposed to replace Martin as Chairman when he stands down next month are Alice and me.

Answer: In formal English, sentence A is correct. Reverse the sentence: *Alice and I are* the members proposed to replace Martin as Chairman when Martin stands down next month. Verdict: Fine. If you reverse sentence B, you get *Alice and me are.* So sentence B is not a good idea, though it is acceptable in conversational English. (See Chapter 1 for more information on formal and conversational English.)

Using Pronouns as Direct and Indirect Objects

Previously in this chapter, we've concentrated on subject pronouns, but now it's time to turn to the receiver of the sentence's action – the object. Specifically, it's time to turn to *object pronouns*. (For more information on finding the object, see Chapter 6.) Pronouns that may legally function as objects include *me, you, him, her, it, us, them, whom* and *whomever*. Here are some examples of direct and indirect object pronouns, all in italics:

> Bibi hit *him* right in the eye for taking the dinosaur away. (*Hit* is the verb; *Bibi* is the subject; *him* is the object.)

> Mortimer took *us* to the new restaurant despite its reputation for being extremely expensive. (*Took* is the verb; *Mortimer* is the subject; *us* is the object.)

> Someone sent *me* a very upsetting anonymous *letter*. (*Sent* is the verb; *someone* is the subject; *letter* and *me* are objects.)

A *direct object* receives the action directly from the verb, answering the questions *whom* or *what* after the verb. An *indirect object* receives the action indirectly (clever, those grammar terms), answering the questions *to whom* or *to what* after the verb. In the previous example sentence, *letter* is the direct object and *me* is the indirect object. For more information on direct and indirect objects, see Chapter 6.

Which sentence is correct?

A. Without bothering to investigate, the head punished we, the innocent, for the food fight that broke out at lunchtime yesterday.

B. Without bothering to investigate, the head punished us, the innocent, for the food fight that broke out at lunchtime yesterday.

Answer: Sentence B is correct. *Us* is the object of the verb *punished*.

Choosing objects for prepositions

Prepositions – words that express relationships, such as *about, after, among, by, for, behind, since* and others – may also have objects. (For a more complete list of prepositions, see Chapter 9.) Here are some examples:

> Bill, unable to cope with five growing puppies, gave one *to us* yesterday.

> Mortimer's dinner is a problem *for her* because she can't find a suitable dress.

> Rashid's latest performance received a critical review *from them*.

> Natasha didn't like the colour, so she simply painted *over it*.

Notice that the object word answers the usual object questions (*whom? what?*):

Bill, unable to cope with five growing puppies, gave one to whom? Answer: to *us*.

Mortimer's dinner is a problem for whom? Answer: for *her*.

Rashid's latest performance received a critical review from whom? Answer: from *them*.

Natasha didn't like the colour, so she simply painted over what? Answer: over *it*.

Also notice that all the pronouns – *us*, *him*, *her*, *them*, *it* – come from the set of object pronouns.

Which sentence is correct?

A. Conversation between Deborah and I always turns eventually to the subject of Damian.

B. Conversation between Deborah and me always turns eventually to the subject of Damian.

Answer: Sentence B is correct. *Between* is a preposition. *Between* whom? *Between Deborah and me. Me* is one of the objects of the preposition *between*.

For some reason, the phrase *between you and I* has caught on (although no one ever says *between we*!). But *between* is a preposition, so object pronouns follow it. The pronoun *I* is for subjects and *me* is for objects. So, between you and me, *me* is the word you want.

Seeing double causes problems

You'll probably choose the correct object pronoun when there's only one in the sentence, but when pronouns come in groups, combined with other pronouns or with nouns, they sometimes cause problems. The solution is fairly easy: check each pronoun separately. Your ear helps you find the right choice. Here are some examples:

'George's information gives the Inspector and me a new line of inquiry,' said Sergeant Williams.

CHECK: 'George's information gives me a new line of inquiry,' said Sergeant Williams. When you isolate the pronoun, *me* is obviously the correct choice. You're unlikely to accept *George's information gives I a new line of inquiry*.

Try another one.

> Bibi's delighted. Lucinda presented Susie and she with one of Tinkerbell's kittens.

> CHECK: Lucinda presented she with one of Tinkerbell's kittens. Verdict: *presented she?* Nope. The sentence doesn't work. It has to be *presented her.*

> CORRECTED SENTENCE: Bibi's delighted. Lucinda presented Susie and her with one of Tinkerbell's kittens.

Pronouns of Possession: No Exorcist Needed

Possessive pronouns show (pause for a drum roll) possession. Not the movie head-twisting-backwards kind, but the kind where you own something. Possessive pronouns include *my, your, his, her, its, our, their, mine, yours, hers, ours, theirs* and *whose.* Check out the following sample sentences:

> Sure that the computer had beeped *its* last beep, Edgar shopped for a new model.

> He can now start work on *his* second novel confident that the computer won't delete the file.

> Mortimer fired the dancer *whose* stiletto heels had wounded Lucinda.

> Lucinda and Ellie used all *their* persuasive powers to make him relent.

> 'The shoes are actually *mine*,' admitted Lucinda.

The possessive pronouns in these examples show that the beep belongs to the computer, the novel belongs to Edgar, the stilettos belong to the dancer (or so we think), the powers belong to Lucinda and Ellie, and the shoes actually belong to Lucinda.

Note that none of the possessive pronouns have apostrophes. They never do! Ever! Never ever! Putting apostrophes into possessive pronouns is one of the most common errors. (*It's* doesn't mean *belongs to it. It's* means *it is.*)

Why don't possessive pronouns have apostrophes? We have no idea. Logically, you expect possessive pronouns to have apostrophes, because apostrophes show possession for nouns (*Edgar's mug*, for example). But logic and grammar aren't always friends or even acquaintances, and (as you may have noticed) possessive pronouns don't have apostrophes. Ever.

Which sentence is correct?

A. 'I believe the car that George saw on the day of the murder is yours,' said the Inspector.

B. 'I believe the car that George saw on the day of the murder is your's,' said the Inspector.

Answer: Sentence A is correct. No possessive pronoun has an apostrophe, and *yours* is a possessive pronoun.

Dealing with Pronouns and –ing Nouns

The rule concerning possessive pronouns and *–ing* nouns is broken so often that it may be a losing battle. However, the rule is actually logical. Some nouns that end in *–ing* are created from verbs. (In grammarspeak, they're called *–ing nouns* or, traditionally, *gerunds*. See Chapter 24 for more information.) When you put a pronoun in front of one of these nouns, you must be sure that the pronoun is possessive. Here are some examples:

'I've never objected to *his using* the car when I don't need it,' said Mortimer. (not *him using*)

Lucinda's parents are being strict with her, but she knows *their insisting* that she be in by midnight doesn't mean that they disapprove of her friends. (not *them insisting*)

'Will you dislike *my missing* some of your rehearsals when we're married?' asked Alice. (not *me missing*)

'I don't see that *our spending* time together is any of Damian's business since the divorce,' said Deborah. (not *us spending*)

Why possessive? Here's the reasoning. If you put a possessive pronoun in front of the noun, the noun is the main idea. Therefore:

Mortimer doesn't object to the *taking* of the car. Of course he doesn't object to *him* (that was never the issue).

Lucinda knows something about the *insisting* on a curfew. She may not know anything about *them*, and anything she does know is irrelevant because that's not what we're talking about.

Alice is worried that Rashid may dislike her *missing* his rehearsals. She knows that he doesn't dislike *her* (they're getting married).

Damian objects to Deborah *spending* time with . . . well, any man. That doesn't mean he dislikes *us* (Deborah and the men in her life). Though, of course, it may come to that.

Some *–ing* words weren't created from verbs, and some *–ing* words aren't nouns. Don't worry about distinguishing between one and the other. Just apply this simple test: you need a possessive if the meaning of the sentence changes radically when you drop the *–ing* word. Check out this example:

> Martin loves me singing and always invites me to perform at his concerts.

If I drop the *–ing* word, the sentence says

> Martin loves me.

Now there's a radical change of meaning. Clearly the sentence is incorrect. The correct version is

> Martin loves my singing.

Now the focus is on *singing*, not on *me*.

Which sentence is correct?

A. Stunned by Bill's beetroot-coloured suntan, Mike tried to discourage his sitting in the sun any longer.

B. Stunned by Bill's beetroot-coloured suntan, Mike tried to discourage him sitting in the sun any longer.

Answer: Sentence A is correct. Mike nags and nags his brother about sunscreen and the dangers of melanoma (because he worries about him), but doesn't discourage him generally. (In sentence B, he's discouraging *him*, all of him, in everything he does.)

Chapter 18

Fine-Tuning Verbs

. . . .

In This Chapter

▶ Distinguishing between active and passive voice

▶ Choosing the correct verb to describe different events at different times

▶ Reporting information with the proper tense

▶ Describing ideas that are always true

. . . .

*H*ave you ever written a letter and then, after reading it, gone back and crossed out half the words? Do the verbs tie your tongue (or your pen) in knots? Are you constantly struggling with verb problems? If so, this chapter is for you.

Giving Voice to Verbs

Verbs can have two voices. No, not soprano and tenor. Verbs can be either active or passive. Take a look at these two examples:

> 'The window *was broken* yesterday,' reported Rob, carefully tucking his cricket bat under the sofa.

> 'I *broke* the window yesterday,' reported Rob, hoping that his parents wouldn't be too angry.

How do the two versions differ? Well, in one case Rob is hoping he won't be blamed and in the other he's confessing. Grammatically, Rob's statement in version one focuses on the receiver of the action, the *window*, which received the action of *breaking*. The verb is *passive* because the subject is not the person or thing doing the action but instead the person or thing receiving the action. In version two the verb is in the active voice because the subject (*I*) performed the action (*broke*). When the subject is acting or being, the verb is *active*.

To find the subject of a sentence, locate the verb and ask who or what . . . (insert the verb). For more information on subjects, see Chapter 4. For more information on the basics of verbs, see Chapter 2.

Here are some active and passive verbs:

Bill *gives* a free-tattoo coupon to Lucinda. (active)

Lucinda *is convinced* by Damian to get a tattoo. (passive)

Mortimer *talks* Lucinda out of it. (active)

Damian *is tattooed* by Bill. (passive)

Making the Better Choice? Active or Passive Voice

We know that you're desperately keen to know all the latest stylistic contro-versies, so here's one. Some people loathe the passive voice. They insist that the active voice is direct, honest and more powerful, and that the passive is evasive and takes more words. We'll show you how the passive works (and give you word counts for all the examples), and you can decide for yourself whether to use it in your writing. Let's look at some examples.

Everyone accepts that if you don't know the facts the passive comes in handy:

The police have made little progress in their investigation of the murder of Ms Stakes, the local teacher who *was battered* to death with her own garden gnome a year ago today. (Passive: 32 words)

We can't give any specific information about the murderer because he (or she) hasn't been identified yet, but we've given all the information we have. The sentence is in the passive. In fact, you can put this sort of sentence in the active voice too:

The police have made little progress in their investigation of the murder of Ms Stakes. An unknown assailant *battered* the local teacher to death with her own garden gnome a year ago today. (Active: 33 words – OK, 31 if you say *someone* instead of *an unknown assailant*)

What about these?

The English language has been murdered in Lucinda's diary. (Passive: 9 words)

Lucinda murders the English language on a routine basis in her diary. (Active: 12 words – OK, 8 if you leave out *on a routine basis*)

We know whose diary it is in both cases. The first sentence isn't a very good sentence. The second sentence is better. It tells us much more directly that Lucinda, and Lucinda alone, is to blame for the fact that she can't understand her own diaries when she reads them. And the anti-passive league is clearly winning on length: they're a word ahead in each example so far.

But their strongest argument is that the passive is evasive – it deceives the reader by avoiding giving information. Look at these sentences:

> It *has been recommended* that the servicing of the boiler be postponed until next year. (Passive: 15 words)

> Rashid *recommended* that the servicing of the boiler be postponed until next year. (Active: 13 words)

In the first (passive) sentence, no one is taking responsibility for this action. If the central heating breaks down. In the second (active) sentence, the building's residents know exactly who to blame if they're freezing in the winter.

Are you convinced that the active voice is better than the passive? Good. Now look at these sentences:

> The teacher failed Isolde because Isolde tore up the grammar book before opening it. (Active: 14 words)

> Isolde was failed because he tore up the grammar book before opening it. (Passive: 13 words)

The passive allows us to leave out the teacher, so it's *shorter* than the active sentence. Have we deceived the reader by omitting the teacher? Or does this focus attention exactly where it belongs – on Isolde and the reason why she failed?

Now go back to the sentence about the boiler. The active sentence tells us who to blame if the heating breaks down. But if we complain to Rashid he will point out that the service date for the boiler was moved by the company who just installed the new heating system because the new boiler doesn't need servicing yet. (Rashid just wrote the memo to inform the maintenance staff.) The breakdown was nothing to do with the service date.

So the writer who used the passive may have been trying to avoid saying who made the decision (or may not know, or may be presenting the decision of a group of people), but the other may be inciting you to shout at Rashid because he wants to get him fired. In each case the important thing is not the use of the active and passive, but the (perhaps deliberately) misleading use of the word *postponed*.

In short, the active *may* be more appropriate in a novel, and the passive *may* be useful in report writing. The active may be shorter (it isn't always), but length isn't necessarily the most valuable criterion by which to judge a piece of prose. If you want to make your writing short and pithy, you'll need to look at a lot more than your use of active and passive voice.

What's really important is that it is possible for a reader to be deceived and manipulated in both the active and the passive voice, if a writer is intent on deception. This section has deliberately tried to manipulate your opinion by the way in which it presented its argument. (Did you notice the use of the active voice there? *This section . . . tried to manipulate your opinion*. It use the active voice, yet it's deliberately hiding whose opinions have been presented here.)

OK, this is where I (that's the English author of the book you're reading) have to come clean. I've been referring to the authors as *we* throughout this book to keep things simple. Both of us (the original American author and the English author who has been making changes to the book) know that English and American grammar are slightly different, so we (that's the publisher) didn't think it was necessary to point out which bits have been written by me. But here we (the authors) have a serious difference of opinion. The American prefers the active voice. The Brit is biased in favour of the passive.

This book is about grammar, but the whole of this section isn't about grammar at all. (It hasn't told you how to avoid mistakes in using the passive.) It's about *style*. If you take anything useful from this section at all it should be that you need to be critical as a reader. And, in anything you're writing, ask yourself whether you can say it in a shorter, clearer and more direct way. You will find yourself using the passive: it's so much a part of the language that it's hard to avoid. If you think you've said what you want to say in the best way, that's all that counts.

Label the verbs in these sentences as active or passive.

    A. The omelette was made with egg whites, but the yolks were discarded.

    B. Bibi slobbers when she eats eggs.

Answer: Sentence A is passive (*was made*, *were discarded*), and sentence B is active (*slobbers*, *eats*).

Try one more. Which is active and which is passive?

    A. A nail has been hammered into that sign.

    B. Mortimer is building a conservatory onto his country house.

Answer: Sentence A is passive (*has been hammered*), and sentence B is active (*is building*).

Putting It in Order: Sequence of Tenses

All verbs express information about three time periods: the present, the past and the future. Unfortunately, human beings have a tendency to want more specific information about timing. Enter about a million shades of meaning, closely followed by about a million rules.

For information on the basic tenses of verbs, see Chapter 3. In this chapter we focus on some special cases – which verbs to use when more than one thing is happening.

To clarify what's happening when, timelines accompany some of the examples in this section. Match the events on the timeline to the verbs in the sentence to see where in time each tense places an action.

Case 1 – Simultaneous events: main verbs

Look at the italicised verbs in each of these sample sentences:

> Grandma Robinson *swiped* a handkerchief and daintily *blew* her nose. (*swiped* and *blew* = two events happening at almost the same moment; both verbs are in the past tense)

> Grandma *will be* in court tomorrow, and the judge *will rule* on her case. (*will be* and *will rule* = two events happening at the same time; both verbs are in the future tense)

> Grandma *is* extremely sad about the possibility of a criminal record, but she *remains* hopeful. (*is* and *remains* = states of being existing at the same time; both verbs are in the present tense)

If two actions take place at the same time (or nearly the same time), use the same tense for each verb.

Case 2 – Simultaneous events: –ing participles

In the following sentences, check out the italicised words. The first is an *–ing* form of the verb and the second is the main verb. Note that the *–ing* form matches with present, past and future verbs and places the two actions at the same time or close enough in time to make the difference irrelevant. Also note that none of the *–ing* forms is associated with the word *have* or *had*. (*Have* and *had* help express actions taking place at different times. See Case 6 later in this section.)

> *Swiping* a handkerchief, Grandma daintily *blows* her nose. (The *swiping* and the *blowing* take place at nearly the same time – in the present.)
>
> *Swiping* a handkerchief, Grandma daintily *blew* her nose. (The *swiping* and the *blowing* took place at nearly the same time – in the past.)
>
> *Swiping* a handkerchief, Grandma *will* daintily *blow* her nose. (The *swiping* and the *blowing* will take place at nearly the same time – in the future.)

Another variation:

> *To blow her nose daintily*, Grandma swipes a handkerchief. (The *blowing* and the *swiping* take place at nearly the same time – in the present.)
>
> *To blow her nose daintily*, Grandma swiped a handkerchief. (The *blowing* and the *swiping* took place at nearly the same time – in the past.)
>
> *To blow her nose daintily*, Grandma will swipe a handkerchief. (The *blowing* and the *swiping* will take place at nearly the same time – in the future.)

In the preceding sample sentences, *swiping* is the –*ing* form of a verb (or present participle), and *swiping a handkerchief* is a participial clause describing *Grandma*. The action expressed by the present participle takes place at the same time (or nearly the same time) as the action expressed by the main verb. For more information on participles, see Chapter 24.

To blow is an infinitive, the basic form of a verb. Infinitives never function as the main verb in the sentence. In the sample sentences, *to blow her noise daintily* is an infinitive clause describing Grandma. For more information on infinitives, see Chapter 2. For tips on using infinitives creatively, see Chapter 24.

Case 3 – Events at two different times in the past

Everything in the past happened at exactly the same moment, right? Oh, if only this statement were true. History tests would be much easier, and so would grammar. Sadly, you often need to talk about events that took place at different times in the past. The verb tenses you use create an order of events – a timeline – for your reader. Check out the italicised verbs in this sentence:

> Grandma *had* already *swiped* the handkerchief when she *discovered* the joys of honesty.

There are two events to think about, one taking place before the other. (Unfortunately for Grandma, the joy of honesty came after the theft, for which she has been arrested.) Note the timeline:

For two events in the past, write the earlier event with *had* and the more recent event in simple past tense (without *had*). (Verbs written with *had* are in the past perfect tense. See Chapter 3 for definitions of tenses.)

Check out these examples:

> Because of Susie's skill with a needle, where a hole in the sock *had gaped*, a perfect heel now *enclosed* Bibi's little foot. (Event 1: the hole in the sock gapes; event 2: the mended sock covers the foot.)

> When Damian's accomplice *had inserted* the drugs, he *sewed up* the hole in the now illegal teddy bear. (Event 1: Damian's accomplice inserts the drugs in the teddy bear; event 2: he sews up the bear.)

> Because her mother *had been arrested*, Vicky refused to leave the house. (Event 1: Vicky's mother is arrested; event 2: Vicky refuses to leave the house.)

> After the song *had been played* at least 12 times, someone *shouted*, 'Enough!' (Event 1: the song is played 12 times; event 2: someone protests because he can't stand to hear it again.)

A common error is using *had* for everything. Wrong! Don't use *had* unless you're consciously putting events in order:

> WRONG: Grandma had dried her eyes, and then she had gone to see the judge.

> RIGHT: After Grandma had dried her eyes, she went to see the judge.

Also, sometimes you may want to talk about events in the past without worrying about specific times. You *went* on vacation, *had* a great time, *sent* some postcards, *ate* a lot of junk food, and *came* home. No need for *had* in this description because the order isn't the point. You're just making a general list. Use *had* when the timing matters. Don't overuse it – it's boring!

Note that you may encounter one other use of *had:* the subjunctive. See Chapter 22 if you have to know absolutely everything about *had* – and trust us, you don't.

Which sentence tells you about events that happened at different times?

A. Slipping the magistrate a fifty-pound note, Grandma hoped for mercy.

B. Although she had slipped the judge only one fifty-pound note, Grandma hoped for mercy.

Answer: Sentence B reports events at different times. Grandma tried the bribe at 10 a.m. and spent the rest of the day planning a trip to Rio (cancelled when her prison sentence was announced). In sentence A, Grandma bribes and hopes at the same time.

One more question. Which sentence reports events happening at two different times?

A. To prepare for her trial, Grandma bought a copy of *Be Your Own Lawyer!*

B. Grandma had bought a copy of *Be Your Own Lawyer!* when the trial began.

Answer: Sentence B has two events, one earlier than the other. The purchase of the book (*had bought*) happened before the trial (*began*). In sentence A, the two events (*to prepare*, *bought*) happen at the same time.

Case 4 – More than two past events, all at different times

This rule is similar to the one described in Case 3. Apply this rule when you talk about more than two events in the past:

Vicky *had baked* a cake and *had put out* her best china before Susie arrived for tea.

Now the timeline is as follows:

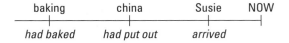

What do you notice? The most recent event (*arrived for tea*) is written without *had*. In other words, the most recent event is in the simple past tense. Everything that happened earlier is written with *had* – that is, in the past perfect tense. For more information on tenses, see Chapter 3.

Here are some examples:

> Sandy *had checked* all the boat's equipment carefully and *had held* a party to say goodbye to all her friends before she *left* on her voyage round the world. (Events 1 and 2: Sandy prepares to leave; event 3: she leaves.)

> Alice's parents *had planned* the wedding, and Rashid's *had* even *planned* the honeymoon, by the time Alice *agreed* to marry Rashid. (Events 1 and 2: Rashid and Alice have their lives planned for them; event 3: they decide to get married anyway.)

> Rob *had volunteered* his services as a babysitter, *given* Susie Mike's phone number and *arranged* for them to have dinner together before Mike realised what he was doing. (Events 1, 2 and 3: Rob sets Susie and Mike up with a date; event 4: Mike discovers that he has a date with Susie.)

In the last example three verbs – *volunteered*, *given* and *arranged* – form a list of the actions that Rob managed to do before Mike caught on. They all have the same subject (*Rob*). The word *had* precedes only *volunteered*, the first verb of the three. You may omit the word *had* in front of *given* and *arranged* because they are part of the same list and they all have the same subject. The reader knows that the word *had* applies to all three of the verbs. In other words, the reader understands that *Rob had volunteered*, *had given* and *had arranged*.

Identify the events in this sentence and put them in order.

> A supermarket now stood where Mortimer and Clarence had grown up and their parents had spent their entire married life.

Answer: Events 1 and 2: A couple build a home and raise their sons; event 3: years later, the sons visit their old home only to find that it has been knocked down. (Did the order of the information confuse you? You should still have been able to work out the answer by looking for the telltale word *had*.)

Case 5 – Two events in the future

Leaving the past behind, it's time to turn to the future. Read this sentence:

> Yasmin *will have completed* all her term's essays before they are due.

Yasmin works hard and plans her time, so her essays will be done before the deadline. *Deadline* is the important word here, at least regarding verb tense. The *have* form of the future, also called *future perfect tense*, involves a deadline. You don't necessarily have two verbs in the sentence, but you do have two events:

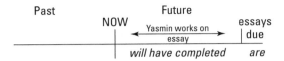

Use the future perfect tense to talk about the earlier of the two events. Look at these examples:

> Susie *will have put* Bibi to bed before Rob arrives to babysit. (The deadline in the sentence is the arrival of Rob.)

> By the time the spare parts for his computer arrive, Edgar *will* probably *have finished* his novel on the back of envelopes. (The deadline in the sentence is the delivery of spare parts.)

Case 6 – Different times, different verb forms

Remember those *–ing* forms from Case 2, earlier in the chapter? When they express different times, an auxiliary verb (*having* or *have*) is involved. Check out this sentence:

> *Having sealed* the envelope containing his mother's birthday card, Edgar *realised* that he hadn't written anything on the card.

In other words, unless he rips open the envelope, his card will be anonymous because the *sealing* of the letter took place before the *remembering* that he hadn't written the card.

Here are additional examples:

> *Having finished* his homework, Rob *turned* on the television to watch the horror film. (Event 1: Rob finishes his homework while babysitting; event 2: he watches the film his parents had said he wasn't to watch.)

> *Having accepted* a job at the theatre, Lucinda paid back the money her mother had lent her. (Event 1: Lucinda gets paid employment; event 2: she does the right thing and pays her debts.)

The *–ing* form (or present participle) – *finishing*, for example – combines with present, past and future verbs to show two events happening at the same time or at nearly the same time. The *–ed* form (the past participle) with *having – having finished*, for example – combines with present, past and future verbs to show two events happening at different times.

She done him wrong

The word *done* is never a verb all by itself. A true party animal, this verb form insists on being accompanied by auxiliary verbs. In grammars-peak, *done* is a past participle of the verb *to do*. Naked, shivering, totally alone participles never function as main verbs in sentences. Here are some examples:

WRONG: He done all he could, so he stopped worrying.

RIGHT: He had done all he could, so he stopped worrying.

WRONG: She done him wrong.

RIGHT, BUT A BAD SENTENCE: She has done him wrong.

BETTER SENTENCE: What she has done to him is wrong.

You may blame the fact that so many people create sentences like *He done all he could* on one of the many joys of English grammar: some past participles – those of regular verbs – look exactly the same as the plain past tense. Consider the verb *to walk:*

PLAIN PAST TENSE: I *walked* twenty miles.

PRESENT PERFECT TENSE: I *have walked* twenty miles.

WHAT THESE TWO SENTENCES HAVE IN COMMON: The word *walked*, which is a verb in the first example and a past participle – part of a verb – in the second example.

WHY ENGLISH DOES THIS: We have no idea.

BOTTOM LINE: You may use *walked* alone or with an auxiliary verb because the same word may be both a past tense verb and a participle. You may not use *done* by itself as a verb, however, because it's not the past tense of *to do*. The past tense of *to do* is *did*.

Infinitives may also show events happening at two different times. The present perfect infinitive (*to have finished*, for example) is the one that does this job. Don't worry about the name; just look for the *have*. Here's an example:

It was helpful *to have bought the cookbook* before the dinner party. (Event 1: pre-party, panicked trip to the bookshop; event 2: Rashid and Alice arrive, unaware that his mother will be serving Alfalfa-sprout Surprise.)

Which sentence shows two events happening at the same time, and which shows two events happening at different times?

A. Running up the road, Vicky escaped from the reporter.

B. Having run up the road, Vicky escaped from the reporter.

Answer: Sentence A shows two events happening at the same time. Vicky is running and escaping from the reporter. Sentence B shows two events happening at different times. Vicky has arrived at her house and is now escaping from the reporter (note that the word *having* is involved, indicating that different events are occurring at different times).

Mix and Match: Combining the Past and Present

Tears *rolled* down his cheeks as he *explained* what had happened. He *was* upset when Mortimer *showed* him the anonymous letter, so he *borrowed* the car as Mortimer *did*n't *need* it. Then he *got* stuck in traffic on the M25 and *missed* having tea with his aunt. The dogs *barked* so loudly as he *drove* past Barker's house on the way home that he *stopped* to complain about them keeping him awake, but he *went* to the wrong house.

The butler's story is indirect speech. We're not quoting him directly. If we were, we'd insert some of his exact words:

'I don't know what came over me!' he sobbed.

In the story, the verbs are all in the past tense. It's also possible to talk about past events in the present tense. Sporting commentators do it. Novels do it. You probably do it when you talk to friends. The present tense adds an extra dose of drama. Here's the Sergeant telling the Constable about Tilson's confession:

. . . So he*'s* so stressed out he *flips* when he *hears* all the dogs. He *marches* up the path, *hammers* on the door and *gets* a faceful of Emmeline Stakes! It*'s* the wrong house! She *starts* screeching something about murder, so he *picks up* the nearest hard object – that would be the gnome – and *hits* her with it. And *keeps* hitting her. Sad, really!

When storytelling, either present or past tense is acceptable. However, mixing tenses when you're talking about past events is *not* acceptable. Don't move from one to the other.

Correct the verb tense in this paragraph. The verbs are in italics.

She first *begins* to like him when Damian *took* her to the charity ball. Damian *had drunk* too much, as usual, and when she *slips* while dancing the tango she *goes* flying and he *did* nothing to help. So she *was lying* in a heap at Mortimer's feet and he *says* 'Your shoes *are* nice'. All she *could think* of to say *is* yes! He *must think* she*'s* totally senseless.

Answer: The story is in two different tenses, past and present. To correct it, choose one of the two. (But the speech doesn't count, as we're reporting exactly what was said at the time.) Here is the past tense version, with the changed verbs underlined:

She first *began* to like him when Damian *took* her to the charity ball. Damian *had drunk* too much, as usual, and when she *slipped* while dancing the tango she *went* flying and he *did* nothing to help. So she *was lying* in a heap at Mortimer's feet and he *said* 'Your shoes are nice'. All she *could think* of to say *was* yes! He *must have thought* she *was* totally senseless.

Here is the present tense version, with the changed verbs underlined:

She first *begins* to like him when Damian *takes* her to the charity ball. Damian *drinks* too much, as usual, and when she *slips* while dancing the tango she *goes* flying and he *does* nothing to help. So she*'s lying* in a heap at Mortimer's feet and he *says* 'Your shoes are nice'. All she *can think* of to say *is* yes! He *must think* she*'s* totally senseless.

Habits: Using the present tense

You can make a general statement about something that always happens (someone's custom or habit) using the present tense. And you can combine such a statement with a story about events in the past tense. Therefore, a story may begin in the present tense and move to the past tense in this way:

George works on his allotment every Saturday morning. He always asks Vicky what vegetables she'd like before he goes, and he always remembers and brings exactly what she asks for.

Up to here in the story, all the verbs are in the present tense because the story tells of George's habits. The story isn't reporting what happened on one specific day. In the next sentence, the story switches to the past tense because it examines one unusual day in the past.

Last Saturday, Vicky knew that something had upset George because he brought her a cabbage and some potatoes, but she'd asked for a cauliflower and some carrots. Nothing was said as they ate lunch, but over a cup of tea afterwards George saw the way she was looking at him and knew he'd have to tell her. He put his cup down, sighed and took the anonymous letter out of his pocket.

Eternal truths: Statements that are always in the present tense

What's wrong with these sentences?

Susie explained that one plus one *equalled* two.

The professor challenged them to prove that the earth *was* round.

Lucinda didn't believe that diamonds *were made* of carbon.

Well, you may be thinking,

Equaled two? What does it equal now? Three?

Was round? And now it's a cube?

Were made of carbon? Now they make diamonds from something else?

In others words, the verb tense is wrong. All these statements represent eternal truths – they are timeless statements that will never change. When you write such statements, you should always write them in the present tense, even if the statement was made in the past:

Susie explained that one plus one *equals* two.

The professor challenged them to prove that the earth *is* round.

Lucinda didn't believe that diamonds *are made* of carbon.

News from the front

You are also allowed to slip the present tense in with the past tense if the thing you're talking about is still happening (even if it isn't an eternal truth). For example:

Mike *said* that he *agrees* with the firm hand Dr Mackenzie is taking with her son. (We expect that he still agrees and that Dr Mackenzie is still taking a firm hand.)

'That was Edgar,' said his mother. 'He says that his book is number one in the bestseller list!' (It hasn't stopped being number one since she put the phone down, and he's still telling anyone who'll listen.)

Which sentence is correct?

A. Edgar said that Yasmin had meningitis when she was 6.

B. Edgar says that Yasmin has meningitis.

C. Edgar said that Yasmin has meningitis.

Answer: All are correct in different circumstances. (Sorry, we're mean like that.) Sentence A is talking about a past event. Sentence B is talking about events as they happen. (News is just reaching her friends that Yasmin is in hospital fighting for her life.) In each case, the tenses match. Sentence C would be correct if Edgar told you an hour ago, but this is the first chance you've had to tell anyone else. (Yasmin *still* has meningitis.)

Try one more. Which of these are correct?

> A. Tinkerbell brings Lucinda dead mice. Last week she brought her three.
>
> B. Yasmin tried to explain to Isolde why water *runs* downhill.
>
> C. Everyone was relieved that the killer had been caught at last and they can relax.

Answer: Sentences A and B are correct. Sentence A tells us about Lucinda's cat's habitual act of bringing her gifts (*brings* is in the present tense) and then switches to the past tense (*brought*) to tell us of one particular past event. In Sentence B, Yasmin *tried* (past tense) to explain the basic laws of the universe to Isolde, but these are eternal truths so we use the present tense for *runs*. Sentence C is wrong because it's just telling a story and the present and past tenses are mixed. It should be either *Everyone was relieved that the killer had been caught at last and they* could *relax* or *Everyone* is *relieved that the killer* has *been caught at last and they can relax.*

Chapter 19

Saying What You Want to Say: Descriptive Words and Phrases

In This Chapter

▶ Placing descriptions so that the sentence says what you mean

▶ Beginning a sentence with a participle: danglers

▶ Avoiding double meanings for descriptive words

*O*nce upon a time, most English words had many forms, including one to show that the word received an action and one to show that it performed an action. Because the words themselves carried so many aspects of meaning, you could arrange them in many ways and still say the same thing. Word order was less important in Old English than it is in Modern English.

The good news is that speakers of Modern English don't have to learn dozens of forms of words. The bad news is that Modern English speakers have to be careful about word order. Most people do all right with nouns and verbs, but descriptive words are another matter. In this chapter, we show you how placing a description in the wrong spot can completely wreck your sentence.

Ruining a Perfectly Good Sentence: Misplaced Descriptions

Can you spot what's wrong with this sentence?

> Damian put a ring into his pierced lip that he had bought last week.

The way the sentence is now, *that he had bought last week* describes *lip*. The Internet sells plenty of unusual items, but not lips (yet). Here's the correction:

> Into his pierced lip, Damian put a ring that he had bought last week.

Now, *that he had bought last week* follows ring, which Damian really did buy last week.

The description *that he bought last week* is a relative clause. It modifies the noun *ring*. For more information on relative clauses, see Chapter 24.

Here's another description that wandered too far from home:

> Lucinda bought a genuine, 1950-model, fluorescent pink hula-hoop with a credit card.

According to news reports, toddlers and dogs have received credit card applications, but not hula-hoops – at least as far as we know. Yet the sentence says that the hula-hoop comes with a credit card. How to fix it? Move the description:

> Using a credit card, Lucinda bought a genuine, 1950-model, fluorescent pink hula-hoop.

Granted, most people can figure out the meaning of the sentence, even when the description is in the wrong place. The human brain is a wonderful thing. But there's a real danger that occasionally you will write a sentence that doesn't say what you mean at all.

The rule concerning description placement is simple: place the description as close as possible to the word that it describes.

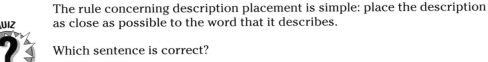

Which sentence is correct?

A. George put the paper into his pocket with the shopping list written on it.

B. George put the paper with the shopping list written on it into his pocket.

Answer: Sentence B is correct because the paper has the shopping list written on it, not the pocket.

Try another. Which sentence is correct?

A. Natasha pedalled to Mortimer's house on her ten-speed bicycle with a complete set of paint samples.

B. Natasha pedalled on her ten-speed bicycle to Mortimer's house with a complete set of paint samples.

C. With a complete set of paint samples, Natasha peddled on her ten-speed bicycle to Mortimer's house.

Answer: Sentence C is correct. In sentence A, the bicycle has ten speeds, two tires and a set of paint samples. In sentence B, Mortimer's house has a complete set of paint samples. Perhaps so, but the sentence revolves around Natasha, so the more likely meaning is that Natasha has the samples. Only in sentence C does Natasha have the samples. By the way, the renovations to Mortimer's country house are progressing well.

Keeping Your Audience Hanging: Danglers

In the never-ending human quest to save time, words are often chopped out of sentences. The assumption is that the listener or reader will be able to supply the missing piece. Check out these examples:

> After sleeping for exactly 33 minutes, Mike yawned and woke up.

> Although screaming with rage, Damian managed to keep an eye on the clock.

Do you understand what these sentences mean? Yes, of course. You can fill in the missing pieces from the information given in the rest of the sentence. Right there after the comma is the information you need. With all the words present, the sentences read as follows:

> After *Mike had been* sleeping for exactly 33 minutes, Mike yawned and woke up.

> Although *Damian was* screaming with rage, Damian managed to keep an eye on the clock.

But what happens if the information isn't where we expect it to be? Read this sentence:

> Eating a sausage butty, the cholesterol really builds up.

Who is eating? You? Mortimer? Everyone in the local diet club? In the sentence above, no one is eating.

What about this sentence?

> Watching the football on TV, Deborah caught Bill breaking his diet.

We're waiting to find out who's watching the match and . . . there's the answer: Deborah! Well, no, actually it was Bill who was watching the match and Deborah came in unexpectedly and caught him bingeing on pizza. So what's going on in this sentence?

Verb forms that have nothing appropriate to describe are called *danglers* or *dangling modifiers* (or *hanging* or *misrelated* or *unattached* modifiers – there's nothing experts like more than terms proliferation). They latch on to the nearest possible subject and make it their own. To correct the sentences, make sure that the subject is right there where we need it:

> Eating a sausage butty, *Mortimer* smiled and waved to his GP.
>
> OR: *Mortimer* was eating a sausage butty, but smiled and waved to his GP.
>
> OR: Mortimer smiled and waved at his *GP*, who was eating a sausage butty. (if it was the GP who was doing the eating)
>
> As *Bill* was watching the football on TV, Deborah caught him breaking his diet.
>
> OR: Watching the football on TV, *Bill* was bingeing on pizza when Deborah walked in and caught him.

It's very easy to start a sentence without saying what you're talking about. In itself, this isn't a problem, but these hungry words kidnap the first thing they find and force it to act as their subject. For those of you who like grammatical terms, the problem word is often a participle (an *–ing* form or *–ed* form of a verb). (For more information on participles, see Chapter 24.) In sentences beginning with a participle, the subject of the sentence must perform the action mentioned in the participle. (For more information on identifying the subject of a sentence, see Chapter 4.) So watch out if any of your sentences start with an *–ing* word and make sure that you're saying what you mean.

Here's another example:

> WRONG: Sitting on the park bench, the swimming ducks delighted Bibi.(Oh really? The ducks are sitting on a bench and swimming at the same time?)
>
> RIGHT: Sitting on the park bench, Bibi was delighted by the swimming ducks. (Now *Bibi* is the subject of the sentence, so the introductory description applies to her, not to the ducks.)
>
> ALSO RIGHT: The swimming ducks delighted Bibi, who was sitting on the park bench. (Now the descriptive words *sitting on the park bench* are placed next to Bibi, who in fact is the one sitting and being delighted by the ducks.)

A dangler can also be an infinitive (*to* + a verb) that begins a sentence.

> WRONG: To avoid eye strain, George bought Vicky a better light to sew by. (Who's avoiding eye strain? George? No.)

> RIGHT: So that she wouldn't strain her eyes, George bought Vicky a better light to sew by.

However, this sentence is not wrong.

> To sew well, strong light is necessary.

Who is sewing? The sentence doesn't say, but the meaning is obvious: for *you*, *me* or *anyone* to sew well. In a true dangler, we wait to find out what the subject is and the sentence gives us the wrong one.

Which one is correct?

A. Sailing swiftly across the sea, Sandy's boat was surely a beautiful sight.

B. Sailing swiftly across the sea, the feel of the beautiful boat made Sandy sob.

Answer: Sentence A is correct. *Sailing swiftly across the sea* describes Sandy's boat. Sandy's boat is performing that action. Sentence B is wrong because in sentence B *feel*, the subject, is sailing. (And, of course, a *feel* can't sail.)

Avoiding Confusing Descriptions

Take a look at the following example:

> The teacher Rob annoyed often gave him a detention.

What does the sentence mean? Did Rob *often annoy* the teacher? Perhaps the teacher *often gave* Rob a detention.

The problem is that *often* is between *annoyed* and *gave* and can be linked to either of them. The sentence violates a basic rule of description: don't put a description where it can have two possible meanings.

How do you fix the sentence? You move *often* so that it's closer to one of the verbs (usually in front of it), thus showing the reader which of the two words it describes. Here are two correct versions, each with a different meaning:

The teacher Rob often annoyed gave him a detention. (*Often* clearly belongs to annoyed, so Rob was behaving badly and the teacher finally flipped and gave him a detention.)

The teacher Rob annoyed gave him a detention often. (There's no doubt that *often* belongs to *gave*. The teacher has decided 'not to take anything from that little brat' and gives him a detention every time he sees him, on principle.)

The most commonly misplaced descriptions are single words: *only*, *just*, *almost* and *even*.

Correct or incorrect? You decide.

The man who had two homes only bought the villa in Spain.

Answer: incorrect. You don't know if we mean *the man who had only two homes* or that he *only bought the villa* or that he *bought only the villa*. Here's how to correct the sentence:

The man who had only two homes rented the villa in Spain. (The man with four homes said that he already had a villa in Spain and was looking for a cottage in France.)

OR: The man who had two homes bought only the villa in Spain. (He said that he already had two homes and thought he was being extravagant buying the villa in Spain so he wasn't interested in the cottage in France as well.)

OR: The man who had two homes didn't buy anything except the villa in Spain. (But he rented the cottage in France for six months.)

You may be tempted to fix a description by tucking it inside an infinitive:

Ellie's song is strange enough to *intensely* captivate her audience.

Some people insist that you shouldn't split an infinitive (to + a verb – *to captivate* in this sentence). They will insist that *to captivate intensely* is right and *to intensely captivate* is wrong. This rule is definitely on the way out. But if you're writing for a super-stickler be careful not to split an infinitive. Know what they are and how to recognise them, and avoid them if your boss or teacher dislikes them.

Chapter 20

Good, Better, Best: Comparisons

*I*s your knowledge of comparisons *more better* or *less worse?* If you chose one of those two alternatives, this chapter is for you – because *more better* and *less worse* are both incorrect. English has two ways of creating comparisons, but you can't use them together and they're not interchangeable. In this chapter, we show you how to tell the difference between the two types of comparisons, how to use each correctly, and how to avoid some of the common errors of comparisons. We don't, however, tell you which comparisons to avoid altogether, such as *Which dress makes me look fat?* and *Am I a better dancer than your last date?* You have to figure out those dilemmas yourself.

Ending It with –er or Giving It More

Bill is *more outgoing* than his twin brother, but Mike is *thinner*.

Damian searched for the *least energy-efficient* sports car, believing that global warming is *less important* than having the *sexiest* image.

Edgar's *most recent* book is proving *more successful* than his *earlier* novel.

Mortimer's *younger* brother is even *wealthier* than Mortimer, but Mortimer is *more contented*.

Bill's *latest* tattoo is *bigger* than Damian's, but Damian just wants the *most outrageous* location for his tattoo and doesn't care about size.

The dictionary is your friend

You can learn a lot from the dictionary, with only a little boredom. The following is a list of what the average dictionary entry tells you about each word:

- The part of speech

- The pronunciation

- The definitions of the word, listed in order of importance

- Some common expressions using the word

- Other forms of the word

- Something about the history of the word – its earlier forms or its linguistic ancestors

- A ruling on whether the word is acceptable in formal English

All that information is packed into only an inch or two of writing! But, to fit in everything, the publishers rely on abbreviations. Therefore, reading a dictionary entry may resemble a trip to a foreign country – one where everyone else seems to know the language and customs and is happy to leave you out of the picture.

Let us put you in the picture. Here's a very special dictionary entry, with the parts decoded for the average reader. (By the way, don't look for this word in a real dictionary – it's made up especially for you.) Just match the letters in the dictionary entry with the explanations below.

A. chukblok B. (chuck–blok) **C.** n. **D.** *pl.* chuk-bloks. **E.** 1. The state currency of Belrovia. 2. The national bank of Belrovia. 3. In economics, a very high protective tariff: a *chukblok* against imported bananas. **F.** 4. *Informal* extremely rich person: he's a walking *chukblok.* **G.** 5. *obs.* A coin made of gold. **H.** – *adj.* 1. rich: She put a *chukblok* icing on that cake. 2. illegal: The *chukblok* plan was bound to backfire. **I.** [ML *chublah*; OL *chubare* a coin.] **J. Syn.** n. coins, money, cash, dough. *adj.* well-heeled, well-off, illicit. **K.** – **to see chukbloks in the trees** *Slang.* To assume that one is about to get rich. – **to flip one's chukblok** *Informal.* To bet all of one's money on the throw of the dice.

Here are the letter identifications:

A. The word

B. The pronunciation. The symbols here are a little confusing, but most dictionaries provide a key in the front of the book. The key explains the pronunciation symbols by showing you the same sound in some easily recognisable words.

C. The part of speech.

D. The abbreviation *pl.* means *plural*, and this part of the entry tells you how to form the plural of this word.

E. The definitions. The most commonly used definitions are first.

F. *Informal* tells you that you shouldn't use that particular meaning in formal writing. If the word isn't labelled, it's acceptable in formal writing.

G. *Obs.* means *obsolete* and tells you that a meaning is no longer used.

H. Another part of speech. The *adj.* abbreviation tells you that you can also use *chukblok* as an adjective, in addition to using it as a noun. The meanings listed after *adj.* explain what the word means when it's used as an adjective. Again, the definitions are in order from the most common meaning to the rarest.

I. These symbols tell you the family tree of the word *chukblok*. The abbreviation *ML* refers to *Middle Lunian*, a language we invented. *OL* is another abbreviation; it refers to *Old Lunian*, another language that we made up. In the brackets, you learn that you can trace the history of *chukblok* to the Middle Lunian word *chublah*, which in turn may be traced to an Old Lunian word *chubare*, meaning *coin*.

J. Another abbreviation. *Syn.* means *synonym*. Following this symbol are words that mean the same as the noun and adjective versions of *chukblok*.

K. The meaning of common expressions with the word *chukblok*. One is slang and the other informal; neither is acceptable in formal writing.

What did you notice about the comparisons in these examples? Here's the stripped-down list: *more outgoing, thinner, least energy-efficient, less important, sexiest, most recent, more successful, earlier, younger, wealthier, more contented, latest, bigger, most outrageous.*

Some of the comparisons were expressed by adding *–er* or *–est*, and some were expressed by adding *more, most, less* or *least* to the quality that's being compared. How do you know which is appropriate? (Or, to use a comparison, how do you know which is *better*?) The dictionary is the final authority, and you should consult one if you're in doubt about a particular word. However, here are some general guidelines:

✔ Add *–er* and *–est* to most one-syllable adjectives.

✔ If the word already ends in the letter *e*, don't double the *e* by adding *–er* or *–est*. Just add *–r* or *–st*.

✔ *–Er* and *–est* endings are not usually appropriate for words ending in *–ly* or for words of more than two syllables.

Table 20-1 is a chart of some common descriptions, with both the *–er* and *–est* forms.

Table 20-1	**Common Descriptions**	
Description	*–er form*	*–est form*
able	abler than Lucinda	ablest of all the budding scientists in her year
bald	balder than an eagle	baldest of the professors
cute	cuter than an elf	cutest of all the two-year-olds
dumb	dumber than a sea slug	dumbest of US presidents

(continued)

Table 20-1 *(continued)*

Description	–er form	–est form
edgy	edgier than caffeine	edgiest of the addicts
friendly	friendlier than a flatterer	friendliest person in the street
heavy	heavier than a 'before' ad for a diet book	heaviest of all the sumo wrestlers
itchy	itchier than she was before Rob covered her in itching powder	itchiest of all the dermatologist's patients

Note that, when the last letter is *y*, you must often change the *y* to *i* before you tack on the ending.

Table 20-2 contains even more descriptions, this time with *more, less, most* and *least* added.

Table 20-2 Two-Word Descriptions

Description	More/Less form	Most/Least form
jerkily	more jerkily than an arthritic horse	most jerkily of all the marionettes
knock-kneed	less knock-kneed than an old sailor	least knock-kneed of all the beauty contest entrants
lily-livered	less lily-livered than the saloon owner in an old movie	least lily-livered of all the florists
magnificent	more magnificent than a work of art	most magnificent of all the mothers
notorious	more notorious than a footballer	most notorious of the gangsters
oafish	less oafish than the young prince	least oafish of all the traffic wardens
prune-faced	less prune-faced than her teacher	least prune-faced of the students
queenly	more queenly than Elizabeth I	most queenly of all the movie stars
rigid	less rigid than a grammarian	least rigid of the train managers

These two tables give you a clue about another important comparison characteristic. Did you notice that the second column is always a comparison between *two* people or things? The addition of *–er* or *more* or *less* compares two things. In the last column of each chart, the comparison is with a group with more than two members. When the group is larger than two, *–est* or *most* or *least* creates the comparison and identifies the extreme.

To sum up the rules:

> ✔ Use *–er* or *more/less* when comparing only two things.
>
> ✔ Use *–est* or *most/least* when singling out the extreme in a group that's larger than two.
>
> ✔ Never combine two comparison methods, such as *–er* and *more*.

The *–er* or *less/more* form of comparison is called the comparative and the *–est* or *least/most* form of comparison is called the superlative.

Which sentence is correct?

A. Lucinda, relaxing over a decaf. skinny latté, was the more cheerful of all her friends in the coffee bar.

B. Lucinda, relaxing over a decaf. skinny latté, was the most cheerful of all her friends in the coffee bar.

Answer: Sentence B is correct. The sentence singles out Lucinda as the extreme in a group, so you need *most* here, not *more*.

Try another:

Which sentence is correct?

A. Edgar's design for a new carton is simpler than the one the professor came up with.

B. Edgar's design for a new carton is more simpler than the one the professor came up with.

Answer: Sentence A is correct. Never combine two forms of comparison. Sentence B combines the *–er* form with the word *more*.

Last one. Which sentence is correct?

A. Of all the cars in the parking lot, Edgar's is the newer.

B. Of all the cars in the parking lot, Edgar's is the newest.

Answer: Sentence B is correct. Edgar's car is being compared with more than one other car.

Breaking the Rules: Irregular Comparisons

Whenever English grammar gives you a set of rules that make sense, you know it's time for the irregulars to show up. Not surprisingly, then, you have to create a few common comparisons without *–er*, *–est*, *more/less* or *most/least*. Look at the following examples:

> Martin's performance is *good*, but Ellie's is *better* and, according to Alice, Rashid's is the *best* of all.

> Bibi's constant sneezing is *bad*, but Bill's tendency to crack jokes is *worse*. Damian's habit of drinking and driving is the *worst* habit of all.

> Ellie has a *good* piano. Mortimer's is *better* than Ellie's, but he never uses it. The piano that Edgar bought Yasmin when she got out of hospital is the *best* of all the pianos available.

Got the idea? Here is a list of the irregular comparisons:

- ✔ good, better, best
- ✔ bad, worse, worst
- ✔ well, better, best
- ✔ little, less, least
- ✔ many (or much), more, most

These irregulars break the rules, but they are easy to remember. Three of the irregulars judge quality (good, bad, well) and two judge quantity (little, many). The comparative form compares one thing with another, and the superlative form identifies the extreme in the group.

Answer this question in correct English and then correct the question itself.

> Who's the baddest kid in the playground?

Answer: The *worst* (not *baddest*) kid in the playground is Rob. The correct question is *Who's the worst kid in the playground?*

Here's another:

> Who plays more better jazz?

Answer: No one. Use *more* or *better*, but not both, to make the comparison. Other ways to word the question include:

Who plays better jazz?

Who plays the best jazz?

Who plays jazz best?

Of the two saxophonists, who plays better jazz?

Last one. Which sentence is correct?

A. Rob says that he is feeling worse today than yesterday, but his mother must consider the fact that today is the day of the algebra test.

B. Rob says that he is feeling more bad today than yesterday, but his mother must consider the fact that today is the day of the algebra test.

Answer: Sentence A is correct. *More bad* is incorrect; use *worse*.

Watch out with *less* and *least*. In formal writing, these should not be used when you're talking about things that you count: use *fewer* (and *fewest*, but that's not needed much). For example:

George is eating fewer cakes now that Vicky's putting less sugar in them.

Use *fewer* for the cakes (because you count them) but *less* for the sugar (because you don't count sugar when you're making a cake – you weigh it).

Never More Perfect: Using Words That You Can't Compare

Is this chapter more unique than the previous chapter? No, definitely not. Why? Because nothing is *more unique*. The word *unique* means 'one of a kind'. Either something is one of a kind or it's not. Yes or no, true or false, one or zero (when you're speaking in computer code). No halfway point, no degrees of uniqueness, no . . . well, you get the idea. You can't compare something that's unique with anything but itself. Check out the following examples:

WRONG: The vase that Edgar broke was more unique than the Grecian urn.

ALSO WRONG: The vase that Edgar broke was fairly unique.

WRONG AGAIN: The vase that Edgar broke was very unique.

RIGHT: The vase that Edgar broke was unique.

ALSO RIGHT: The vase that Edgar broke was unique, as was the Grecian urn.

RIGHT AGAIN: The vase that Edgar broke was more unusual than the Grecian urn.

WHY IT'S RIGHT: *Unusual* is not an absolute term, so you can use it in comparisons.

The word *unique* is not unique. Several other words share its absolute quality. One is *perfect*. Something is perfect or not perfect; nothing is *very perfect* or *unbelievably perfect* or *quite perfect*.

WRONG: Yasmin is *extremely perfect* when it comes to grammar.

WHY IT'S WRONG: *Perfect* is absolute. There are no degrees of perfection.

RIGHT: Yasmin is *nearly perfect* when it comes to grammar.

WHY IT'S RIGHT: You can approach an absolute quality, comparing how close someone or something comes to the quality. Yasmin approaches perfection but doesn't achieve it.

ALSO RIGHT: Yasmin is *perfect* when it comes to grammar.

WHY IT'S RIGHT: You may approach *perfect*, as in *nearly perfect*. You may also be *perfect*, without any qualifiers.

As some of these RIGHT examples illustrate, you can't compare absolute qualities, but you can compare how close people or things come to having those qualities. Look at these examples:

Lucinda thinks that her new earrings are an *almost perfect* accessory.

Clarence's style of relaxation *approaches uniqueness*.

One more word causes all sorts of trouble in comparisons: *equally*. You hear the expression *equally as* quite frequently. You don't need the *as*, because the word *equally* contains the idea of comparison. For example:

WRONG: Sandy and her sister are *equally as* good at tennis.

RIGHT: Sandy and her sister are *equally* good at tennis.

ALSO RIGHT: Sandy's sister is *as* good at tennis *as* Sandy is.

Which sentences are correct?

A. Mortimer's recent drama is even more unique than his last play.

B. Mortimer's recent drama is even more unusual than his last play.

C. Mortimer's recent drama is more unusual compared with his last play.

D. Mortimer's recent drama is unique, as was his last play.

Answer: Sentences B and D are correct. Sentence A incorrectly compares an absolute (*unique*). In sentence B *more unusual* is a correct comparison. Sentence C uses *more* (a comparative word) and *compared with* (another comparative expression) – you don't need both. Sentence D tells you that Mortimer's recent drama is unique and that his last play was also unique. The absolute is not being compared but simply applied to two different things.

Which is correct here?

A. Edgar's chess game is as good as the grand master's.

B. Edgar's chess game is equally as good as the grand master's.

Answer: Sentence A is correct. Do not say *equally as* because the words *equally* and *as* both express the concept of comparison. You don't need both.

Leaving Your Audience in Suspense: Incomplete Comparisons

What's wrong with this sentence?

Gloria screamed more chillingly.

Maybe these hints will help:

Gloria screamed more chillingly. 'Uh oh,' thought Olivier, 'yesterday I thought she would burst my eardrum. If she screamed more chillingly today, I'd better get my earplugs out.'

or

Gloria screamed more chillingly. Mortimer, rushing to aid Ellie, whose scream had turned his blood to ice, stopped dead. 'Gloria sounds even worse,' he thought. 'I'd better go to her first.'

or

Gloria screamed more chillingly. 'Please,' said the director, 'I know that you have just completed take 99 of this extremely taxing scene, but you'll have to put a little more into it. Try again!'

Now the problem is clear. The comparison in the examples is incomplete. Octavia screamed more chillingly than . . . than what? Until you finish the sentence, your readers are left with as many possibilities as they can imagine. Bottom line: don't stop explaining your comparison until you get your point across. Look at the following example:

WRONG: Gloria screamed more chillingly.

RIGHT: Gloria screamed more chillingly than the cat did the day Bibi drove her toy truck over her tail.

ALSO RIGHT: Gloria screamed more chillingly than she had in the previous takes, but the director decided to cut the scene.

Here's another comparison with a fatal error. Can you spot the problem?

Clarence loves golf more than Mortimer.

Need another hint? Read on:

Clarence travels to golf courses all over the world and plays every weekend. Mortimer plays golf when he needs to talk to important movie people and that's the only way he can get their attention.

or

Clarence turned down the invitation to his brother's 30th birthday party because he had golfing plans.

See the problem? *Clarence loves golf more than Mortimer* is incomplete. Your reader can understand the comparison in two different ways, as the two stories illustrate. The rule here is simple: don't omit words that are necessary to the meaning of the comparison.

WRONG: Clarence loves golf more than Mortimer.

RIGHT: Clarence loves golf more than he loves Mortimer.

ALSO RIGHT: Clarence loves golf more than Mortimer does.

Remember: in making a comparison, be clear and complete.

Which sentence is correct?

A. Tinkerbell chases bluebottles more quickly.

B. Tinkerbell chases bluebottles more quickly than Poppet.

Answer: Both are wrong. (Sorry! Trick question.) The meaning is unclear in both A and B. In sentence A, the reader is left asking *more quickly than what?* In sentence B, the sentence may mean *Tinkerbell chases bluebottles more quickly than she chases Poppet* (Bibi's kitten) or *Tinkerbell chases bluebottles more quickly than Poppet chases bluebottles.* Neither comparison is complete.

Try another. Which sentence is correct?

A. Martin played the tuba solo as emotionally as Edgar did, but with fewer mistakes.

B. Martin played the tuba solo just as emotionally, despite the fact that he has no real feeling for the piece.

Answer: Sentence A is correct. In sentence B, the reader wonders about the basis of comparison. Did Martin play *as emotionally as the other works on his programme* or did he play the solo *as emotionally as Edgar*, who has less technical skill but a deep love of the piece? Sentence A tells us everything we need to know.

Spock was Better than any First Officer in Star Fleet: Illogical Comparisons

What's wrong with this heading? It takes Spock out of the group of first officers. It makes him a *non*-first officer. To keep him in this group, add *other*:

RIGHT: Spock was better than any *other* first officer in Star Fleet.

The rule for comparisons here is very simple: use the word *other* or *else* when comparing someone or something with other members of the same group. Check out the following examples:

WRONG: The movie star Gloria Griddle talks louder than anyone in the cast.

WHY IT'S WRONG: The sentence makes it clear that Gloria is in the cast, but the comparison implies that she's not in the cast. Illogical!

RIGHT: The movie star Gloria Griddle talks louder than anyone *else* in the cast.

WRONG: That robot short-circuits more frequently than any mechanical device.

WHY IT'S WRONG: A robot is, by definition, a mechanical device, but the comparison takes the robot out of the group of mechanical devices.

RIGHT: That robot short-circuits more frequently than any *other* mechanical device.

Here's another problem. Can you find it?

WRONG: Alice and Rashid were late for lunch because roadworks made their journey take longer than last week.

WHY IT'S WRONG: This sentence says that their journey took longer than last week. No wonder they were late for lunch! Don't compare a journey time with a week – unless the journey took a week. Compare journey times with other journey times and weeks with weeks and don't mix them.

RIGHT: Alice and Rashid were late for lunch because roadworks made their journey take longer than it took last week.

ALSO RIGHT: Alice and Rashid were late for lunch because roadworks made their journey longer than last week's.

One more example:

WRONG: The flavour of George's home-grown vegetables is better than the supermarket vegetables.

WHY IT'S WRONG: It's comparing flavours with vegetables. It needs to compare flavours with flavours or vegetables with vegetables.

RIGHT: There's more flavour in George's home-grown vegetables than in supermarket vegetables.

ALSO RIGHT: George's home-grown vegetables taste better than supermarket vegetables.

Here's the bottom line:

✔ Make sure that your comparisons are logical.

✔ Check to see that you have compared what you want to compare – two things that are at least remotely related.

✔ If the first part of the comparison involves a possessive noun or pronoun (showing ownership), the second part of the comparison probably needs a possessive too.

Two for the Price of One: Double Comparisons

No one will misunderstand you if you break this rule, but sticklers everywhere will hunt you down and berate you. When you're making two comparisons at the same time, finish the first one before you begin the second. In other words, don't say

> Sandy's sister is as dumb, if not dumber than Lucinda.

In this sentence, you're really trying to say two different things:

1. Sandy's sister is as dumb as Lucinda.
2. Sandy's sister may be dumber than Lucinda.

First of all, and completely apart from grammar, you ought to make a decision. Just how dumb is Lucinda? Don't leave your reader in suspense. Take the plunge and express your real opinion. Grammatically, you may sit on the fence, but only if you finish the first comparison before going on to the second. Here's how you finish:

> Sandy's sister is as dumb as Lucinda, if not dumber.

What a difference an *as* makes! Now the sentence is complete after the word *Lucinda*, so the *if* statement is an add-on, as it should be.

Chapter 21

Keeping Your Balance

. . . .

In This Chapter

▶ Constructing properly balanced sentences

▶ Being consistent in form, tense and voice

▶ Using pairs of conjunctions correctly

. . . .

*W*e all need to keep our balance in life, and in speech and writing we need to create sentences that aren't lopsided. We're talking about why Hamlet says, 'To be or not to be' instead of 'Being or not to be'. In this chapter, we show you how to avoid several everyday errors of balance.

Constructing Balanced Sentences

Clarence wanted with all his heart to find a bride who was intelligent, beautiful and had as much money as he did.

Not counting Clarence's matrimonial ideas, the sentence has another problem: it's not balanced. Concentrate on the part of the sentence following the word *was*. Clarence's dream bride was supposed to have these characteristics:

✔ Intelligent

✔ Beautiful

✔ Had as much money as he did

Do you see that these three descriptions don't match? The first two are adjectives. The third consists of a verb (*had*) and an object (*as much money as he did*). (For more information on adjectives, see Chapter 8. For more information on verbs and objects, see Chapters 2 and 6.) But all three descriptions are doing the same job in the sentence – describing Clarence's dream bride. Because they're doing the same job, they should match, at least in the grammatical sense.

Another way of thinking of this is to try to end the sentence with each description in turn:

> RIGHT: Clarence wanted with all his heart to find a bride who was intelligent.

> RIGHT: Clarence wanted with all his heart to find a bride who was beautiful.

> WRONG: Clarence wanted with all his heart to find a bride who *was had* as much money as he did.

Here's one revised list:

> ... who was *intelligent, beautiful, rich* and *short-sighted*. (We added this one because we've actually seen Clarence.)

And here's another:

> ... who had *intelligence, beauty, a large fortune* and *bad eyesight*.

Both lists are fine. In the first set, all the characteristics of Clarence's bride are adjectives. In the second set, all the characteristics are nouns. You can use either list. Just don't take some elements from one and some from another. Here's another way to solve the problem:

> Clarence wanted with all his heart to find a bride with intelligence, beauty and bad eyesight, who also had a large fortune.

Here, the error is corrected by finishing off the list at *and bad eyesight* and adding *had a large fortune* in a separate clause.

Now for another lopsided sentence. Can you spot the problem?

> To climb Everest, swimming the Channel and starting her own gym were Sandy's goals.

Perhaps a list will help you. Sandy's goals are as follows:

- ✔ To climb Everest
- ✔ Swimming the Channel
- ✔ Starting her own gym

Which one doesn't match? *To climb Everest.*

To climb is an infinitive, but the next two items in the list are not. *Swimming* and *starting* are gerunds. For more information on infinitives and gerunds, see Chapter 24.

All three of Sandy's goals are subjects of the sentence. Because they're doing the same job in the sentence, they should be the same grammatically. Here are two possible corrections:

> ... *climbing* Everest, *swimming* the Channel and *starting* her own gym.

> ... *to climb* Everest, *to swim* the Channel and *to start* her own gym.

Items in a sentence with the same job (function) should have the same grammatical identity. Whenever you have more than one subject, object, verb, or other element of the sentence, make a list and check it carefully.

Here's another example:

> WRONG: The new member of Mortimer's domestic staff, a gourmet cook and renowned for his delicious omelettes, thinks that French cooking is overrated.

> WHAT'S WRONG: The *and* joins two descriptions of the new member of staff. One is a noun (*cook*) and one is a verb form (*renowned*).

> RIGHT: The new member of Mortimer's domestic staff, a gourmet cook renowned for his delicious omelettes, thinks that French cooking is overrated.

> WHY IT'S RIGHT: Once you remove the *and*, the problem is solved. Now the verb (*renowned*) describes the noun (*cook*).

Which is correct?

A. Alice found the honeymoon suite restful, exotic, tasteful and in the quiet part of the hotel.

B. Alice found the honeymoon suite restful, exotic and tasteful. It was located in the quiet part of the hotel.

C. Alice found the honeymoon suite restful, exotic, tasteful and quiet.

Answer: Sentences B and C are correct. The qualities of the honeymoon suite listed in sentence A are

✔ Restful

✔ Exotic

✔ Tasteful

✔ In the quiet part of the hotel

The first three are adjectives, but the last is a prepositional phrase. (For more information about prepositional phrases, see Chapter 9.) Because they don't match, the sentence is not properly balanced. In sentence B, the three adjectives are alone in one sentence – the prepositional phrase is in its very own sentence. Sentence C expresses all the characteristics of the honeymoon suite as adjectives.

To avoid these errors, you don't have to know the correct grammatical terms. Even without the fancy grammatical names, the list shows you the odd man out. Just use your common sense and listen.

Shifting Grammar into Gear: Avoiding Stalled Sentences

If you have learned to drive, you will probably remember that your first few miles were far from smooth. If something was just a little off, the car would move in jerks and jumps. The same thing is true in sentences. You can, at times, shift in tense, voice, or person, but even the slightest mistake stalls your sentence. In this section, we explain how to avoid unnecessary shifts and how to check your sentence for consistency.

Steering clear of a tense situation

Check out this sentence with multiple verbs:

> Mortimer asks Lucinda to marry him, offers her his heart and everything he owns, and finally won her hand.

Now make a list of the verbs in the sentence:

- ✔ Asks
- ✔ Offers
- ✔ Won

The first two verbs are in the present tense, but the third shifts into the past for no valid reason. Stall! If the verbs in this sentence were gears in your car, your car would conk out. All three verbs should be in the present tense or all three should be in the past tense. Here are the corrected versions of the sentence:

> Mortimer asks Lucinda to marry him, offers her his heart and everything he owns, and finally wins her hand. (All three verbs are in the present tense.)

OR: Mortimer asked Lucinda to marry him, offered her his heart and everything he owns, and finally won her hand. (All three verbs are in the past tense.)

For more information on mixing tenses – when it's legal and when it isn't – see Chapter 18. For the basics of tenses, see Chapter 3.

Knowing the right person

Ah, loyalty. One of the most celebrated virtues, in life as well as in grammar! Loyalty in grammar relates to consistency of person. You shouldn't start out talking about one person and then switch to another in a sentence, unless you have a valid reason for doing so. Here's an example of an unnecessary shift in person:

To celebrate his marriage, Mortimer promised all his employees a day off because you need to do something spectacular on such occasions.

The first part of the sentence talks about *Mortimer*. The second part of the sentence, which begins with the word *because*, shifts to *you*. This is wrong because we're not talking about Mortimer any more. In grammatical terms, we've switched from the third person (*Mortimer* and *he* are in the third person) to the second person (*you*).

In grammar, there are three *persons*. In the *first person*, the subject narrates the story. In other words, *I* or *we* acts as the subject of the sentence. In the *second person*, the subject is being spoken to, and *you* (either singular or plural) is the subject. In the *third person*, the subject is being spoken about, using *he*, *she*, *it*, *they* or any other word that talks *about* someone or something.

Making the correction is simple:

To celebrate his marriage, *Mortimer* promised all his employees a day off because *he* needed to do something spectacular to celebrate the occasion.

OR: To celebrate his marriage, *Mortimer* promised all his employees a day off because *everyone* needs to do something spectacular on such occasions.

Both of these sentences are correct. Why? In the first, *Mortimer* is the subject of the first part of the sentence and *he* (referring to Mortimer) is the subject of the second part. No problem. In the second correction, *Mortimer* (third person) is matched with *everyone* (a third person pronoun). *Everyone* includes *Mortimer*, but *you* doesn't.

Here's another example:

> WRONG: *I* am planning to do as much overtime as possible next month; *you* can't pass up the extra money!

> WHY IT'S WRONG: The first part of the sentence is in the first person (*I*) and the second part of the sentence shifts to *you*, the second person form. Why shift?

> RIGHT: *I* am planning to do as much overtime as possible next month; *I* can't pass up the extra money!

Make sure that your sentences are consistent in person. Unless there's a logical reason to shift, follow these guidelines:

- ✔ If you begin with the first person (*I* or *me*), stay in the first person.
- ✔ If you begin with the second person (*you*), stay in the second person.
- ✔ If you begin with the third person, talking *about* someone or something, make sure that you continue to talk *about* that someone or something.

Which sentence is correct?

A. Whenever a person breaks a grammar rule, you get into trouble.

B. Whenever a person breaks a grammar rule, he or she gets into trouble.

C. Whenever a person breaks a grammar rule, they get into trouble.

Answer: Sentences B and C are correct. In sentence A, *a person* does not match *you*. The sentence shifts from the third to the second person for no logical reason. In sentence B, *a person* matches *he or she* because both talk about someone. Sentence C stays in the third person, talking about someone, using *they* to avoid the clumsy *he or she*. (For more information on singular and plural pronouns, see Chapter 10.)

Try one more. Which is correct?

A. Everybody loves somebody sometime because all you need is love.

B. Everybody loves somebody sometime because all anybody needs is love.

Answer: Sentence B is correct. Sentence A shifts from the third person (*everybody*) to the second (*you*) with no reason other than a pathetic attempt to quote song lyrics. Sentence B stays in the third person (*everybody*, *anybody*).

Seeing Double: Conjunction Pairs

Most joining words fly solo. Single words – *and, but, nor, or, because, although, since* and so on – join sentences or parts of sentences. Some joining words, however, come in pairs. (In grammarspeak, joining words are called *conjunctions.* Double conjunctions are called *correlatives.*) Here are some of the most frequently used double conjunctions:

- ✔ Not only . . . but also
- ✔ Either . . . or
- ✔ Neither . . . nor
- ✔ Whether . . . or
- ✔ Both . . . and

Some of these words show up in sentences without their partners. No problem! Sometimes they show up and don't act as conjunctions. Again, no problem. Just make sure that, when they do act as conjunctions, they behave properly. Here's the rule: whatever fills in the blanks after these pairs of conjunctions must match. The conjunctions have partners, and so do the things they join. You may join two nouns, two sentences, two prepositional phrases – two whatevers! Just make sure the things that you join match. Look at this example:

> Not only Mortimer but also his bride wanted to honeymoon in Hawaii. (The conjunction pair joins two nouns, *Mortimer* and *his bride.*)

> Either you or I must break the news of the engagement to Clarence. (The conjunction pair joins two pronouns, *you* and *I.*)

Nouns and pronouns are equals when it comes to balance. Because pronouns take the place of nouns, you may mix them without ill effect:

> Neither Ellie nor I can think what to buy Mortimer and Lucinda as a wedding present. (The conjunction pair joins a noun, *Ellie,* and a pronoun, *I.*)

Here's another example:

> Both *because he will be away playing golf* and *because he doesn't like Lucinda,* Clarence refused to be best man. (This conjunction pair joins two subject–verb combinations.)

A helpful test is the deletion test. Cross out the double conjunctions and everything between them and see what happens to the sentence. When there's an error, the sentence collapses – it doesn't work. To help you spot these errors in sentences with conjunction pairs, here are a few mismatches, along with their corrections:

WRONG: Either Mortimer will take Lucinda to Amsterdam to buy her engagement ring or to Paris to buy her trousseau.

APPLY THE TEST: Delete everything from *Either* to *or*. You're left with *to Paris to buy her trousseau.* That's not a complete sentence, so there's an error.

RIGHT: Mortimer will take Lucinda either to Amsterdam to buy her engagement ring or to Paris to buy her trousseau.

APPLY THE TEST: Delete *either* to *or* and you're left with *Mortimer will take Lucinda to Paris to buy her trousseau.* That's a complete sentence, so the original sentence is fine.

WRONG: Both her mother and father thought they made a lovely couple.

APPLY THE TEST: Delete *both* to *and*. You're left with *Father thought they made a lovely couple.* But you were trying to say *her father.* So it's not quite right.

RIGHT: Both her mother and her father thought they made a lovely couple. (Now the test leaves us with *Her father thought they made a lovely couple.*)

ALSO RIGHT: Her mother and father thought they made a lovely couple. (Now there's no double conjunction to go wrong.)

Which sentence is correct?

A. Mortimer took Lucinda not only to see a diamond being cut but also bought her a Rolex.

B. Mortimer not only took Lucinda to see a diamond being cut but also bought her a Rolex.

Answer: Sentence B is correct. In sentence A, *not only* precedes an infinitive (*to see*) and *but also* precedes a past tense (*bought*). In sentence B, *not only* and *but also* both precede a past tense (*took* and *bought*). Applying the deletion test gives us *Mortimer took Lucinda bought her a Rolex* in sentence A (not quite a complete sentence), but *Mortimer bought her a Rolex* in sentence B (a complete sentence).

Either way I need a verb: subjects with either/or statements, neither/nor statements and questions

Suppose you're talking about Rashid and Alice, and Rob. Your sentence starts like this:

> Either Rob or Rashid and Alice . . .

What comes next? *Is* or *are?* In a sentence with a singular subject – *Rob*, for example – the choice is easy. *Rob is*, because *Rob* is a singular subject. If the sentence has a plural subject – say, *Rashid and Alice* – the choice is also easy. *Rashid and Alice are.* But what if a singular and a plural subject are in the same sentence? Then what do you do?

When you have a pair of subjects, one singular and one plural, separated by *or*, grab a ruler. OK, you don't actually need a ruler, but you do have to measure. Which subject is closer to the verb? The closer subject determines the type of verb that you need. If the closer subject is singular, use a singular verb. If the closer subject is plural, use a plural verb. Thus,

> Either *Rob* or *Rashid and Alice* are going to baby-sit for Susie next week.

The closest subject is *Rashid and Alice*, a plural, so you need the plural verb *are.* If you rearrange the sentence, you get the following:

> Either *Rashid and Alice* or *Rob* is going to baby-sit for Susie next week.

The closest subject now is *Rob*, a singular, so you need the singular verb *is.*

The same goes for pairs of subjects connected by *neither* and *nor.*

Now for questions. To change a statement into a question in English, you have to fool around with the word order of the sentence.

Also, questions in English are usually constructed with two-word verbs – a main verb and an auxiliary verb. The hard part comes when you're choosing a subject for a question with an *either . . . or* pair. Such sentences have two subjects. What if one subject is singular and one is plural? Which one should you match? The answer is easy. Take out your ruler. Find the subject that's closer to the part of the verb that changes (the auxiliary verb) and make a match. For example:

> *Does* either *Damian* or his ex-wives own the house?

The singular subject *Damian* is closer to the auxiliary verb *does. Does* is the part of the verb that matches a singular subject.

Here's another version of the same question, with the order changed:

> *Do* his *ex-wives* or Damian own the house?

The plural subject *ex-wives* is closer to the auxiliary verb *do. Do* is the part of the verb that matches the plural subject.

You may use the same trick when you're writing a question with *neither . . . nor* in it. We don't often hear *neither . . . nor* questions. Still, if you're burning with curiosity or dying to make a *neither . . . nor* question, here are two:

> This book is a disgrace! *Do* neither the *authors* nor the editor know anything at all about grammar?

> This book is a disgrace! *Does* neither *the editor* nor the authors know anything at all about grammar?

Try another. Which sentences are correct?

A. Natasha has finished the redecorations in both Mortimer's penthouse and in his country house.

B. Natasha has finished the redecorations in both Mortimer's penthouse and his country house.

C. Natasha has finished the redecorations both in Mortimer's penthouse and in his country house.

Answer: Sentences B and C are correct. In sentence A, the deletion test gives us *Natasha has finished the redecorations in in his country house.* Two *in*'s so something's wrong. In sentences B and C, the deletion test gives us *Natasha has finished the redecorations in his country house.*

Part V
Rules Even Your Great-Aunt's Grammar Teacher Didn't Know

'Hi – I'm Gerry & I teach English grammar – Gerry is short for Gerund by the way.'

In this part . . .

Learned philosophers in the Middle Ages used to argue about the number of angels that could dance on the head of a pin. That debate was only a little less complicated than the grammar rules in this part. Chapter 22 explains the moods of verbs (yes, they have moods). Chapter 23 shows you how to choose the proper pronoun for all sorts of weird sentences. The next chapter deals with the inner workings of the sentence – dependent and independent clauses. Chapter 25 gives you a master's degree in punctuation.

The bottom line is that if you want to learn some of the pickiest grammar rules ever devised, this part's for you.

Chapter 22

The Last Word on Verbs

Bill storms in, slams the door and grabs the remote. As he raises the volume on the wrestling match to supersonic level, Deborah asks politely, 'Is anything wrong?' In reply, Bill frowns and glares silently. Deborah shrugs and goes out to spread the word: Bill is in one of his Moods. Beware.

*V*erbs have moods too, but they're a lot more polite about showing them than Bill. A little change of form, and hey presto: the verb is in a different mood.

Modern English verbs have three moods: indicative, imperative and subjunctive. Indicative is the most common; you'll encounter the two other moods – imperative and subjunctive – only occasionally. In this chapter, we give you the lowdown on these so you're sure to know the mood of any verb without consulting a mind-reader.

Getting a Feel for Everyday Verbs: The Indicative Mood

Almost all verbs are in the indicative mood. *Indicative* is the everyday, this-is-what-I'm-saying mood, good for questions and statements. All the lessons about verbs in this book – aside from those later in this chapter – discuss verbs in the indicative mood. (This fact, by the way, is totally useless. Forget it immediately.)

Rising to the occasion

Rise and *raise* are two very confusing verbs. *Rise* is a self-contained action: the subjects act upon themselves. It means 'to stand', 'to get out of bed', or 'to move to a higher rank' under one's own power. So George *rises* early every morning, and Sandy was cut off by the *rising* tide last week.

Raise means 'to lift something or someone else up' or 'to bring up children or animals'. The action that begins with one person (or thing) and moves to another person or thing. So Bill *raises* puppies, but Damian won't *raise* a finger to help anyone.

The indicative verbs are italicised in the following sentences:

> Ellie *displayed* her musical range when she *sang* a Mozart aria and a heavy-metal hit in the same concert.

> Mike *will be* perfectly happy as soon as Susie *agrees* to marry him.

> Bill often *dreams* about bacon.

Commanding Your Verbs: The Imperative Mood

Don't worry about imperatives – they're fairly simple. *Imperative verbs* give commands. Most imperative verbs don't have a written (or spoken) subject. Instead, the subject in an imperative (command) sentence is *you*. The word *you* usually doesn't appear before the imperative verb. The reader or listener simply understands that *you* is implied.

Here are a few examples to get you thinking:

> *Eat* a balanced diet.

> *Climb* every mountain.

> *Calculate* the odds.

Sentences with *let* or *let's* are also commands:

> *Let* me do that for you.

> *Let's* go out for dinner. (*Let's* is short for *let us*.)

There's almost nothing you can do wrong in creating an imperative sentence, so this topic is easy. *Go* fishing or, if you're in the mood to torture yourself, *move on* to the subjunctive.

Discovering the Possibilities: The Subjunctive Mood

Headache time! The subjunctive mood is dying, but while it's hanging on it draws errors like a magnet. Master this topic and you'll qualify for the title Grammarian of the Year. Subjunctive verbs show up when you state something that is contrary to fact. They may also express indirect commands and wishes. We'll tackle each of these situations in the following sections.

Using subjunctives with 'were'

Tevye, the main character in the musical *Fiddler on the Roof,* sings 'If I Were a Rich Man' with the sadness of a man who knows that he'll never be anything but poor. Tevye's song is about a *condition contrary to fact* – something that's not true. Take note of the verb in the title: *were.* Normally (that is to say, in an indicative sentence) the subject–verb pair would be *I was.* But Tevye sings *If I were* because he isn't a rich man. The verb *were* is in the subjunctive mood.

Unless someone is going to test you on it, don't worry about the terminology. Just know that if you're expressing a condition contrary to fact, you need the verb *were* for present and future ideas. (The past tense is different. See the next section, 'Using subjunctives with *had*'.) Here are some examples of the present and future tenses:

SUBJUNCTIVE: If Damian *were* a caring human being, he wouldn't keep wrecking his marriages.

WHY IT'S SUBJUNCTIVE: Damian isn't a caring human being, and women are always going to find this out eventually.

WHAT THE NORMAL SUBJECT–VERB PAIR WOULD BE: Damian was.

SUBJUNCTIVE: If Edgar *were* less talented, he would lead a quieter life.

WHY IT'S SUBJUNCTIVE: Edgar isn't talent-free; he's a genius – the kind of student who actually *enjoys* tests.

WHAT THE NORMAL SUBJECT–VERB PAIR WOULD BE: Edgar was.

To sum up, in subjunctive sentences, *were* is usually all you need (unlike in the Beatles song, where love is all you need). Here are a few details about the subjunctive for present and future statements of conditions contrary to fact:

- ✔ Use *were* for all subjects in the part of the sentence that expresses what is not true. (If she *were* convinced that Rob had done his homework . . .)

- ✔ For the other part of the sentence, use the auxiliary verb *would*. (. . . his mother *would leave* him to watch TV in peace.)

- ✔ Never use the auxiliary verb *would* in the untrue part of the sentence. (You'll hear Americans do this on TV a lot. Don't catch the habit.) For example:

  WRONG: If I would have been prime minister, I would reduce taxes.

  RIGHT: If I were prime minister, I would reduce taxes.

Which sentence is correct?

- A. Damian would have been happier if he would have been able to give up gambling.

- B. Damian would have been happier if he were able to give up gambling.

- C. Damian would be happier if he could give up gambling.

Answer: Sentences B and C are correct. In sentence B, the *if* part of the sentence contains a subjunctive verb (*were*) because it expresses something that is not true. The *if* part of the sentence should never contain the helping verb *would*. Sentence C is also right. It doesn't use the subjunctive, and is a much more common way of saying the same thing. (That's why you don't need to know this stuff.)

Using subjunctives with 'had'

The other subjunctive that pops up from time to time is created with the helping verb *had*. For past tense sentences, the *had* belongs in the part of the sentence that is contrary to fact. The contrary-to-fact part of the sentence may begin with *if*, or the *if* may be understood.

Normally – that is, in non-subjunctive sentences – the past tense would be expressed by a single-word past-tense verb. The *had* form, in a non-subjunctive sentence, is used only to show one action happening before another. (See Chapter 18 for more information.) Here are a few examples of the past subjunctive:

Now I lie me down to sleep . . .

Whoever invented the verbs *lie* and *lay* had an evil sense of humour. *Lie* means 'not to tell the truth', but that meaning isn't a problem. *Lie* also means 'to rest or to plop yourself down, ready for a snooze' or 'to remain'. *Lay* means 'to put something down, to place something'. Look at this example:

> Vicky *lies* down for an hour after lunch. Before she *lies* down, she *lays* a blanket on the sofa.

So far, this topic isn't too complicated. The problem – and the truly devilish part – comes in the past tense. The past tense of *lie* (to rest, to recline, to remain) is *lay*. The past tense of *lay* (to put or place) is *laid*. Check out this example:

> Vicky *lay* down for an hour after lunch yesterday. As usual, she *laid* a blanket on the sofa.

One more complication. When you add *has*, *had* or *have* to the verb *lay* (to put or place), you say *has laid*, *had laid*, *have laid*. When you add *has*, *had* or *have* to the verb *lie* (to rest, to recline, to remain), the correct form is *has lain*, *had lain*, *have lain*. In other words:

> Vicky *has lain* down for an hour after lunch every day of her married life. For the last 20 years, she *has laid* a blanket on the sofa first.

To recap, that's *lie, lay, have lain*, but *lay, laid, have laid*. (If you're feeling uncomfortable with *lain*, you can do what most people do and avoid *has lain* and *had lain* by using *has been lying* and *had been lying*. This will get you out of most tricky situations.)

SUBJUNCTIVE WITH THE WORD *IF:* If Deborah *had known* how moody Bill was, she wouldn't have started dating him.

SUBJUNCTIVE WITHOUT THE WORD *IF: Had* Deborah *known* about Bill's moods, she wouldn't have started dating him.

WHY IT'S SUBJUNCTIVE: Deborah knew nothing about his moods; Bill seemed perfect compared with Damian.

WHAT THE NORMAL SUBJECT–VERB PAIR WOULD BE: Deborah knew.

Which sentence is correct?

A. If Edgar would have played the tuba better, he could have joined the university orchestra.

B. If Edgar had played the tuba better, he could have joined the university orchestra.

Answer: Sentence B is correct. Edgar plays the tuba very badly, so the subjunctive is appropriate. The word *would* is never part of an *if* statement.

When *if* doesn't need a subjunctive

As you're reading about the subjunctive *if*, you may think that all sentences with the word *if* need a subjunctive verb. Nope. Some *if* sentences don't express a condition contrary to fact; they express a possibility – something that may happen. The *if* sentences that express a possibility take a plain old normal indicative verb. Here are some examples:

NON-SUBJUNCTIVE *IF* SENTENCE: If Grandma Robinson goes to prison again, she will take a cookbook with her.

WHY IT'S NOT SUBJUNCTIVE: Prison is a possibility.

NON-SUBJUNCTIVE *IF* SENTENCE: If Damian remarries, he will divorce within a year.

WHY IT'S NOT SUBJUNCTIVE: Remarriage is a possibility. In fact, Damian is already looking around.

In an *if* sentence, if something is possible, use a normal everyday verb to say it. If something is untrue, use a subjunctive verb.

Using subjunctives with commands, wishes and requests

Clarence loves to exercise power:

> Clarence decrees that all his employees *be* at their desks by 6 a.m.

> He insists that each head of department *give* him a full daily report on the department's activities.

> He further insists that his secretary *remain* in the office until he goes home, however late that is.

The italicised verbs are all subjunctive. These sentences need subjunctives because they express wishes, requests, or indirect commands. (Commands that are given directly to the person who is supposed to follow them are in the imperative mood. See 'Commanding Your Verbs: The Imperative Mood', earlier in this chapter.)

In the example sentences, the normal subject–verb pairs (the indicative pairs) would be *employees are*, *head of department gives*, *secretary remains*. In these subjunctive sentences, all subjects take the same form of the verb – the bare infinitive (the infinitive without *to*). (For more information on infinitives, see Chapter 2.) Thus you have

> to be: subjunctive = be

> to give: subjunctive = give

> to remain: subjunctive = remain

and so forth.

Try and figure these out: when you need an infinitive

Now that you've read the heading above, do you see what's wrong with it? *Try and* means that you are going to do two different things: *try* (first task) and *figure out* (second task). But you don't have two tasks in mind, do you? *Try and* is a common expression, but not a correct one. Here's what you really mean: *try to figure this one out. Try to* follows the normal English pattern of a verb and an infinitive:

George and Vicky *plan to go* to Barcelona for a holiday. (*plan* = verb, *to go* = infinitive)

Bibi *likes to talk* to strangers. (*likes* = verb, *to talk* = infinitive)

Alice *hates to cry* in public. (*hates* = verb, *to cry* = infinitive)

By the way, infinitives look like verbs, but they never act as the main verb in a sentence. In the sample sentences above, all the infinitives are direct objects. (For more information on direct objects, see Chapter 6; for more information on infinitives, see Chapter 24.)

To sum up: *try to remember* the verb–infinitive rule and *try to forget* about *try and*.

In everyday communication, many speakers of perfectly good English avoid the subjunctive and use an infinitive or the auxiliary verb *must* or *should* instead. Here are Clarence's demands with *must* or *should* or an infinitive instead of subjunctive verbs:

Clarence insists that all his employees *must be* at their desks by 6 a.m. (*Must be* is a plain old normal verb.)

He demands that each head of department *should give* him a full daily report on the department's activities. (*Should give* is a plain old normal verb.)

He also requires his secretary *to remain* in the office until he goes home, however late that is. (*To remain* is a plain old infinitive.)

Which sentence is correct?

A. Clarence insists that his employees are paid by the hour.

B. Clarence insists that his employees must be paid by the hour.

C. Clarence insists that his employees be paid by the hour.

Answer: All the sentences are correct, but they aren't necessarily saying the same thing. Sentence C uses the subjunctive verb (*be*) to tell us what Clarence wants. (The infinitive *to be* minus the *to* equals the subjunctive.) Sentence B avoids the subjunctive by saying *must be*. It's also telling us what

Clarence wants. Sentence A may not be saying the same thing. It could mean that, whether his employees are paid by the hour or not, Clarence says that they are. But it is increasingly being used, at least in informal speech, to mean the same as Sentence C. (That's what happens when a whole chunk of grammar dies.) The context may help, of course, but the moral is – as always – be sure that your meaning is clear.

If you've read all the preceding sections on the subjunctive mood, by now you're probably in a mood yourself – a bad mood. Take heart! Although it may seem as if the subjunctive were all over the English language, in reality you need it only occasionally. If you speak another language – Spanish or French, for example – you've probably noticed by now that the subjunctive is a much bigger deal and far more common in those languages. One last thought: if the rules for the subjunctive in this chapter seem overwhelming, forget about them. The grammar police won't execute you if you completely ignore the subjunctive. Many literate, educated people work around it, and errors of the subjunctive are not nearly so serious as, say, littering.

I Can't Help But Think This Rule Is Crazy: Deleting Double Negatives

In some lucky languages, the more negatives the better. In English, however, two negatives are a no-no. (By the way, no-no is *not* a double negative! It's just slang for something that's prohibited.) We explain several basic forms of double negative in Chapter 8. Here we'll tell you about some of the less obvious forms of double trouble.

One of the most common double negatives doesn't look like one: *cannot help but.* How many times have you heard someone say something like

> Martin *cannot help but* act in that dramatic style because he was trained by a real ham.

Sometimes, *help* is left out:

> Edgar *cannot but* think that it's his job to bring home the bacon.

Unfortunately, both of these sentences are wrong because they both contain double negatives. The *not* and the *but* both express negative ideas. Use one or the other. Don't use both. Here are correct versions:

> Martin *cannot help acting* in that dramatic style because he was trained by a real ham.

> Edgar *can* but think that it's his job to bring home the bacon.

This last sentence sounds terrible, doesn't it? These are is much better:

> Edgar *can* only think that it's his job to bring home the bacon.

> OR: Edgar *cannot help* thinking that it's his job to bring home the bacon.

> OR: Edgar *thinks* that it's his job to bring home the bacon.

Ironically, in English two negatives make a positive. When you say *cannot help but*, you actually convey the opposite of what you imagine you're saying (or writing). For example:

> Susie told her boss, 'I cannot help but ask for a raise.'

> WHAT SHE THINKS SHE SAID: I have to ask for a raise.

> WHAT SHE REALLY SAID: I can't ask for a raise.

> The boss told Susie, 'I cannot help but say no.'

> WHAT THE BOSS THINKS SHE SAID: No.

> WHAT THE BOSS ACTUALLY SAID: Yes. (Susie still didn't get the raise, though.)

Which sentence is correct?

> A. I cannot help but think that this double negative rule is ridiculous.

> B. I cannot help thinking that this double negative rule is ridiculous.

Answer: Sentence B is correct.

Can't Hardly Understand This Rule: Yet Another Double Negative

No matter what you do, avoid saying or writing *can't hardly* when you are using formal English. *Can't* is short for *cannot*, which contains the negative *not*. *Hardly* is another negative word. If you combine them, by the logic of grammar, you've said the opposite of what you intended – the positive instead of the negative. Look at this example:

> Deborah commented, 'Bill can't hardly count his tattoos.'

> WHAT DEBORAH THINKS SHE SAID: Bill can't count his tattoos.

> WHAT DEBORAH ACTUALLY SAID: Bill can count his tattoos.

A variation of this double negative is *can't scarcely* (or *aren't scarcely* or *isn't scarcely*). Once again, *can't* is short for *cannot*, clearly a negative. *Aren't* and *isn't* are the negative forms of *are* and *is*. *Scarcely* is also negative. Use them together and you end up with a positive, not a super-negative.

Here's another double negative, in a couple of forms: *hadn't only, haven't only, hasn't only, hadn't but, haven't but* and *hasn't but*. All express positive ideas because the *not* (*n't*) part of the verb and the *only* or *but* are both negatives:

> WRONG: Susie *hadn't but* ten minutes to catch the bus.

> WHY IT'S WRONG: As it reads now, the sentence says that Susie had more than ten minutes to catch the bus, but the bus was already coming down the road and she was about to miss it and be late for work.

> RIGHT: Susie *had but* ten minutes to catch the bus.

> ALSO RIGHT: Susie *had* only ten minutes to catch the bus.

Which sentence is correct?

> A. Lucinda can't hardly understand those pesky grammar rules.

> B. Lucinda can't help but be confused by those pesky grammar rules.

Answer: Both are wrong. (Teachers are required to play annoying tricks on students.) In sentence A, *can't hardly* is a double negative. In sentence B, *cannot help but* is a double negative.

What about these?

> A. Lucinda can scarcely understand those pesky grammar rules.

> B. Lucinda can't help being confused by those pesky grammar rules.

Answer: Sentences A and B are both correct. In sentence A, Lucinda has only a little understanding of grammar. In sentence B she is confused.

It takes two to make a mistake

English has three *to*'s, all sounding exactly alike but spelled differently. (Words that sound alike but are spelled differently are known as *homonyms*.) *To* may be part of an infinitive (*to speak, to dream*) or it may show movement towards someone or something (*to the shops, to me*). *Two* is the number (*two eyes, two ears*). *Too* means also (*Are you going too?*) or more than enough (*too expensive, too wide*). In other words:

If you *two* want *to* skip school and go *to* the arcade, today's a good day because the teacher will be *too* busy *to* check.

Two things you should always remember before you decide *to* break a grammar rule: it is never *too* late *to* learn proper English and you are never *too* old *to* get in trouble with your teacher.

Chapter 23

The Last Word on Pronouns

In This Chapter

▶ Deciding between who/whoever and whom/whomever

▶ Matching pronouns to the nouns they replace

▶ Understanding pronoun use in complicated sentences

▶ Decoding the meaning of *who, which* and *that*

▶ Choosing the proper pronoun for groups

▶ Avoiding vague pronouns

*Y*ou've come to it at last: the dreaded pronoun chapter where you find out the intricate details of who/whom and the like. Be warned: in three nanoseconds, you can easily find something to do that is more interesting than these concepts – training fleas for circus duty, for example.

You're still reading? OK, you asked for it. Here is the last word on pronouns, including who/whom sentences and a host of other really picky pronoun points. People have led perfectly pleasant (albeit grammatically incorrect) lives without knowing this stuff. But if you insist. . . .

Knowing the Difference Between Who/ Whoever and Whom/Whomever

'*Whom?*' you're thinking. 'I'd never say *whom*. And *whomever?* You're joking!' Yes, we know. Most young people don't use *whom* (and *whomever*) much, if at all. The words are quietly disappearing from the language. You will read newspapers that don't use them because they think that their readers will be put off by them, and novels that don't use them because the characters would never speak like that. So you can skip this if you like. Only read on if you occasionally need to write in very formal English.

The rule for knowing when to use *who* and *whom* is simple; applying the rule is not. First, the rule:

- ✔ *Who* and *whoever* are for subjects.

- ✔ *Who* and *whoever* also follow and complete the meaning of linking verbs. In grammarspeak, *who* and *whoever* serve as linking-verb complements.

- ✔ *Whom* and *whomever* are for objects – all kinds of objects (direct objects, indirect objects, objects of prepositions, objects of infinitives and so on).

For more information on subjects, see Chapter 4. For more information on objects and linking-verb complements, see Chapter 6.

Before applying the rule concerning who/whoever and whom/whomever, check out these sample sentences:

> *Whoever* needs help from Damian is going to wait a long time. (*Whoever* is the subject of the verb *needs*.)

> *Who* is calling Lucinda at this time of night? (*Who* is the subject of the verb *is calling*.)

> 'I don't care *whom* you ask to the dance,' exclaimed Deborah. (*Whom* is the direct object of the verb *ask*.)

> The gold sash is for *whomever* he designates employee of the month. (*Whomever* is the direct object of the verb *designates*.)

> For *whom* are you bellowing? (*Whom* is the object of the preposition *for*.)

Now that you know the rule and have seen the words in action, here are two tricks for deciding between *who/whoever* and *whom/whomever*. If one trick seems to work, use it and ignore the other. Here goes. . . .

Trick 1: Horse and carriage

According to an old song, 'love and marriage go together like a horse and carriage'. Grammarians may sing that song with slightly different lyrics: 'subject and verb go together like a horse and carriage'. (What do you think? Grammy material?) To use Trick 1, follow these steps:

1. Find all the verbs in the sentence.

2. Don't separate the auxiliary verbs from the main verb. Count the main verb and its auxiliary verbs as a single verb.

3. Now pair each of the verbs with a subject.

4. If you have a verb flapping around with no subject, chances are *who* or *whoever* is the subject you're missing.

5. If all the verbs have subjects, check them one more time. Do you have any linking verbs without complements? (For more information on complements, see Chapter 6.) If you have a lonely linking verb with no complement in sight, you need *who* or *whoever*.

6. If all subjects are accounted for and you don't need a linking verb complement, you've reached a final answer: *whom* or *whomever* is the only possibility.

Here's a sample sentence, analysed using Trick 1:

SENTENCE: *Who/Whom* shall I say is calling?

The verbs are *shall say* and *is calling*.

The subject of *shall say* is *I*.

The subject of *is calling* is . . . OK, here we go. We need a subject for *is calling* but we're out of words. There's only one choice: *who*.

CORRECT SENTENCE: *Who* shall I say is calling?

Now you try. Which word is correct?

Bill buys chocolate for Deborah, *who/whom* he adores even though they've split up.

Answer: *Whom*, because it's the direct object of *adores*. *Bill buys* and *he adores* are subject–verb pairs. Both are action verbs, so no subject complement is needed.

Trick 2: Getting rhythm

This trick relies on your ear for grammar. Most English sentences follow one pattern: Subject–Verb–Object (or Subject–Verb– Complement). Trick 2 is to say the parts of the sentence in this order, even if you have to rearrange the words a little. Here are the steps to follow:

1. Identify the verb in the sentence that seems connected to the *who/whom* choice. Usually it's the verb nearest *who/whom*. It's also the verb logically connected by meaning – that is, in the same thought as *who/whom*.

2. Say (aloud, if you don't mind scaring the people nearby, or silently, if you plan to keep a reputation for sanity) the three parts of the sentence.

Anything before the verb is *who* or *whoever.*

If you're working with an action verb, anything after the verb is probably *whom* or *whomever.*

If you're working with a linking verb, anything after the verb is probably *who* or *whoever.*

Here is a sample sentence analysed with Trick 2:

Who/Whom will Bill hire for the vacancy in his shop?

The verb is *will hire.*

Will hire is an action verb, so forget about linking-verb complements.

Say aloud: Bill will hire *who/whom.*

Choose *whom* because the word is after the verb.

Whom is the direct object of *will hire.*

CORRECT SENTENCE: *Whom* will Bill hire for the vacancy in his shop?

Which word is correct?

Who/Whom do you like better, Alice or Ellie?

Answer: *Whom* is correct. Change the order of the words to *you do like whom.* Choose *whom* after an action verb. In this sentence, *whom* is the direct object. (By the way, it's a silly question – it's impossible to choose between Alice and Ellie.)

Studying Improper Antecedents

The *antecedent* of a pronoun is the word that the pronoun replaces. You should be able to replace the pronoun with its antecedent (or the antecedent with the pronoun) without changing the meaning of the sentence. To follow this rule, you must make sure that the pronoun has an antecedent to replace. If the pronoun has no antecedent, the pronoun flaps around loose. And the pronoun is a picky little part of speech: it refuses to replace any old word. If an antecedent is almost but not quite right, every self-respecting pronoun just turns up its nose. (For more information on pronouns and their antecedents, see Chapter 10.) Here are some examples:

WRONG: She's a lawyer, and I want to study it.

What does *it* replace? *Law,* perhaps. But the word *law* is not in the sentence; *lawyer* is. *Law* and *lawyer* are close, but not close enough.

> RIGHT: She's a lawyer, and I want to be one too.
>
> WHY IT'S RIGHT: *One* refers to *lawyer.*
>
> ALSO RIGHT: I'd like to study law, as she did.
>
> WHY IT'S ALSO RIGHT: There's no floating pronoun in the sentence.

Another (trickier) example is:

> WRONG: In Edgar's poetry, he frequently uses cow imagery.

Who's *he?* Edgar, I imagine. But *Edgar* isn't in the sentence. *Edgar's* – the possessive noun – is in the sentence. You can replace *Edgar's* by *his* (because *his* is a possessive pronoun), but not by *he.*

> RIGHT: Edgar frequently writes poetry with cow imagery.
>
> WHY IT'S RIGHT: There's no pronoun in the sentence.
>
> ALSO RIGHT: Stay away from Edgar's poetry readings unless you are really, really, really fond of cows.

Which sentence is correct?

A. Deborah has always been interested in archaeology because she thinks that they spend a lot of time digging up interesting things.

B. Deborah has always been interested in archaeology because she thinks archaeologists spend a lot of time digging up interesting things.

Sentence B is correct. In sentence A, no proper antecedent exists for *they.* Sentence B replaces *they* with the noun *archaeologists.*

Matching Verbs to Pronouns in Complicated Sentences

Singular pronouns must be paired with singular verbs, and plural pronouns must be paired with plural verbs. Easy rule, right? *He says. They say.* No problem. But not all pronouns are as simple as *he* and *they.* Some pronouns – *who, which* and *that* – are chameleons. (See Chapter 25 for details on punctuating sentences with *which* and *that*.) They always look the same, but they may be either singular or plural depending on their antecedents. You have to decode the sentence to decide whether the antecedent is singular or plural. Then you must match the verb to the antecedent. In some sentences with simple structures, the choice is fairly obvious. For example:

> *English Grammar For Dummies* is the book that you're reading. (*that* = book = singular)

> The books that fell off the shelf broke my favourite mug. (*that* = *books* = plural)

In complicated sentences, the choice is not so obvious. To pair the pronoun with the correct verb, use your reading comprehension skills to figure out the meaning of the pronoun. After you know the meaning of the pronoun, the choice between a singular and plural verb is clear. Check out the following examples:

> SENTENCE A: Bill is the only one of my friends who *has/have* more than 11 tattoos.

> The *who* statement is about having more than 11 tattoos. According to the sentence, how many friends are in that category? One or more than one? Only one. Choose the singular verb (*has*).

> CORRECT SENTENCE: Bill is the only one of my friends who *has* more than 11 tattoos.

> SENTENCE B: Isolde is one of the members of Rob's class who *has/have* a tattoo.

> The *who* statement is about having a tattoo. How many of Rob's class-mates have a tattoo? Several. Isolde is only one of them. *Who* is plural, referring to all the class members who have a tattoo. Choose the plural verb (*have*).

> CORRECT SENTENCE: Isolde is one of the members of Rob's class who *have* a tattoo.

Which word is correct?

> Alice claims she is one of the many women who *has/have* been rejected by Damian.

Answer: *Have.* Damian has rejected more than one woman, according to the sentence, so the verb must be plural.

This, That and the Other: Clarifying Vague Pronoun References

One pronoun may refer to one noun. A plural pronoun may refer to more than one noun. But no pronoun may refer to a whole sentence or a whole paragraph. Consider the following scenario:

> Rob's friend Isolde likes to arrive at school around 11 each day because she thinks that getting up at any hour earlier than 10 is barbaric. The principal, not surprisingly, thinks that arriving at school over two hours late each day is not a good idea. *This* is a problem.

This certainly is a problem, and not because of Isolde's sleeping habits or the principal's beliefs. *This* is a problem because the antecedent of the word *this* is unclear. What does *this* mean? The fact that Isolde arrives around 11? That Isolde thinks getting up before 10 is out of the question? Or that the principal and Isolde are not, to put it mildly, in sync? Or all of the above?

The writer probably intends *this* to refer to *all of the above*. Unfortunately, *all of the above* is not a good answer to the question, 'What does the pronoun mean?'

Thus:

> WRONG: The red dye looked horrible, and the new curling tongs had singed her hair. *This* persuaded Lucinda to take Mortimer's advice and use a professional hairdresser in future.
>
> WHY IT'S WRONG: *This* is referring to the 14 words of the preceding sentence, not to one noun.
>
> RIGHT: Because the red dye looked horrible and the new curling tongs had singed her hair, Lucinda decided to take Mortimer's advice and use a professional hairdresser in future.
>
> WHY IT'S RIGHT: Eliminating *this* eliminates the problem.

In ordinary speech (conversational English) you may occasionally use *this*, *which* or *that* to refer to more than one word, as long as your meaning is clear. For example:

> Clarence refused to let everyone go home early on Christmas Eve, which angered all his employees.

In the paper it says . . .

Are you writing about literature or what's in the paper? If so, beware of *it* and *they*. Some common errors follow those pronouns. Check out these examples:

> In *Hamlet*, it says that Claudius is a murderer.

Oh really? What does *it* mean? The play can't speak, and the author of the play (Shakespeare) is a *who*. Actually, in *Hamlet*, the ghost says that Claudius is a murderer, but even the ghost is a *he*. In other words, *it* has no antecedent. Reword the sentence:

> In *Hamlet*, Claudius is a murderer.

> In *Hamlet*, the ghost declares that Claudius is a murderer.

> My teacher says that in *Hamlet* Claudius is a murderer.

Here's another example:

> In today's paper *they* say that more and more people want to drop Shakespeare's plays from the curriculum because they can't understand the language.

(We should probably say, before we get back to grammar, that we actually *like* Shakespeare's plays. Now, back to pronouns.) Who is *they*? Perhaps the authors of an article, but the sentence doesn't make that fact clear. It's possible that the author of the sentence thinks that *they* is a good all-purpose pronoun for talking about anonymous or nameless authors. In other words, the antecedent of *they* is "I don't know and I really don't care". Wrong! The antecedent of *they* must be a real, identifiable group of people. Some possible corrections include:

> Today's paper reports that more and more people want to drop Shakespeare's plays from the curriculum because they can't understand the language.

> In today's paper, education critic I.M. Ignorent says that Shakespeare's plays should be dropped from the curriculum because no one can understand the language.

The pronoun *which* here refers to the fact that Clarence refused to give everyone the afternoon off (despite the fact that they didn't have any work to do). Your audience grasps the meaning easily.

In both conversational and formal English, avoid vagueness. Never use a pronoun that may refer to two or more ideas; don't leave your reader or listener wondering what you mean. For example:

> Isolde's history essay was ten days late and ten pages short. This earned her an F.

What convinced the teacher to fail the essay – the lateness or the fact that she wrote exactly 34 words on "The French Revolution: its causes and effects in relation to the concept of democracy"? One of these factors? If so, which one? Or both? Enquiring minds want to know, and the pronoun doesn't tell. Possible corrections include the following:

Because Isolde's history essay was ten days late and ten pages short, the teacher failed her. (Now you know that both factors influenced the grade.)

Isolde's history essay was ten days late, so the teacher failed her. (Even if it had arrived on time, the fact that it was ten pages short would have earned her an F.)

To sum up this simple rule: be clear when using pronouns.

Its or Their? Selecting Pronouns for Collective Nouns

Collective nouns present a problem when it comes to choosing the right pronouns (and verbs). Collective nouns (*committee*, *team*, *squad*, *army*, *class* and the like) refer to groups. It used to be that all collective nouns were considered to be singular (unless there were two or more of them – one orchestra was singular but two orchestras were plural), but now a lot of people are happier treating them as plural.

So, if this is one of those areas where the language is changing, can't you choose which you prefer and make them all singular or all plural? This is a possibility, but unfortunately if you do this you will inevitably find yourself with some sentences that feel very uncomfortable. So you will need to look at what collective nouns you're using and how you're using them to try to decide a consistent policy for your document. And you'll have to think it through all over again when you write the next thing. Sorry. Anyway, here are some tips.

We have collective nouns because these groups often act as a unit, doing the same thing at the same time. If that's the case, treat the noun as singular and make sure that the pronouns that refer to it are also singular. Like this:

The audience rises and is ready to leave after a stirring performance of Mortimer's new film.

In this sentence, we paired the subject, *audience*, with singular verbs – *rises* and *was* – because the audience acts together (a collection of people all doing the same thing together) and because we don't know any of them individually.

So, if the audience is a unit, should the audience clap *its* hands or *their* hands? At first glance *its* would seem appropriate, because *its* is singular, and *audience* is paired with singular verbs. However, the audience doesn't own a big, collective hand. Every person in the audience has two individual hands. Body parts, no matter how unified the group, must belong to separate people. Dump the collective noun and substitute *members of the audience*. Now insert *their*:

The members of the audience rise to *their* feet and clap *their* hands.

Members is now the subject. *Members* is plural, so the verbs and pronouns are all plural also.

Are there any sentences in which *its* is correct? Yes. Here's one:

The cast will hold *its* traditional opening night party tonight.

Its is appropriate in this sentence because the party belongs to the cast as a whole, not to the individual members of the cast.

Here's another sentence to figure out:

As the orchestra raises *its/their* instruments, the conductor searches for his music.

Orchestra is another collective noun. The verb is singular, because the orchestra acts in unison, but *its instruments* sounds strange. OK, maybe the *orchestra* owns all the tubas, violins and other instruments of destruction. (You should hear them play.) So if the sentence is talking about ownership, *its* would fit:

The orchestra insures *its* instruments with Lords of Luton.

However, the orchestra can't raise a collectively owned instrument. Each musician raises their own. So *their* and *musicians* make more sense:

The musicians in the orchestra raise *their* instruments and prepare to murder Beethoven.

To sum up the general rules on pronouns that refer to groups:

- ✔ Collective nouns may take singular or plural verbs, but you can't mix the two for the same word.
- ✔ Treat collective nouns as singular if the group is acting as a unit.
- ✔ If the members of the group are acting as individuals, you can use a plural verb, but it's better to drop the collective noun.

Which paragraph is correct?

A. The class will hold its annual picnic during the winter because the teachers were on strike in the summer. The class always enjoy their day out.

B. The class will hold its annual picnic during the winter because the teachers were on strike in the summer. The class always enjoys its day out.

C. The class will hold their annual picnic during the winter because the teachers were on strike in the summer. The class always enjoy their day out.

D. The annual class picnic will take place during the winter because the teachers were on strike in the summer. The children always enjoy their day out.

Answer: Paragraphs B, C and D are all correct. The problem collective noun is *class*. Sentence A is definitely wrong because it begins by treating *class* as singular (*its* picnic) but then switches to plural (*enjoy their* day out). Paragraph B treats *class* as singular. Paragraph C treats it as plural. They're both correct. Experts may not like your choice, but they won't argue with it as long as you're consistent. But paragraph D is the best: it avoids using *class* as a noun (it's an adjective in *annual class picnic*) and uses *children* instead in the second sentence.

Pronouns, Inc.: Using Pronouns with Company Names

What about businesses? Is Harrods having *its* sale or *their* sale?

Some people insist that, even if the business's name looks plural, the business is a singular noun because one company is, after all, just one company. Therefore, the verb is singular. The business is an *it*, not a *they*, because a company is just a company. You may find this difficult because the way the name sounds doesn't help you to get the verbs and pronouns right.

Other people prefer to treat a company as plural, partly because it sounds more natural with some company names but also because they think of a company as consisting of all the people who work there.

So you can choose. But remember that you have to be consistent.

Harrods *is* having *its* sale today.

M&S *are* having *their* sale tomorrow.

A historic or historical occasion

If something is *historical*, it happened and is now history. If something is *historic*, it happened and was important, influencing the course of history. Consider the following:

The little-known Elizabethan courtier, Sir Archibald D'Arcy-Pemberton, whose duties included cleaning all the windows in the Queen's palaces, was married to the equally obscure lady-in-waiting, Ethel Goodbody.

This information is *historical*: you can look it up in Lady Ethel's diary. Other *historical* events in Sir Archibald's life include his trek through the New Forest the time his horse died and the week he spent at Greenwich Palace before he realised that everyone else was at Hampton Court.

Despite his long life in public service, Sir Archibald was not involved in any *historic* events whatsoever. Even when he was expected to attend important ceremonies, he had a knack of being taken ill the day before – he was a martyr to colds. Thus, Sir Archibald was a *historical* (not imaginary) figure who did not participate in any *historic* events. (OK, we confess, he wasn't historical at all – we made him up.)

Which sentence is correct?

    A. Barker & Sons say that they stock only the best in their hardware shops.

    B. Barker & Sons says that it stocks only the best in their hardware shops.

    C. Barker & Sons says that it stocks only the best in its hardware shops.

Answer: Sentences A and C are both correct. You can choose which you prefer. Sentence A treats the company as plural (*they say, they stock, their shops*). Sentence C treats the company as singular (*it says, it stocks, its shops*). Sentence B can't make its mind up. It starts out singular (*it says, it stocks*), but switches to plural (*their shops*). That's wrong.

Chapter 24

The Last Word on Sentence Structure

Say you get a new car. What do you do? Check the engine, or hop in and drive it away? The engine-checkers and the drive-awayers are the two sub-groups of car owners. The engine-checkers have to know what's going on inside the machine. The other group doesn't care what's going on inside: they just want the car to run.

You can also divide speakers of English into two groups. Some people want to understand what's going on inside the sentence, but most just want to communicate. In this chapter we provide some information for both the check-the-engine group and the take-it-for-a-drive group. The first part of this chapter digs into the structure of the sentence; the second part shows you how to make your writing more interesting by varying sentence patterns.

Understanding the Basics of Clause and Effect

No matter what food you put between two pieces of bread, you've got a sandwich. That's the definition of *sandwich:* bread plus filling. Clauses have a simple definition too: subject plus verb. Any subject–verb combination creates a clause. The reverse is also true: no subject or no verb, no clause. You can throw in some extras (descriptions, joining words, lettuce, tomato . . . whatever), but the basic subject–verb combination is the key. Some sentences have one clause (in which case the whole sentence is the clause) and some have more than one.

Be sure to check your sentences for completeness. Each sentence should contain at least one complete thought, expressed in a way that can stand alone. In grammarspeak, each sentence must contain at least one main clause (check out 'Getting the goods on main and subordinate clauses', later in this chapter). For more information on complete sentences, see Chapter 5.

Here are a few examples of one-clause sentences:

> Has Mike cracked the case of the anonymous letters? (subject = *Mike* verb = *has cracked*)
>
> Sandy sailed safely round the world single-handed. (subject = *Sandy,* verb = *sailed*)
>
> Clarence and his employees have not reached a new pay agreement. (subjects = *Clarence* and *his employees* verb = *have reached*)
>
> George fixed the dripping tap and changed a lightbulb. (subject = *George,* verbs = *fixed* and *changed*)

Note that one of these sentences has two subjects and one has two verbs, but each expresses one main idea.

Here are a few examples of sentences with more than one clause:

> SENTENCE: Bibi loves Mike, and she likes him to read to her.
>
> CLAUSE 1: Bibi loves Mike (subject = *Bibi*, verb = *loves*)
>
> CLAUSE 2: she likes him to read to her (subject = *she*, verb = *likes*)

> SENTENCE: Rob had finished most of his homework, so his mother said that he could watch his favourite television programme.
>
> CLAUSE 1: Rob had finished most of his homework (subject = *Rob,* verb = *had finished*)
>
> CLAUSE 2: his mother said that he could watch his favourite television programme. (subject = *his mother*, verb = *said*)
>
> CLAUSE 3: that he could watch his favourite television programme (subject = *he*, verb = *could watch*)

There is something odd about the second of these sentences. Clause 3 is actually part of clause 2. It's not a misprint. Sometimes one clause is actually entangled in another. (This topic is deep in the pathless forests of grammar! Get out now, while you still can!)

Here's one more example that's really complicated:

> SENTENCE: Whoever marries Damian next will be disappointed.
>
> CLAUSE 1: Whoever marries Damian next (subject = *whoever,* verb = *marries*)

CLAUSE 2: Whoever marries Damian next will be disappointed. (subject = *whoever marries Damian*, verb = *will be*)

Yes, one clause is the subject of another clause. Good grief! What a system! (For those who truly love grammar: the subject clause is a noun clause. See 'Knowing the three legal jobs for subordinate clauses', later in this chapter, for more information.)

Getting the goods on main and subordinate clauses

Some clauses are mature grown-ups. They have their own home, pay the mortgage and wash the dishes occasionally. These clauses have made a success of life.

Other clauses are like the middle-aged son in a sitcom who still lives at home with his mother. These clauses are not mature; they don't cook or do their own laundry. These clauses may be called *dependent clauses* or *subordinate clauses*. (The terms are interchangeable.)

Following are two sets of clauses. Both have subject–verb pairs, but the clauses in the first set make sense alone and the clauses in the second set don't.

Main clauses:

> Bibi blasted Tinkerbell with her new water pistol.
>
> Mike was sad to discover that she was the author of the anonymous letters.
>
> Did Mortimer donate the painting to the local art gallery?

Subordinate clauses:

> When her mother wasn't looking
>
> Because he liked Mildred
>
> Which he bought at the auction

Main clauses are OK by themselves, but writing too many in a row makes your paragraph choppy and monotonous. Subordinate clauses, however, are not OK by themselves because they don't make complete sentences. To become complete, they have to tack themselves onto main clauses. Subordinate clauses add life and interest to the sentence (just as the guy crashing on your sofa adds a little zip to the household). But don't leave them alone, because disaster will strike. A subordinate clause all by itself is a grammatical crime – a sentence fragment.

The best sentences combine different elements in all sorts of patterns. In the following examples, the main clauses are combined with subordinate clauses to create longer, more interesting sentences:

> Bibi blasted Tinkerbell with her new water pistol when her mother wasn't looking.

> Because he liked Mildred, Mike was sad to discover that she was the author of the anonymous letters.

> Did Mortimer donate the painting, which he bought at the auction, to the local art gallery?

Combine the ideas in each of these sets into one sentence.

Set A:

> Bibi was frightened by the snakes at the zoo.

> Bibi screamed.

> Bibi dropped her ice cream.

Set B:

> Yasmin solved a significant problem in physics.

> Her professor had been working on the problem for three years.

Set C:

> Edgar gave away copies of his books.

> He gave them to his friends.

> He only gave them to people who wanted them.

Answer: Several combinations are possible. Here are three:

A. Bibi screamed and dropped her ice cream when she was frightened by the snakes at the zoo.

B. Yasmin solved a significant problem in physics that her professor had been working on for three years.

C. Edgar gave copies of his books to whichever of his friends wanted them.

Knowing the three legal jobs for subordinate clauses

OK, subordinate clauses can't stand alone. What can they do? They really have three main purposes in life, as we explain in the following sections.

Describing nouns and pronouns

Yep, subordinate clauses can describe nouns and pronouns. That is, the subordinate clause may give your listener or reader more information about a noun or pronoun in the sentence. Here are some examples, with the subordinate clause in italics:

> The diary *that Mr Witherby-Jones kept during his years in government* is on the bestseller list. (*That Mr Witherby-Jones kept during his years in government* describes the noun *diary.*)

> Anyone *who knows him well* will read the book. (*Who knows him well* describes the pronoun *anyone.*)

> The book includes some information *that will prove embarrassing to his friends.* (*That will prove embarrassing to his friends* describes the noun *information.*)

Subordinate clauses that describe nouns or pronouns are called *adjectival clauses* or *adjective clauses.*

Describing verbs, adjectives and adverbs

Subordinate clauses can also describe verbs, adjectives and adverbs. These subordinate clauses tell you *how, when, where* or *why.* Here are some examples, with the subordinate clause in italics:

> *Because Witherby-Jones tells us nothing about his early years in politics,* the book contains nothing about his decision to change his party allegiance. (*Because Witherby-Jones tells us nothing about his early years in politics* describes the verb *contains.*)

> We may find out more *when the film of the book is released.* (*When the film of the book is released* describes the verb *find.*)

> The government may prohibit sales of the book *wherever international tensions make it dangerous.* (*Wherever international tensions make it dangerous* describes the verb *may prohibit.*)

> Witherby-Jones is so stubborn *that he may sue the government.* (*That he may sue the government* describes the adverb *so.*)

Subordinate clauses that describe verbs are called *adverbial clauses* or *adverb clauses*. Subordinate clauses that describe adjectives or adverbs (mostly in comparisons) are also *adverbial clauses*. Adverbial clauses do the same job as single-word adverbs. They describe verbs, adjectives or other adverbs.

Acting as subjects or objects inside another clause

This one is a bit more complicated. Subordinate clauses may do any job that a noun does in a sentence. Subordinate clauses sometimes act as subjects or objects inside another clause. Here are some examples, with the subordinate clause in italics:

> *When Edgar finds the time to write his books* is a mystery. (*When Edgar finds the time to write his books* is the subject of the verb *is*.)

> No one knows *where Yasmin and Edgar are getting married*. (*Where Yasmin and Edgar are getting married* is the object of the verb *knows*.)

> Edgar signed copies of his books for *any of his mother's friends who bought a copy*. (*Any of his mother's friends who bought a copy* is the object of the preposition *for*.)

Noun clauses are subordinate clauses that perform the same functions as nouns – subjects, objects, appositives and so on.

Check out the italicised clause in each sentence. Is it the main clause or the subordinate clause?

A. *Even though they scored six goals*, Bill's team lost the match.

B. *Lucinda danced for a while*, but then she said that her head was splitting and sat down.

Answer: In sentence A, the italicised clause is subordinate. In sentence B, the italicised clause is a main clause.

Untangling main clauses and subordinate clauses

You have to untangle one clause from another only occasionally – when deciding which pronoun or verb you need or whether commas are appropriate. (See the next section, 'Deciding when to untangle clauses', for more information.) When you do have to untangle them, follow these simple steps:

1. Find the subject–verb pairs.

2. Use your reading comprehension skills to determine whether the subject–verb pairs belong to the same thought or to different thoughts.

3. If the pairs belong to different thoughts, they're probably in different clauses.

4. If the pairs belong to the same thought, they're probably in the same clause.

Another method also relies on reading comprehension skills. Think about the ideas in the sentence and untangle the thoughts. By doing so, you've probably also untangled the clauses.

Check out these examples:

SENTENCE: The acting award that Ellie received comes with a substantial cash prize.

SUBJECT–VERB PAIRS: *award comes, Ellie received*

UNTANGLED IDEA 1: The award comes with a substantial cash prize.

UNTANGLED IDEA 2: Ellie received the award.

CLAUSE 1: The acting award comes with a substantial cash prize (main clause)

CLAUSE 2: that Ellie received (subordinate clause)

SENTENCE: When Lucinda makes up her mind, it stays made up.

SUBJECT–VERB PAIRS: *Lucinda ,makes up, it stays*

UNTANGLED IDEA 1: Lucinda makes up her mind.

UNTANGLED IDEA 2: It stays made up.

CLAUSES 1: When Lucinda makes up her mind (subordinate clause)

CLAUSE 2: It stays made up (main clause)

Untangle this sentence into separate clauses.

Natasha's bicycle, which she bought second-hand, has a bent wheel.

Answer: Clause 1: *Natasha's bicycle has a bent wheel.* Clause 2: *which she bought second-hand.*

Try another. Untangle the following sentence.

No one knows when Damian sleeps.

Answer: Clause 1: *no one knows.* Clause 2: *when Damian sleeps.*

Deciding when to untangle clauses

Why would you want to untangle clauses? Not just because you have nothing better to do. You should untangle clauses when you're choosing pronouns, verbs and punctuation. Read on for the whole story.

When you're picking a pronoun

When you're deciding whether you need a subject or an object pronoun, check the clause that contains the word. Don't worry about what the entire clause is doing in the sentence. Untangle the clause and ignore everything else. Then decide which pronoun you need for that particular clause.

Many of the decisions about pronouns concern *who* and *whom*. (For tricks to help you make the *who/whom* choice, see Chapter 23. For a general discussion of choosing the correct pronoun, see Chapters 10 and 17.)

Here's one untangling example, with the pronoun problem in parenthesis:

> SENTENCE: Susie wasn't sure (who/whom) would want one of Poppet's kittens.
>
> UNTANGLED CLAUSE 1: Susie wasn't sure.
>
> UNTANGLED CLAUSE 2: (who/whom) would want one of Poppet's kittens
>
> RELEVANT CLAUSE: (who/whom) would want one of Poppet's kittens
>
> CORRECT PRONOUN: *who* (subject of *would want*)

When you're deciding on the correct verb

When you're deciding subject–verb agreement in one clause, the other clauses are distractions. In fact, if you're writing (not speaking), it can help to cross out or cover the other clauses for a moment. Check the clause that worries you. Decide the subject–verb agreement issue, and then erase the crossing-out line or remove your hand. (For more information on subject–verb agreement, see Chapter 11.)

Here's one untangling example, with the verb choices in parenthesis:

> SENTENCE: Damian, who is thinking of marrying again, (needs/need) no introduction.
>
> UNTANGLED CLAUSE 1: Damian (needs/need) no introduction.
>
> UNTANGLED CLAUSE 2: who is thinking of marrying again
>
> RELEVANT CLAUSE: Damian (needs/need) no introduction.
>
> CORRECT VERB: *needs* (*Damian* = singular, *needs* = singular)

When you're figuring out where to put commas

Sometimes you have to untangle clauses to decide whether or not you need commas. Go through the untangling steps explained earlier in the chapter (see 'Untangling main clauses and subordinate clauses') and then flip to Chapter 25 to see how to use commas correctly.

Putting your subordinate clauses in the right place

Finding the correct place to put a subordinate clause is simple. Clauses acting as subjects or objects nearly always fall in the proper place automatically. Don't worry about them!

Put the subordinate clause that describes a noun or pronoun near the word that it describes. (For lots more detail on placing descriptions in their proper places, see Chapters 8 and 19.)

If the subordinate clause describes the verb, it may land at the front of the sentence or at the rear. On rare occasions, the clause settles down in the middle of the sentence. Here are some examples, with the subordinate clause in italics:

> *Although Isolde understood the equation*, she chose to put a question mark on her answer sheet.

> She wrote the question mark *because she wanted to make a statement about the mysteries of life*.

> Isolde failed the test but, *until her mother found out about the question mark*, Isolde was not distressed.

Choosing the content for your subordinate clauses

Although this topic is fairly easy, a few traps are sprinkled here and there. For example, what to put in each clause is generally a question of personal choice. Most writers believe that putting the important idea in the main clause and the other ideas in subordinate clauses is best. Here are some examples:

> IMPORTANT IDEA: Natasha ran over Alice's mother.

> LESS IMPORTANT IDEA: Alice's mother was wearing a green dress.

> GOOD SENTENCE: Natasha ran over Alice's mother, who was wearing a green dress.

> NOT-SO-GOOD SENTENCE: Alice's mother was wearing a green dress when Natasha ran over her.

IMPORTANT IDEA: Mike just won the lottery.

LESS IMPORTANT IDEA: Mike never wins anything.

GOOD SENTENCE: Mike, who never wins anything, just won the lottery.

NOT-SO-GOOD SENTENCE: Mike, who just won the lottery, never wins anything.

For more discussion on joining main and subordinate clauses, see Chapter 7.

Playing Truant

Wouldn't life be boring if we could never try anything new? Words, just like people, like to do something different occasionally. In this section, we'll tell you about some of the things they get up to.

Appreciating gerunds

Verbs like to play at being nouns occasionally. When they do this, they're called *gerunds*. Gerunds can't quite forget that they're verbs really:

- They end in –ing and look like verbs – *swimming, dripping, being, dancing, singing* and so on.
- They may be described by words or phrases that usually describe verbs – swimming *swiftly*, dripping *noisily*, being *in the moment*, dancing *to the rhythm of a great new song*, singing *yesterday* and so on.
- The types of clause that usually describe verbs may also describe gerunds – swimming *after the race ended*, dripping *when the cap is not tightened*, being *wherever you should be*, dancing *although you are tired*, singing *whenever you feel happy*.
- They may have objects or subject complements – swimming *lengths*, dripping *drops of gooey glop*, being *president of the Book Club*, dancing *the night away*, singing *ancient love songs* and so on.

But they have to remember to play the part of nouns. That means that:

- They may be subjects, objects and anything else that a noun can be.
- Words that usually describe nouns or pronouns – adjectives – may also describe gerunds (*my* swimming, *noisy* dripping, *choral* singing and so on). That's why we say *I hope you don't mind my asking* rather than *I hope you don't mind me asking*.

Here are a few examples, with the gerund and all the words associated with it (the *gerund phrase*, in grammarspeak) italicised:

> *Swimming the Channel* was not foremost in Sandy's mind when she got back from sailing round the world. (*swimming the Channel* = subject of the verb *was*)

> Ms Stakes, a neat person in every possible way, hated *my spilling tea on the rug*. (*my spilling tea on the rug* = direct object of the verb *hated*)

> The importance of *being earnest in one's playwriting* cannot be over-emphasised. (*being earnest in one's playwriting* = object of the preposition *of*)

> After *scratching Bibi on the nose*, Poppet took off at about 100 mph. (*scratching Bibi on the nose* = object of the preposition *after*)

> Bill gave *leaving the country* serious consideration. (*leaving the country* = object of the verb *gave*)

Working with infinitives

The *infinitive* is another happy wanderer. (See Chapter 2 for more information on infinitives.) The infinitive can't forget that at heart it's a verb:

- ✔ Infinitives look like verbs, with the word *to* tacked on in front – *to dance, to dream, to be, to dally* and so on.

- ✔ Words or phrases that usually describe verbs may also describe infinitives – to dance *divinely*, to dream *daily*, to be *in the kitchen*, to dally *for hours* and so on.

- ✔ Similarly, the type of clause that usually describes verbs may also describe infinitives – to dance *until the cows come home*, to dream *when your heart is breaking*, to be *wherever you want to be*, to dally *even though homework awaits* and so on.

- ✔ Infinitives may have objects or subject complements – to dance *a jig*, to dream *an impossible dream*, to be *silly* and so on.

But it can't resist having a go at everybody else's job too. You can catch it behaving as:

- ✔ A noun (acting as a subject, object or subject complement)

- ✔ An adjective (describing a noun)

- ✔ An adverb (describing a verb)

Here are a few examples of infinitives in their natural habitat, the sentence. The infinitive and the words associated with it (the *infinitive phrase*, in grammarspeak) are in italics:

> *To sing on Broadway* is Ellie's lifelong dream. (*to sing on Broadway* = the subject of the verb *is*)

> During rehearsals, Mortimer likes *to listen with his eyes closed*. (*to listen with his eyes closed* = the object of the verb *likes*)

> Rob's goal is *to be an engineer*. (*to be an engineer* = the subject complement of the verb *is*)

> Dr Mackenzie went to the nightclub *to find her son*. (*to find her son* describes the verb *went*)

> The book *to read* is the one by Dr Jones. (*to read* describes the noun *book*)

Participating with a participle

Last but not least is the participle. *Participles* are actually parts of verbs (hence the amazingly original name). So:

- ✔ Participles look like verb parts, though they may have several different forms. Some end with *–ing*, some with *–ed* and some with other letters. Also, they may have auxiliary verbs. *Driven*, *coping*, *exhausted*, *having crossed* and *gone* are a few examples of participles.

- ✔ Words or phrases that usually describe verbs may also describe participles (driven *home*, coping *bravely*, exhausted *by overwork*, having crossed *illegally*, gone *with the wind* and so on).

- ✔ Similarly, the types of clause that usually describe verbs may also describe participles (driven *although he has two perfectly good feet*, coping *bravely when tragedy strikes*, exhausted *because he doesn't delegate*, having crossed *where no man has crossed before* and so on).

- ✔ Participles may have objects or subject complements (driven *mad*, exhausted *the possibilities*, having crossed *the road* and so on).

But they like to moonlight as adjectives, and when they do they may appear in several different spots in the sentence:

- ✔ They may precede the noun or pronoun that they describe: *tired* feet (the participle *tired* describes the noun *feet*), *sneezing* dwarfs (the participle *sneezing* describes the noun *dwarfs*), *burped* baby (the participle *burped* describes the noun *baby*).

- ✔ They may follow a linking verb, in which case they describe the subject. (A linking verb is a form of the verb *to be* or a sensory verb. See Chapter 2 for more information.) For example:

Lucinda is *exhausted.* (The participle *exhausted* follows the linking verb *is* and describes *Lucinda.*)

Ellie's song sounded *enchanting.* (The participle *enchanting* follows the linking verb *sounded* and describes *song.*)

✔ They may follow the noun or pronoun that they describe. In this position, participles often include descriptive words or objects. The participles and the words associated with them – the *participial* or *non-finite clauses* – are italicised here:

Yasmin, *having ordered the wedding cake*, went to discuss the invitations with George. (*Having ordered the wedding cake* describes *Yasmin.*)

I want to read the new book *published last week.* (*Published last week* describes *book.*)

✔ Participles may begin the sentence, in which case they must describe the subject of the sentence:

Poked in the tummy, the doll immediately said, 'Watch it, Buster!' (*Poked in the tummy* describes *doll.*)

Crushed against the door of the train, Lucinda swore never to travel on the Underground again. (*Crushed against the door of the train* describes *Lucinda.*)

Spicing Up Boring Sentences

Subordinate clauses, gerunds, infinitives and participles put a lot of information into little packages, which makes your sentences more interesting. They also help you vary the pattern of your sentences. Here's a before-and-after example. Which paragraph sounds better?

Mortimer bought a new camera. The camera was smaller than a matchbox. Mortimer gave the camera to Lucinda. Lucinda can be rather forgetful. She is especially forgetful now. Lucinda is planning a trip to New Zealand. Lucinda accidentally dropped the camera down the side of an armchair. The armchair was at her mother's house. The camera was lost for five months. Mortimer bought another camera. Then George found the first camera.

Mortimer bought a new camera, which was smaller than a matchbox, and gave it to Lucinda. She can be rather forgetful – especially now that she's planning a trip to New Zealand – and she accidentally dropped it down the side of an armchair at her mother's house. The camera was lost for five months before George found it, and by then Mortimer had bought another one.

You need to practise if you want to get a licence

Are you confused by the two spellings of license/licence and practise/practice? Allow us to advise you. It's really quite simple if you follow our advice. The verbs are spelled with an *s* and the nouns with a *c* (just as in *advise* and *advice*, which you probably have no difficulty with because they don't sound the same).

You probably said that the second paragraph was better. It's a bit shorter (65 words instead of 71), but length isn't the issue. The first paragraph is composed of 11 short, choppy sentences. The second one flows. It has only three sentences. Grammatically, the difference between the two is simple. The second paragraph has more subordinate clauses than the first.

You don't necessarily need to know how to find or label clauses, but you should read your writing aloud from time to time to check how it sounds. Are your sentences monotonous? Are they all more or less the same length? Do all your sentences follow the same pattern? Is everything subject–verb–object or subject–verb–complement? Have you strung a lot of short sentences together with *and* or a similar joining word? If so, your sentences need some first aid. Tucking more than one idea into a sentence saves words and makes your writing less choppy.

Combine these ideas into one or more sentences:

> Clarence bakes infrequently. He does bake with enthusiasm. His favourite recipe is for cake. The mixture must be stirred for three hours. Clarence orders his cook to do the stirring. The cook stirs and Clarence adds the cherries. Sometimes he throws in a spoonful of sultanas.

Answer: Many combinations are possible, including the following:

> Clarence's *baking* is infrequent but enthusiastic. His favourite cake recipe requires three hours of *stirring*, which Clarence orders his cook to do. *Adding* cherries and the occasional spoonful of sultanas is Clarence's job. (The italicised words are gerunds.)

> Clarence, who bakes infrequently but enthusiastically, excels at cooking his favourite cake, which requires three hours of stirring. Ordering his cook to stir, Clarence adds cherries and the occasional spoonful of sultanas. (*who bakes infrequently but enthusiastically* = subordinate clause, *cooking his favourite cake* = gerund, *which requires three hours of stirring* = subordinate clause, *ordering his cook* = participle, *to stir* = infinitive)

Chapter 25

The Last Word on Punctuation

*P*unctuation is one topic that you don't have to worry about when you're speaking. But oh, those little specks of ink do make your life miserable when you're writing. Commas, ellipses (little dots . . .), hyphens, parentheses and brackets can wreak havoc on your mind. And we haven't even mentioned the slash, which isn't the name of a horror film, but it could be.

Despite the terror most people feel when confronted with punctuation dilemmas, the rules actually follow a logical pattern. In this chapter we tackle some advanced punctuation rules. (For the basics of commas, see Chapter 14. For information about semicolons, colons and dashes, see Chapter 15.) With just a little effort, you'll find that your punctuation improves and your writing takes a giant step towards clarity.

Making Your Point Clear with Commas

When you're writing, keep in mind that each comma in your sentence should have a reason for being there. The most important reason, of course, is to make your meaning clear. Commas act as a signal to your reader. Commas separate some words from the rest of the sentence. The reader knows that words enclosed by commas are not part of the main idea of the sentence. Each comma marks a place where the reader may pause slightly, although it doesn't call for as long a pause as a full stop.

Essential or extra? Your commas tell the tale

To begin, here's the rule that tells you when to use commas with descriptions. If a description is essential to the meaning of the sentence, don't put commas round it. If the description is extra, non-essential information, set it off with commas. Consider the following situation. Clarence, who has a constitutional aversion to paying taxes, has been heard to express this opinion:

Taxes, which are a hardship for the people, are not acceptable.

Bert Witherby-Jones, who is a member of parliament, declares himself in complete agreement with Clarence's statement. However, his version has no commas:

Taxes which are a hardship for the people are not acceptable.

What's the difference? Do the commas really matter? Yes. They matter a lot. Here's the deal: *which are a hardship for the people* is a description. If the description is set off from the rest of the sentence by commas, the description is extra – not essential to the meaning of the sentence. You can cross it out and the sentence still means the same thing. Without the commas, the description is essential to the meaning of the sentence. It may not be removed without altering what you are saying. Can you see the difference between Clarence's statement and Bert's? Here's the original and expanded version of each:

CLARENCE'S ORIGINAL STATEMENT: Taxes, which are a hardship for the people, are not acceptable.

MEANING OF CLARENCE'S STATEMENT: The government should not impose taxes. Taxes are a problem for the people (meaning me). They (meaning I) have little enough money as it is. No taxes – that's the bottom line.

Because Clarence's original sentence includes commas, the description *which are a hardship for the people* is extra information. You can omit it from the sentence. Thus Clarence is against all taxes.

BERT'S ORIGINAL STATEMENT: Taxes which are a hardship for the people are not acceptable.

MEANING OF BERT'S STATEMENT: The government is against any taxes which are a hardship for the people. Of course we don't want to place a burden on working families. However, the new taxes introduced in the budget will not be a hardship; they allow the people to show their patriotism by contributing to government funds (and paying for the large increase in my salary). This particular new tax is acceptable.

Bert's proposal is much less extreme than Clarence's. Without commas, the description is a necessary part of the sentence. It gives the reader essential information about the meaning of *taxes*. Bert opposes only some taxes – those taxes that he believes are a burden. He isn't against all taxes. This description doesn't simply add a reason, as Clarence's does. Instead, it identifies the taxes that Bert opposes.

The pronouns *which* and *that* confuse a lot of people. Which one you should use depends on the same rules as the use of commas. *That* introduces information that the sentence can't do without – essential information that isn't set off by commas. However, if you need commas (because the information is non-essential), you need *which*. (You can't put commas round *that* clauses.)

So far so good, but this is where it gets confusing. (So stop now if you're still getting to grips with the 'tax' sentences – you can come back to this later.) You are also allowed to use *which* where *that* would be correct. (Lots of people prefer the sound of *which* and think it gives their sentences better style.) Just be sure to get the commas right, and don't be frightened by your computer – if the grammar checker puts a green underline under things, it will underline every *which* that hasn't got a comma in front of it for you to check. This doesn't automatically mean that it's wrong. Be careful to use *that* if there's any risk that your readers will misunderstand, though.

Sometimes, long sentences contain two essential clauses. According to the straightforward *which*/*that* rules, both should begin with *that*. However, English doesn't like to repeat words unnecessarily, and because *that* and *which* are interchangeable in essential clauses we have a neat alternative: use *that* for the first clause and *which* for the second. Here's an example:

> Lucinda returned the dress that was too tight and which scratched her neck. (She kept the one that fitted perfectly and the one that was tight but didn't scratch as she figured she'd get into it if she stuck to her diet for a couple of weeks.)

If you're re-reading this section because you're struggling to work out whether commas are necessary in one of your sentences and whether you need a *which* or a *that*, you've just discovered the big secret about language that experts don't want to admit: *language doesn't follow the rules*. Sometimes, what you're trying to say isn't obviously one thing or the other. (Wouldn't it be neat and tidy if it was!) If so, relax. Leave out the commas and use *which*.

If you want the grammatical terms, essential and non-essential clauses are sometimes called *defining* and *non-defining* clauses; they're also sometimes called *restrictive* and *non-restrictive* clauses. It's OK – you can forget that now.

Check out these additional examples, with the description in italics:

> SENTENCE: The students *who are planning a sit-in tomorrow* want to be paid for doing homework.

PUNCTUATION ANALYSIS: The description is not set off by commas, so you may not omit it.

WHAT THE SENTENCE MEANS: Some of the students – those who are planning a sit-in – want to be paid for doing homework. Not all the students want to be paid. The rest are perfectly content to do homework for absolutely no money.

SENTENCE: The employees, planning industrial action, have given the television network exclusive rights to cover their work-to-rule.

PUNCTUATION ANALYSIS: The commas indicate that the description is extra, non-essential information.

WHAT THE SENTENCE MEANS: All the employees are involved. They're quite upset, and all have prepared statements for the press.

Which sentence means that there won't be any flights to take you to Manchester for your cousin's wedding?

A. The pilots who are going on strike demand that music be piped into the cockpit.

B. The pilots, who are going on strike, demand that music be piped into the cockpit.

Answer: Sentence B means that all the pilots are going on strike. The description between the commas may be omitted without changing the meaning of the sentence. In sentence A, only the pilots who like music are going on strike (so you probably won't have to take a train).

Do your commas have appositive influence?

If you're seeing double when you read a sentence, you've probably encountered an *appositive*. An appositive is a noun or a pronoun that's exactly the same as the noun or pronoun that precedes it in the sentence. Some appositives are set off by commas and some aren't. The rule is that if the appositive is more specific, don't use commas; if it's less specific, use commas.

Now put the rule into practice. What's the difference between these two sentences?

Mortimer's play *Dinner for Two* is the least understandable of all the plays that he has produced.

Dinner for Two, Mortimer's play, is the least understandable of all the plays that he has produced.

In the first sample sentence, *Dinner for Two* is the appositive of *Mortimer's play.* In the second sample sentence, *Mortimer's play* is the appositive of *Dinner for Two.*

To put the rule another way, if you're sure that your readers will know what you're talking about before they get to the appositive, set off the appositive with commas. If you're not sure your readers will know exactly what you're talking about by the time they get to the appositive, you should not use commas. If the appositive gives identifying, essential information, don't use commas. If the appositive gives extra information, do use commas.

In the first example, the reader doesn't know which one of Mortimer's plays is being discussed. The appositive supplies the name. Hence, the appositive is essential and isn't set off by commas. In the second sentence the reader already knows the name of the play. The fact that it's Mortimer's play is extra information and must therefore be surrounded by commas.

Here are a few more examples:

> SENTENCE: Natasha has five sisters, but her sister Olga is definitely her favourite.
>
> APPOSITIVE: *Olga* is the appositive of *sister.*
>
> PUNCTUATION ANALYSIS: Because Natasha has five sisters, you don't know which sister is being discussed until you have the name. *Olga* identifies the sister and shouldn't be placed between commas.
>
> SENTENCE: Mortimer has only one sibling. His brother, Clarence, does not approve of Mortimer's marriage.
>
> APPOSITIVE: *Clarence* is the appositive of *brother.*
>
> PUNCTUATION ANALYSIS: Because Mortimer has only one sibling, the reader knows that he has only one brother. Thus the words *his brother* pinpoint the person being discussed in the sentence. The name is extra information, not identifying information. Therefore, you should place the name between commas.

Which sentence is correct?

A. Lucinda's mother, Vicky, doesn't approve of her daughter's recent extravagance.

B. Lucinda's mother Vicky doesn't approve of her daughter's recent extravagance.

Answer: Sentence A is correct. Lucinda has only one mother, so the name is extra, not identifying information.

Try another. Which sentence about Edgar's third book is correct?

A. Edgar's book *Monster for Hire* reprinted twice within three months of its publication.

B. Edgar's book, *Monster for Hire*, reprinted twice within three months of its publication.

Answer: This question is a bit tricky. How many books has Edgar written? If he had written only one, sentence B would be acceptable. But he has written more than one (*Monster for Hire* is his third), so sentence A is the better choice because the title supplies identifying information.

Punctuating independently

When you join two complete sentences with the conjunctions *and*, *or*, *but*, *nor*, *yet*, *so* or *for*, it can help your readers if you put a comma before the conjunction. Here's an example:

> Mike may ask Susie to marry him when they have dinner together next week, or he may ask her at the weekend.

For more information on punctuation with conjunctions, see Chapter 7. For more information on complete sentences, see Chapter 5.

Some sentences have one subject (who or what you're talking about) and two verbs joined by *and*, *or*, *nor* or *but*. Don't put commas between the two verbs. You aren't joining two complete sentences, just two words or groups of words. Here are two examples:

> WRONG: When Mike asked her to marry him, Susie said nothing, and cried for an hour.

> WHY IT'S WRONG: The sentence has one subject (Susie) that has two verbs (*said* and *cried*). You aren't joining two complete sentences here, so you shouldn't place a comma before *and*.

> RIGHT: When Mike asked her to marry him, Susie said nothing and cried for an hour.

> WRONG: Mortimer wanted to take Lucinda away for a holiday, but has been too busy to take time off.

> WHY IT'S WRONG: The sentence has one subject (Mortimer) and two verbs (*wanted* and *has been*). The word *but* joins the two verbs, not two complete sentences. You don't need a comma.

> RIGHT: Mortimer wanted to take Lucinda away for a holiday but has been too busy to take time off.

Which sentence is correct?

   A. Susie opens envelopes with a letter opener, but Bibi opens them with her teeth.

   B. Rashid answers every letter on the day he receives it but doesn't pay any bills immediately.

Answer: Both sentences are correct. In sentence A, the conjunction *but* joins two complete sentences. A comma before the conjunction *but* is allowed (and often helpful to the reader). In sentence B, *but* joins two verbs (*answers* and *does pay*), so you mustn't put a comma before the conjunction.

Saving Time with Ellipsis

We sometimes don't bother to say (or write) words that are obvious from the context. This is called ellipsis. The rule is that the missing word (or words) must be present in the sentence in the correct form for the reader to fill in the missing words accurately. Look at this sentence:

> WRONG: When Bill is in one of his moods, he goes for long walks, wearing an old raincoat and frequently all the dogs.

Obviously what we mean is that he frequently *takes* all the dogs. Unfortunately the word *takes* or *taking* isn't present anywhere in the sentence. The word we're being offered to fill in the hole is *wearing*. So Bill frequently goes for walks *wearing* all the dogs!

> RIGHT: When Bill is in one of his moods, he goes for long walks, wearing an old raincoat and frequently taking all the dogs. (Nothing is left out.)

Try this one:

> WRONG: 'I don't and never have needed anyone to protect me,' shouted Hazel.

What Hazel means is 'I don't *need* anyone. I never have needed anyone.' This time we have the correct verb, but it's not in the right form: we're only given *needed*, not *need*.

> RIGHT: 'I don't need and never have needed anyone to protect me,' shouted Hazel. (Nothing is left out.)

Try one more:

> RIGHT: Natasha assured Mike that the decorating would be completed by Wednesday and the carpets laid early the next week.

The complete sentence would be this:

> ALSO RIGHT: Natasha assured Mike that the decorating would be completed by Wednesday and the carpets *would be* laid early the next week.

In the first version, we left out the words *would be*. But the missing words are nearby in the sentence and we can fill them in for ourselves, so it's OK to leave them out.

With this sort of ellipsis we don't need to indicate where the words are missing. People are good at understanding language and don't need any help as long as the missing bits are used somewhere nearby.

Indicating missing words in quotations

There's another kind of ellipsis, where the words exist (because a person has spoken them or written them) but we decide to omit them when reporting them later. When you're quoting someone else's words, you can't leave bits out without saying so. It's just plain rude! So place three dots (and only three dots – never five or six or more) wherever you've left out words from the original. The dots are also called *ellipses*. (One set is an *ellipsis.*)

If you delete the end of a sentence, use four dots: three for the ellipsis and one for the full stop. (Most people agree that this is more correct than using just three dots and assuming that the full stop is included with the deleted words.) Some people like to make the space before the fourth dot bigger (like this: ... .) or smaller (like this: . . ..) to make it clearer that the fourth dot is the full stop at the end of the sentence like this. Others prefer to space all the dots equally (.... or . . . .) These are just style choices.

For more about the rules on leaving bits out of quotations, see Chapter 13.

Here's Isolde's description of what she did last night as written in her diary. The parts that she'll leave out when she explains to her teacher why she hasn't done her homework are in italics. Rewrite the paragraph omitting the italicised words and punctuate the quotation properly.

> I sat down at the computer last night to write the essay. I truly love writing essays, *I don't think,* and I certainly want to do well in this class *if I can get good grades without doing a stitch of work.* I began to write shortly before eight o'clock, but *the phone rang almost immediately. I spoke with my friends for no more than three hours. Then my mother asked me if I wanted a snack. I said yes. I ate two or three large pizzas and settled down at the computer.* Then my stomach hurt, and I was very tired. I had to go to bed. I'll do the essay tonight.

Answer:

> I sat down at the computer last night to write the essay. I truly love writing essays, . . . and I certainly want to do well in this class. . . . I began to write shortly before eight o'clock, but . . . my stomach hurt, and I was very tired. I had to go to bed. I'll do the essay tonight.

The first ellipsis has three dots because the missing words are from the middle of the sentence. The second ellipsis has four dots: three for the missing words and one for the full stop at the end of the sentence. The third ellipsis has three dots covering a multitude of sins – whole sentences missing and bit of sentences, allowing the text on both sides of the deleted text to be connected as a sentence. The only way to do this is with three dots.

We've been having some fun, leaving out key information here. But Isolde's being dishonest and you shouldn't follow her example! One of the most important issues in writing is credibility. If you change the meaning of what you're quoting by leaving out crucial details, your readers will figure this out eventually, and then they won't trust anything you say. (Also, your teacher may fail you.) Check the passage you're quoting before and after you've cut it. Does each convey the same message? If not, don't cut it.

Showing hesitation

You can also use ellipses to show hesitation, particularly in dialogue:

> I don't know what to do about that bill! It's already overdue . . . I just don't have enough money to pay it . . . What am I going to do . . . ?

Using ellipses in this way can get really annoying really fast. Think of the dots as bad jokes. Don't overuse them!

H-y-p-h-e-n-a-t-i-n-g Made Easy

You need hyphens to help you manoeuvre through unexpected line breaks and for a couple of other reasons as well – to separate parts of compound words, to write certain numbers and to create one description from two words. This section provides you with a guide to the care and feeding of the humble hyphen.

Understanding the great divide

Computer users have to worry about hyphens less often than other writers. Most of the time, the word processing program moves a word to a new line if there isn't enough room at the end of a line for the entire word. But sometimes, when you're writing by hand or typing on an old-fashioned typewriter, for example, you need to divide a word. And, if you decide to allow your computer to break words at the ends of lines, you'll need to check that it has made sensible breaks. (The computer doesn't check a dictionary to see where to break a word, it follows a set of rules – and the rules don't always get it right.)

Why should you divide a word? Mostly to make your writing look better. If you want to keep both margins straight (*justified* if you want the technical term), breaking words to fill the lines gives you better spacing. The computer can also give you a ragged right margin if you prefer, but if you have a very long word – supercalifragilisticexpialidocious, for example, or Raxacoricofallapatorius – the computer will move it to a new line when you've filled only half of the preceding line. So it can help to avoid very short lines if you break words occasionally.

If you have to divide a word, follow these simple rules:

- Place the hyphen between the syllables or sounds, of a word. (If you're not sure where the breaks should go, check a word-break dictionary.) But if there's a doubled consonant, break the word between them (as in mes-sage).

- Check that the break doesn't make it hard to see what the word is. (Pronoun-cement, for example, and mans-laughter are bad breaks.)

- Don't leave only one letter on a line. If you have a choice, divide the word more or less in the middle.

- Don't divide words that have only one syllable.

- Don't add more hyphens to a phrase that has a hyphen or hyphens in it already: break it at an existing hyphen.

- Don't break the last word in a paragraph or the last word on a page.

- To divide a word, be sure to use a hyphen (-), which is a short line. Don't use a dash (– or —), which is a longer line and a completely different punctuation mark. (See Chapter 15 for more information on dashes.)

There's just one wrinkle in all this. There are actually two systems for breaking words. The rules above describe the most common one (breaking words according to the sound – the syllables) because it's what you're most likely to see in books and it's what your computer will do. But it's also possible to break words according to their derivation. The difference is that the 'syllable' system gives you photog-raphy and democ-racy, but the 'derivation' system gives you photo-graphy and demo-cracy. You can follow the syllable system by applying common sense, but if you want to follow the other system you may need a word-break dictionary to help you get the breaks right. (Try the *Oxford Minidictionary of Spelling and Word-Division*.)

Using hyphens for compound words

Hyphens also separate parts of compound words, such as *ex-wife*, *pro-choice*, *one-way* and so forth. When you type or write these words, don't put a space before or after the hyphen. If you don't know whether a particular expression is a compound word, a single word or two separate words, check the dictionary.

Are you wondering how to capitalise compound words? For information on capitalisation, see Chapter 16.

Placing hyphens in numbers

Decisions about whether to write a number in numerals or in words are questions of style, not of grammar. The authority figure in your life – teacher, boss, probation officer or whatever – will tell you what they prefer.

In general, larger numbers are usually represented by numerals. People just have different ideas about what *large* means. Some stop writing words out after nine, others after ninety-nine. And in a dictionary of your favourite subject you may find there's so little space that all numbers are written in numerals. Follow the style your company or teacher prefers, and if you have a choice decide on your own rule but make sure you're consistent. However, if the number falls at the beginning of a sentence you must use words because no sentence may begin with a numeral. You may also need to write out a fraction (for example, *four-fifths*) or any number that's an approximation (for example, *about three hundred*).

Here's how to hyphenate numbers:

- Hyphenate all the numbers from twenty-one to ninety-nine.
- Hyphenate all fractions used as descriptions (three-quarters full, for example).
- You don't have to hyphenate fractions used as nouns (three quarters of the pizza, one third of students), but some people prefer to.

The well-placed hyphen

Here's another simple rule concerning hyphens: if two words are being used as a single description, put a hyphen between them if the description comes before the word that it's describing. For example:

> We need a long-term solution.

but

> We can't go on doing this in the long term. (because *long term* isn't describing anything here)

The issue is ambiguity. Where people may be confused about whether *long* is describing *term* or *solution*, the hyphen makes it clear that it's describing *term*. Of course, in a lot of cases there's no ambiguity at all, but lots of people like to add the hyphens anyway. That's OK – it's a style choice. (As always, just be consistent.)

There's no need to hyphenate two-word descriptions if the first word is an adverb (most of these ends in –*ly*), as there's rarely any ambiguity:

> nicely drawn rectangle
>
> fully understood idea
>
> completely ridiculous grammar rule

You can't have a *nicely rectangle*, a *fully idea* or a *completely rule* so it's obvious what the meaning is. But, again, some people like to put hyphens here (*nicely-drawn* and so on). Well, if you must, you must, but the hyphen isn't doing anything useful.

Well is also an adverb, but it sometimes causes problems, so most people prefer to keep the hyphen here:

> I like a well-placed hyphen.

(even though no one's really likely to think that you mean a *well hyphen*) but not here:

> That hyphen is well placed.

Place hyphens where they're needed in this paragraph:

> Vicky was recently elected secretary treasurer of her local reading group. Over two thirds of the members voted for her. Some of them think that she can get Edgar to speak to the group, but she also has many kind hearted friends.

Answer: Here's the paragraph with the hyphens inserted, along with explanations in parentheses:

> Vicky was recently elected secretary-treasurer (a hyphen is needed for a compound title) of her local reading group. Over two thirds of the members (no hyphens are necessary for fractions that aren't being used as descriptions, but you can add one if you prefer) voted for her. Some of them think that she can get Edgar to speak to the group, but she also has many kind-hearted friends (most people prefer to add a hyphen to a two-word description).

Slashing Your Sentences

The slash (or solidus in printing terminology) seldom appears in your writing, and/or you're unlikely to need it. The computer has probably done more to increase the number of slashes than any other machine/event/application. Are you tired/irritated/angry with this paragraph yet? Answer yes/no.

OK, here's the deal. You can use the slash (which means *or*) when you need to present alternatives, but try try try to find a way to avoid it.

Slashes have one other important job. If you're writing about poetry and quoting some lines, the slash shows the reader where the poet ended one line and began another. Here's an excerpt from Dr Jones's essay on a poem written by Edgar:

> The exertion of mountain climbing has contributed to the imagery Edwards employs in his poem 'Everest or Nothing': 'and then the harsh/breath of the mountain/meets the harsh/breath of the climber/ I am/the climber.'

The slashes tell us that the lines of Edgar's poem were arranged as follows:

and then the harsh
breath of the mountain
meets the harsh
breath of the climber
I am
the climber.

Part VI
The Part of Tens

'Is that all the help I get? Keep
using the Computer Grammar Checker?
A fine muse you are!'

In this part . . .

This section opens the door to a grammatical life beyond *English Grammar For Dummies*. After you've absorbed the rules of grammar, you've still got to apply them. Chapter 26 provides ten strategies to improve your proofreading. (After reading this chapter, you'll never sign a letter 'Yours turly' again.) Chapter 27 lists ten ways to train your ear for good English, a process that inevitably improves your speech and writing. You may not follow all the suggestions (especially the one that tells you to hang out with nerds), but you'll find at least some appealing.

Chapter 26

Ten Ways ~~Two~~ to Improve Your Proofreading

- -

- -

*Y*ou read it 50 times and finally post it. It's so important that you can't stop checking it even when it's too late to change it. Unable to calm your fears, you sit down to read the text for the 51st time. And that's when you finally see it – an error. Not a little error, but a big one. An embarrassing one. Nothing short of a murder of the English language. Sound familiar? If so, you need some proofreading help. In this chapter, we give you ten tricks to improve that all-important final check.

Read Like a Professional Proofreader

It may come as a shock to you to find out that professional proofreaders don't read all those books they're being paid to proofread. If you asked them questions about what they'd just read, they probably wouldn't know the answers. 'Just like at school,' you're thinking. It is. And the reason is exactly the same – they were thinking about something else. They were looking for the closing bracket to match that opening one, looking at the numbers in that list to see that they were all in order, checking that the verb agreed with the subject in every sentence, checking the punctuation and – above all – looking at the spelling of every word. They spell words out, as though they're only just learning to read, and even mispronounce words (deliberately and only in their heads, at least *most* of the time) in ways that help them remember how to spell them. And they're *very* slow. They even look carefully at every little word, to make absolutely sure that it's the *right* little word. (You may not look at them at all when you're reading for fun.) If you could hear how a proofreader was reading the words, it would go something like this:

Sat ur day morn ing (comma) she *leap ed* (italics) out of bed be fore six a(full stop no space)m(full stop) (space)

They're probably not thinking the words in brackets, but they're *actively* seeing those things and watching to see that they are in all the places that they should be. If an a.m. pops up without its full stops, you can bet they'll notice.

This is a different sort of reading, and you can teach yourself to do it too. All you need is practice. Of course, you will *read* your work as well. But, for the best results, at least one read should be a *proofread*, when you stop looking at the wonderful forest you've created and look instead at each individual tree.

Read Backwards

OK, reading backwards sounds crazy, but sometimes we're so close to the stuff we've written and so concerned about what we're saying that we can't make the switch from reading to proofreading. And, let's face it, however great an author you are, the seventh time you re-read your work you may be just a little bit bored with it and tempted to rush. And proper proofreading has to be *slooooow*. You've got to do something different to break the monotony. If you read backwards (word by word or sentence by sentence), you're in a better frame of mind to catch spelling errors because reading in the wrong direction means that you aren't being distracted by the meaning.

Wait a While

Another way to get some perspective on what you've written is to distance yourself from it by putting it away and doing something else. Go to an aerobics class, remodel the garden or just work on something else for a few days (or weeks). Like those actors who find it unbearably painful to watch the films they've made (because they can see so many ways in which they could have done it better), most authors have (at least once) looked at something they created only a month ago and wondered how they managed to write such utter drivel.

Of course, for this to work, you must leave some time before the deadline. If you finish your report three nanoseconds before the boss wants to see it, you can't use this technique.

Read It Aloud

Reading aloud helps you experience your writing in a different way. So put the radio on or lock yourself in the bathroom (or, if all else fails, explain *calmly* to the nice men in white coats what it is that you're doing). Take the paper and read the words in a normal speaking voice. Did you stumble anywhere? If so, you may have come across an error. Stop, circle the spot and continue. Later, check all the circles. Chances are you'll find something that should be different.

Delete Half the Commas

Most people tend to use too many commas. There are lots of places in English where commas are allowed but not always required, and as your writing becomes more interesting your sentences will get longer and you'll instinctively put more commas in. The problem for your readers is that if you have eight or nine commas in a sentence they can't see which commas form pairs and how the little bits of text relate to each other. If you're not yet confident with commas, aim to limit yourself to one comma or one pair of commas in each sentence. Of course you can have more commas if the sentence really needs them, but if you try to keep them to the minimum you will find some that you can do without, or even places where you can shorten a sentence or use a semicolon or dashes. (But don't overdo them either.)

Swap with a Friend

The best proofreading comes from a fresh pair of eyes. So, always be prepared to read your friend's report, novel, letter home to their parents asking for money, or whatever. You'll see lots of errors in your friend's writing and you'll be able to make all sorts of helpful suggestions for improving it. You'll delete all their irritating mannerisms and find places where you're not sure what they meant. And, of course, you'll find their spelling mistakes and errors of punctuation. This will give you a wonderful warm feeling because you know that you've been a great help to them. So, when they do the same to you, **do not** storm off and refuse to speak to them ever again. Accept their criticism gracefully, in the spirit in which it was intended. You can, after all, ignore their helpful suggestions if you want. But they're probably right.

Let the Computer Help

After you've finished writing, go back and check whatever the stupid machine's grumbling about (the red and green lines or whatever). Don't trust the computer to make the corrections for you: it makes too many mistakes. The computer identifies only *possible* mistakes and misses many errors (any word that's a word but not the right word, in fact). Let your own knowledge of grammar and a good dictionary help you decide whether you need to change something.

Check the Sentence Length

Shorter sentences are easier to manage, so look at each sentence and ask yourself whether it would be better as two. You will find that you make fewer grammatical errors in shorter sentences. And your readers will find the reading easier.

The Usual Suspects

Do you have mistakes that you make a lot? Perhaps a tendency to hold the shift key down a little too long, so many words have TWo CApital LEtters? Are there words that you never type correctly (like becasue)? Some of these aren't a problem because they're EAsy to SEe or because the computer will point them out to you. Others can cause major problems. The computer won't query *from* when you meant *form* or – much worse – *now* when you meant *not* because it doesn't know the difference. Look at these (and other) problem words particularly carefully.

Draw up a Checklist

While you're thinking about this, make yourself a checklist (with boxes to tick) of things to look at separately, like this:

❑ Paragraphs not too long

❑ Verbs agree with subjects

❑ Not too many dashes

❑ Spelled my own name correctly

❑ *and so on*

Your checklist will be unique because it will deal with your peculiar problems. It will grow as you think of new things, but it can get shorter, too, as your writing develops and your grammar improves.

The last thing to do before putting that important letter in the post (or sending that vital e-mail) is to go through your checklist, ticking the boxes, to make sure that you haven't forgotten anything.

Chapter 27

Ten Ways to Learn Better Grammar

*Y*es, we admit it. This book helps you learn grammar, but (sigh) it's not the only way to improve your communication skills. A few other resources may also help you in your quest for perfect language. In this chapter, we suggest ten ways to learn better grammar.

Read Good Books

Good books usually contain good writing and, if you read some, pretty soon your own speech and writing will improve. How do you know whether a particular volume contains good writing? Read the reviews. Read the blurb on the back of the book, looking particularly for comments written by people who don't work for the publisher. Ask at your local bookshop, and chat to book-minded friends. Classics are always a choice (although the older they are, the more old-fashioned their grammar rules will be), but you will also find modern texts, both fiction and non-fiction, written according to the best grammar rules.

Incidentally, there's no law that says you have to finish every book you start. If you read a couple of chapters and don't like the characters, or hate the way the author writes, **stop if you want to**. (Unless, of course, you're going to have to write about it in an exam.) And you don't have to finish it by some imagined deadline. (You do if there's a *real* deadline, set by your boss.) If you borrow a book do give it back as soon as possible (library books, but especially anything you borrow from a friend – unless you want to lose the friend). But if it's your own copy you can take as long as you like and savour it in small pieces while reading other things in between. You don't even have to start at the beginning and read it in order. (We actually know people who like to read the end first, and enjoy a mystery much more if they know who the killer was before they start. You work it out!)

The point is to expose your mind to proper English. When you read, you hear the author's voice. You become accustomed to proper language. After a while correct grammar sounds natural to you, and you detect non-standard English more easily.

Watch Good Television

When we say *good* television, we're talking about programmes in which people actually converse. This doesn't necessarily mean programmes with nothing but experts talking (although they're good). If you find these hard going, try nature programmes and documentaries – even the news. (Watch them in secret if you're afraid of ruining your reputation.) Even thrillers can be helpful if you pick them carefully: go for the ones set among the aristocracy, in the past, or in perfect villages or university towns (or any combination of these), rather than the ones described as 'gritty' in the programme listings. Don't expect to pick up the finer points of grammar on TV (even in the best programmes no one's perfect), but you can get some pointers on the basics.

Read the Newspaper

Well, read *some* newspapers. You already know which papers are considered the classier ones. Maybe you read one of them regularly already. Or maybe you avoid them like the plague. (Or maybe you don't read newspapers at all!) Try an experiment and buy *all* the papers one day in the week when you have nothing special planned for the coming weekend. See how they cover the big stories and compare the writing styles of their contributors. Read with a grammarian's eye (if the thought isn't too frightening for you), absorbing *how* the writer expresses an idea. You may find it interesting. (At least you'll get to see some different cartoons and do a different crossword for a change.)

Flip through Magazines

If all the words in a magazine are in little bubbles above brightly coloured drawings, you may not find complete sentences and proper pronoun usage. However, most published writers have at least the fundamentals of good grammar, and you can learn a lot from reading publications aimed at an educated audience. How do you know whether a publication is aimed at an educated audience? Check the articles. If they seem to address issues that you associate with thoughtful readers, you're okay. Even if they address issues that aren't associated with thoughtful readers, you may still be okay. Reading well-written magazine articles will give you some models of reasonably correct grammar. And, as a side effect, you'll learn something.

Visit Nerd Hangouts

Nerd is a word based on value judgments. What most people deem nerdy (or whatever the current slang equivalent is), others may call *educated*. We're not saying that the locker room or the pub is filled with uneducated people. We're saying that you ought (occasionally) to investigate some spots where people gather when they're in the mood to talk about something other than football. Do you live near a bookshop that runs cultural events? Do you have a local book club? Is anything happening at your library? (Check out their noticeboard.) Have you ever signed up for an evening class? How often do you relax over a coffee at your local cafe and just listen to what the world's saying and how they're saying it? Your ear for good grammar will sharpen over time.

Check Out Strunk and White

The Elements of Style (published by Longman) is small enough to fit in a pocket. Authors William Strunk Jr and E.B. White (yes, the fellow who wrote *Charlotte's Web* and *Stuart Little*) tackle a few grammar issues and make important points about style. You'll spend an hour or two reading it and a lifetime absorbing its lessons.

Listen to Authorities

Listen! Your teacher or boss probably says that word often, and you should (pause to arrange a dutiful expression) always do what your personal authority figures say. Apart from all the other reasons, you should listen in order to learn better grammar. By speaking properly, they are probably giving you English lessons along with the detention or the projected sales figures or whatever.

Review Manuals of Style

No, manuals of style won't tell you whether *aubergine* is one of this year's approved colors or what kind of nose ring Hollywood favours this month. They may tell you, in exhaustive (and exhausting) detail, where to put every punctuation mark ever invented, what to capitalise, how to address an ambassador, and lots of other things that you never really wanted to know. Some universities produce style guidelines for students to follow when writing their thesis or dissertation. And some publications (*The Times* newspaper and *The Economist* magazine, for example) have their own style manuals, which they publish as books *(The Times Style and Usage Guide* and *The Economist Style Guide)*. The company you work for may have a Plain English Policy and a comprehensive style guide of its own. If not, your boss (especially if one of the stickler variety) may have a favourite, and asking what it is can't hurt your career. Use these as a reference for the picky little things and as a guide to the important issues of writing.

Surf the Internet

We can't leave this one out, though the Internet contains as many traps as it does guiding lights. Type *grammar* in a search engine and press Enter. Sit back and prepare yourself for a flood of sites explaining the rules of grammar. Some sites are very good; some are horrible. Look for ones run by universities or good quality publications. And talk to friends to find out which ones they like and have found useful.

Build Your Own Reference Library

There are lots of books on grammar. Some present the subject in some sort of logical order (as *English Grammar For Dummies* does). Others present smaller topics in alphabetical order. These often have the word *Usage* in the title (rather than *Grammar*). A notable one is *Fowler's Modern English Usage*. H.W. Fowler wrote it in 1926 and, when it became necessary for other people to take over keeping it up-to-date, his name slipped into the title. The latest edition (the third, 1996) is edited by R.W. Burchfield.

There are others that we like, but it's time for you to go out on your own and find the books (and websites and people and . . . you know what we mean) that help you. (And that you enjoy.) Don't worry. Every book you dip into will lead you to another . . . and another . . . Good hunting!

Index

● *B* ●

FOR DUMMIES®

Do Anything. Just Add Dummies

ROPERTY

UK editions

Buying and Selling a Home For Dummies
0-7645-7027-7

Renting Out Your Property For Dummies
0-470-02921-8

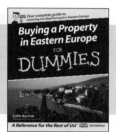

Buying a Property in Eastern Europe For Dummies
0-7645-7047-1

RSONAL FINANCE

Investing For Dummies
0-7645-7023-4

Bookkeeping For Dummies
0-470-05815-3

Sorting Out Your Finances For Dummies
0-7645-7039-0

USINESS

Starting a Business For Dummies
0-7645-7018-8

Marketing For Dummies
0-7645-7056-0

Business Plans For Dummies
0-7645-7026-9

Answering Tough Interview Questions For Dummies (0-470-01903-4)

Arthritis For Dummies (0-470-02582-4)

Being the Best Man For Dummies (0-470-02657-X)

British History For Dummies (0-470-03536-6)

Building Confidence For Dummies (0-470-01669-8)

Buying a Home on a Budget For Dummies (0-7645-7035-8)

Children's Health For Dummies (0-470-02735-5)

Cognitive Behavioural Therapy For Dummies (0-470-01838-0)

Cricket For Dummies (0-470-03454-8)

CVs For Dummies (0-7645-7017-X)

Detox For Dummies (0-470-01908-5)

Diabetes For Dummies (0-7645-7019-6)

Divorce For Dummies (0-7645-7030-7)

DJing For Dummies (0-470-03275-8)

eBay.co.uk For Dummies (0-7645-7059-5)

European History For Dummies (0-7645-7060-9)

Gardening For Dummies (0-470-01843-7)

Genealogy Online For Dummies (0-7645-7061-7)

Golf For Dummies (0-470-01811-9)

Hypnotherapy For Dummies (0-470-01930-1)

Irish History For Dummies (0-7645-7040-4)

Neuro-linguistic Programming For Dummies (0-7645-7028-5)

Nutrition For Dummies (0-7645-7058-7)

Parenting For Dummies (0-470-02714-2)

Pregnancy For Dummies (0-7645-7042-0)

Retiring Wealthy For Dummies (0-470-02632-4)

Rugby Union For Dummies (0-470-03537-4)

Small Business Employment Law For Dummies (0-7645-7052-8)

Starting a Business on eBay.co.uk For Dummies (0-470-02666-9)

Su Doku For Dummies (0-470-01892-5)

The GL Diet For Dummies (0-470-02753-3)

The Romans For Dummies (0-470-03077-1)

Thyroid For Dummies (0-470-03172-7)

UK Law and Your Rights For Dummies (0-470-02796-7)

Winning on Betfair For Dummies (0-470-02856-4)

FOR DUMMIES®

Do Anything. Just Add Dummies

HOBBIES

0-7645-5232-5

0-7645-6847-7

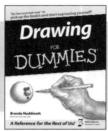

0-7645-5476-X

Also available:

Art For Dummies
(0-7645-5104-3)
Aromatherapy For Dummies
(0-7645-5171-X)
Bridge For Dummies
(0-471-92426-1)
Card Games For Dummies
(0-7645-9910-0)
Chess For Dummies
(0-7645-8404-9)

Improving Your Memory
For Dummies
(0-7645-5435-2)
Massage For Dummies
(0-7645-5172-8)
Meditation For Dummies
(0-471-77774-9)
Photography For Dummies
(0-7645-4116-1)
Quilting For Dummies
(0-7645-9799-X)

EDUCATION

0-7645-7206-7

0-7645-5581-2

0-7645-5422-0

Also available:

Algebra For Dummies
(0-7645-5325-9)
Algebra II For Dummies
(0-471-77581-9)
Astronomy For Dummies
(0-7645-8465-0)
Buddhism For Dummies
(0-7645-5359-3)
Calculus For Dummies
(0-7645-2498-4)

Forensics For Dummies
(0-7645-5580-4)
Islam For Dummies
(0-7645-5503-0)
Philosophy For Dummies
(0-7645-5153-1)
Religion For Dummies
(0-7645-5264-3)
Trigonometry For Dummies
(0-7645-6903-1)

PETS

0-470-03717-2

0-7645-8418-9

0-7645-5275-9

Also available:

Labrador Retrievers
For Dummies
(0-7645-5281-3)
Aquariums For Dummies
(0-7645-5156-6)
Birds For Dummies
(0-7645-5139-6)
Dogs For Dummies
(0-7645-5274-0)
Ferrets For Dummies
(0-7645-5259-7)

Golden Retrievers
For Dummies
(0-7645-5267-8)
Horses For Dummies
(0-7645-9797-3)
Jack Russell Terriers
For Dummies
(0-7645-5268-6)
Puppies Raising & Training
Diary For Dummies
(0-7645-0876-8)

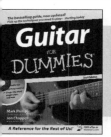

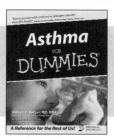

FOR DUMMIES®

Helping you expand your horizons and achieve your potential

INTERNET

The Internet For Dummies
0-7645-8996-2

Blogging For Dummies
0-471-77084-1

Creating Web Pages For Dummies
0-7645-7327-6

Also available:

eBay.co.uk
For Dummies
(0-7645-7059-5)

Dreamweaver 8
For Dummies
(0-7645-9649-7)

Web Design
For Dummies
(0-471-78117-7)

Everyday Internet
All-in-One Desk Reference
For Dummies
(0-7645-8875-3)

Creating Web Pages
All-in-One Desk Reference
For Dummies
(0-7645-4345-8)

DIGITAL MEDIA

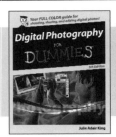

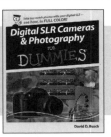

Digital Photography For Dummies
0-7645-9802-3

iPod & iTunes For Dummies
0-471-74739-4

Digital SLR Cameras & Photography For Dummies
0-7645-9803-1

Also available:

Digital Photos, Movies, &
Music GigaBook
For Dummies
(0-7645-7414-0)

Photoshop CS2
For Dummies
(0-7645-9571-7)

Podcasting
For Dummies
(0-471-74898-6)

Blogging
For Dummies
(0-471-77084-1)

Digital Photography
All-In-One Desk Reference
For Dummies
(0-7645-7328-4)

Windows XP Digital Music F
Dummies
(0-7645-7599-6)

COMPUTER BASICS

PCs For Dummies
0-7645-8958-X

Laptops For Dummies
0-470-05432-8

Windows XP For Dummies
0-7645-7326-8

Also available:

Office XP 9 in 1
Desk Reference
For Dummies
(0-7645-0819-9)

PCs All-in-One Desk
Reference For Dummies
(0-471-77082-5)

Pocket PC For Dummies
(0-7645-1640-X)

Upgrading & Fixing PCs
For Dummies
(0-7645-1665-5)

Windows XP All-in-One Des
Reference For Dummies
(0-7645-7463-9)

Macs For Dummies
(0-470-04849-2)

TJI91433-9780470057520-22-08-19